Ergonomic Aspects of
Visual Display Terminals

Ergonomic Aspects
of
Visual Display Terminals

Proceedings of the International Workshop, Milan, March 1980

Edited by

E. Grandjean

Swiss Federal Institute of Technology
Zurich

and

E. Vigliani

Carlo Erba Foundation
Milan

Taylor & Francis Ltd
London
1980

First published 1980 by Taylor & Francis Ltd,
4 John Street, London WC1N 2ET

British Library Cataloguing in Publication Data

Ergonomic aspects of visual display terminals.
   1. Information display systems—Human factors—
Congresses
I. Grandjean, Etienne   II. Vigliani, E.
001.6′443   TK7882.I6

ISBN 0-85066-211-7

Printed and bound in Great Britain by
Taylor & Francis (Printers) Ltd,
Rankine Road, Basingstoke, Hampshire RG24 0PR.

Contents

Preface

Until about 10 to 20 years ago, punch cards were used to feed data into a computer, and the results came back to the operator through a printer. Computer industries accelerated these interactions between operator and computer by introducing

keyboards for data entry, and
cathode-ray-tube (CRT) displays to send data back.

The correct term for this equipment would be 'Visual Display Terminal' (VDT), but since the expression 'Visual Display Unit' (VDU) has become popular, it will be widely used in this publication.

VDU systems are becoming more and more common. They have found a large field of application in commercial enterprises, banking, insurance and printing, in many sections of industry and in various forms of administration. Some experts expect that 10% of all workplaces will be equipped with VDU systems in the near future.

As long as engineers and other highly motivated experts operated VDUs, nobody complained about health impairments. The situation changed a lot with the expansion of VDUs at workplaces where traditional working methods had been applied formerly. At VDU workplaces many employees are now a part of a man–machine-system; psychological problems, sometimes associated with fear and negative attitudes arise from this new situation.

The reports of complaints provoked different reactions: some believe that the complaints are highly exaggerated whereas others consider the health hazard as a serious problem requiring immediate measures to protect operators. The scientists stand between these opposite poles; their duty is to analyse objectively the ergonomic and medical aspects related to VDU workplaces.

This was the aim of the international scientific workshop on ergonomic aspects of VDUs, held in Milan from 17 to 19 March 1980 under the auspices of the Permanent Commission and International Association on Occupational Health and the Carlo Erba Foundation, Occupational and Environmental Health Section.

The workshop and the publication of its proceedings were generously supported by the following sponsors:

Alitalia (Rome, Italy)
Banca d'Italia (Rome, Italy)
Cassa di Risparmio delle Provincie Lombarde (Milan, Italy)

Continental Luxo (Ponte San Pietro, Italy)
Giroflex Entwicklungs-AG (Koblenz, Switzerland)
IBM Europe (Paris, France)
Istituto Bancario San Paolo di Torino (Turin, Italy)
Olivetti (Ivrea, Italy)
Philips NV (Eindhoven, Netherlands)
Siemens AG (Munich, Federal Republic of Germany)
SIP—Italian Telephone Company (Turin, Italy)

Zurich, April 1980

E. Grandjean, Zurich   *E. Vigliani, Milan*

Ergonomics of VDUs: review of present knowledge

By E. GRANDJEAN

Swiss Federal Institute of Technology, Department of Hygiene and Ergonomics,
CH-8092 Zurich, Switzerland

VDUs are a new tool in many workplaces. They show and produce teething troubles due to

  inadequate workplace design;
  not optimally developed technology;
  unadapted work organization;
  psychological attitudes of end-users.

Many therapies are available; others must still be studied and developed. Therapies are useful only if they are applied.

1. The activities of operators at VDU systems

Among the manifold types of VDU operations, two kinds can frequently be distinguished:

The conversational terminal, which is also called the interactive system. The operator gives many data through the keyboard to the computer and watches the results appear after a certain lapse of time on the display. In this kind of work, the gaze of the operator is mostly alternating between source documents and display. Very roughly one can estimate that the gaze is oriented about 50% of the time to the source documents and 50% to the display. The frequency of alternation depends on the task; an alternation every 5 to 10 seconds is often observed. Rather low stroke speeds on the keyboard are another characteristic of work at conversational terminals.

At the data-entry terminal the operator gives a very large quantity of data through the keyboard into the computer. The gaze of the operator is mainly directed to the source documents; only from time to time will he look at the keyboard or the display for periodical control of progress. The operator accommodates his eyes mainly on the text of the source documents but in many cases the display remains in his visual field. Employees at data-entry terminals mostly use only the right hand to operate the keyboard, while the left hand handles the source documents. The working speed is usually very high and 8000 to 12 000 strokes per hour is not exceptional.

Besides these two typical terminal workplaces, there are many others; some of them use the VDU only occasionally for various purposes.

2. Physical properties

Among the many physical characteristics of VDU systems, some which are of importance from the point of view of ergonomics will be mentioned here:

Most of the screens have a utilized surface which is 15 to 20 cm high and 20 to 25 cm wide.

The display is based on an electron beam, which generates alphanumeric and symbolic characters on the screen.

The number of raster scan lines is mostly 9 units per mm.

The character images are today generated

either by strokes, where the shape of the character is formed by a series of connected lines (strokes);

or by a dot matrix in which the shape of the character is formed by an appropriate series of dots in a given rectangular pattern. In general 5×7 dots or 7×9 dots per matrix area are used.

The size of the characters is usually 4–8 mm high and 2–4 mm wide.

The regeneration rate (beam movements per second) is between 25 and 80 Hz.

In front of the screen, there is usually a convex glass plate. In order to reduce the risk of reflections on the glass plate, many apparatuses use a filter device, either in front of, or incorporated in, the glass plate. All filter devices alter the light characteristics and decrease the luminance of the characters.

3. Luminances on screens

Luminances of the characters and the background luminances of the screen itself are important physiological elements for the legibility. Luminances are measured in nits; 1 nit $= 1 \text{ cd/m}^2$.

In general, the following luminance ranges are observed:

characters   7 to 84 nit,
background of screen 1 to 11 nit.

We can deduce that the contrasts between characters and background are in the range of 2:1 to 30:1. The median value is 9:1.

It should be noted here that for black characters on white paper, contrasts of 1:5 up to 1:10 are often observed.

4. The colour of characters

The colour of the characters is generated by the phosphor. It seems that the colour contrast component increases the capacity to distinguish the characters against the reflections on the glass plate. Many operators prefer coloured characters though they cannot give a rational argument.

Some constructors of displays use a colour in the yellow–green range, which is in the middle of the visible spectrum. This seems advisable, since the spectral sensitivity of the eye is higher in this range than at either end of the visible spectrum.

5. The oscillation of luminances of the characters

The type of phosphor is also associated with the so-called persistence of luminance which is in turn an important factor for the oscillation of luminances of characters. The persistence of a phosphor is determined by the time the character remains illuminated after having been excited by the electron beam. The decay time until luminance drops to 10% of the peak level is often used to characterize the persistence of a phosphor. Table 1 shows a few decay times of several phosphor types. It can be seen that the decay times are of the magnitude of milliseconds, and that some phosphors producing green colours are associated with rather longer decay times.

Table 1. Decay time in milliseconds of several types of phosphor according to IBM Corporation (1978).

Phosphor type	Colour	Decay time (ms) to 10% luminance
P1	green	24
P4	white	0·15
P20	yellow	6·5
P22G	green	6
P39	green	400

Figure 1 shows the main characteristics of the oscillation of luminances of characters. The luminances of one character show a rather sharp peak and a decay to a basic level which depends mainly on the luminance of the background of the screen. Furthermore, it should be noted that the proportion of the bright part to the dark part within one cycle is certainly much smaller than in a sinusoidal form of modulation of a fluorescent tube.

The degree of the oscillation is often measured by the 'uniformity figure' UF, which expresses the relation between the lowest and the highest luminance levels of any cycle. Therefore, a low UF means a great degree of oscillation, while a high UF corresponds to a small oscillation.

Above a certain level the oscillation is perceived as a flickering light, while below this level the oscillation is not seen. It is well known that the visible

E. Grandjean

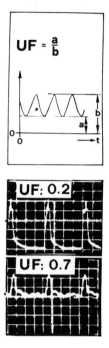

Figure 1. The oscillation of luminances of the characters. Uniformity figure: UF =
a/b. Upper photograph: UF = 0·2. High oscillation due to a dark background
of the screen. Lower photograph: UF = 0·7. Moderate oscillation due to a
brighter background of the screen.

flicker has adverse effects on the eye mainly because it produces an overloading
of the adaptation of the eye, brought about by the repetitive 'over-exposure' of
the retina to light. The main effect of flickering light is similar to that of glare,
more precisely to adaptive glare.

Little is known about the effects of a non-visible flicker, that is, of a non-
perceived light oscillation. It is known that complaints of irritated eyes from
fluorescent tubes were reported as long as there was no suitable equipment to
avoid great modulations. We have good reason to assume that the light
oscillation of characters could—also in the invisible range—have some adverse
effects on the retina. Läubli *et al.* (1980) show some results which support this
assumption. Further research is necessary to clarify the question of whether the
special type of light oscillation of characters has any physiological effects, and
whether or not such effects can be tolerated. Many other questions are still
open in this area of luminance oscillation.

We can summarize the various factors influencing the degree of oscillation
as follows: for the eye, focusing a character on the screen, *the oscillation of the
luminances is increased*:

with high luminances of characters,
with low background luminances of the screen,
with low general illumination level in the workroom,
with short persistence of the phosphor,
with low refreshing rate of the electron beam,
with modulated light of fluorescent tubes.

6. The visual functions involved

The main visual functions involved at VDU workplaces are the accommodation, the convergence, and the adaptation.

Accommodation and convergence are the ability of the eyes to bring into 'sharp focus' characters at varying distances. Nervous mechanisms control (through eye muscles) these functions.

The adaptation is the ability of the retina to adapt its sensitivity to varying illumination levels. The adaptation is based on photochemical and nervous regulations of the retina.

The accommodation is made more difficult and can, therefore, be impaired by a decreased image sharpness, or by low contrasts between characters and background of the screen.

In fact, the boundaries of the character-images are not sharp on CR tubes; there is no sharp edge between character and background as there is in printed texts.

The second function involved at VDU workplaces is the *adaptation of the retina*, which can be strained (*a*) by the large contrasts of the surface luminances between screen and source documents, as well as between screen and some surrounding elements, like windows, walls and light sources, and (*b*) by the oscillation of the character luminances, which may produce a sort of 'repetitive over-exposure' of the retina.

7. Physiological effects of VDUs

Several studies investigated the physiological effects of VDUs on subjects working under practical conditions or in simulated experimental situations (Höller *et al.* 1975, Cakir *et al.* 1978, Laville *et al.* 1980).

We can summarize some of the results as follows: work at VDUs led to a decrease of the accommodation power, produced a decrease of the critical fusion frequency, and was associated with heterophorias.

These authors did not use control groups doing the same type of work with hard-copy texts. Therefore, an important question remains open: are these physiological effects possibly symptoms of a normal degree of fatigue or is it justified to consider them as symptoms of excessive fatigue?

8. Complaints of VDU operators about eye troubles

General experience as well as many field studies indicate that some operators complain about various types of eye troubles (Hultgren *et al.* 1974, Östberg 1975, Meyer *et al.* 1978, Läubli *et al.* 1980).

The following complaints were recorded in several cases: general eye discomfort, eye strain, burning and irritated eyes, lachrymation and red eyes, difficulty in fixing characters, and blurring or double vision.

The proportion of operators with such complaints varies from one study to another over a wide range. The formulation of the question, of course, influences the results strongly.

Roughly we can estimate that 10 to 15% of the operators have almost daily pains or irritations in their eyes, while 40 to 50% report occasional impairments.

Two studies state that these eye impairments persist during the evening until sleeping time (Laville *et al.* 1980, Läubli *et al.* 1980). Apparently, some operators avoid watching television or reading during leisure time.

All these authors conclude that continuous work on VDUs is

for a relevant part of the operators—associated *with a pronounced impairment of the well-being in the sense of excessive fatigue of the eyes often associated with painful reactions and decrements of visual performances.* In general, these impairments are considered rather as reversible and functional troubles than as persistent injuries to health.

Some qualifications must be made to most of the mentioned studies. Comparisons with control groups with similar jobs but without VDU displays are mostly lacking. Since it is well known that office employees frequently have eye troubles (Nemecek and Grandjean 1973), the extension of the same questionnaire to control groups is a 'compulsory procedure'.

In table 2 the eye complaints of various groups of office employees are reported.

Table 2. Complaints about ('almost daily') eye troubles of various groups of office employees according to Läubli *et al.* (1980).

Groups	*n*	'Eye strain' (%)	'Eye pains' (%)
Date entry terminal	53	20	12
Conversational terminal	109	28	11
Typists (full-time)	78	18	7
Traditional office work	55	5	2

This study shows that eye complaints are reported from each group, and also from full-time typists. After all, insufficient lighting and source documents of poor quality are seen at many office workplaces. Nevertheless, there is no doubt that eye troubles are more frequent with VDU operators than in other groups.

Opinion on the real cause of these eye impairments is not unanimous and is based mainly on hypothetical assumptions. Luminance contrasts and unfavourable conditions for easy accommodation as well as visual disorders are often mentioned as most probable reasons. Läubli *et al.* (1980) could show that strong luminance contrasts as well as a great luminance oscillation of characters are associated with a higher incidence of eye complaints.

The following questions remain open:

What are the effects of unsharp boundaries of characters on the accommodation and the visual acuity?

What are tolerable contrasts of surface luminances?

What is the tolerable degree of luminance oscillation of characters?

Only if these questions can be clarified, should it be possible to adapt the physical properties of VDUs to the physiological needs of the operators.

9. Constrained postures at VDU workplaces

Constrained postures are associated with static muscular efforts, which may produce painful fatigue symptoms in the muscles concerned. If the static effort is repeated daily over a long period, more or less permanent aches will appear and may involve not only the muscles but also the joints, tendons and other tissues.

Constrained postures at VDU workplaces are due to the fact that the operators are forced to keep the head as well as the hands more or less permanently in a practically fixed position. The head position is determined by the appropriate visual distance to the screen or to the source documents, and the position of the hands is given by the location of the keyboard or sometimes by the location of the source documents.

A visit to VDU workplaces shows that many operators adopt an unfavourable position, which is often characterized by the following elements:

the trunk is leaning backwards and the neck is bent forwards,
the shoulders are held high,
the arms are extended forwards,
forearms and hands are often high at a level between shoulders and elbows.

Figure 2 shows an example of such a sitting posture at a VDU workplace.

Most experts in ergonomics require the following positions for this type of work:

the neck should not be bent more than 20° (head–neck axis to the main trunk axis),
shoulders must be relaxed,

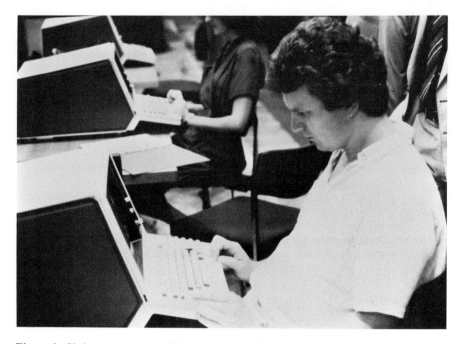

Figure 2. Sitting posture at a VDU workplace. Many operators lean backwards and
bend the head forwards. They have no support on the backrest at the lower part
of the spine.

elbows should be hanging down with an angle range of 80 to 100°,
forearms and hands ought to be in a horizontal position.

It is very rare to find an operator whose posture corresponds to these recommendations. Sometimes it is possible to identify an inadequate workplace dimension as a reason for a bad posture; sometimes there is no visible reason. According to our experience, the following factors are often recognized as the origin:

no proper support for source documents,
keyboard levels too high,
source document levels too low,
no or inadequate supports to rest forearms or hands,
insufficient space for knees and legs.

These postural problems are not peculiar to VDU workplaces; they appear in all jobs with business machines, if keyboards must be operated at such a speed as to impose constrained postures.

A systematic investigation on constrained postures at VDU workplaces was carried out by Hünting *et al.* (1980). Table 3 shows the incidence of some of the physical troubles reported from five different groups of office operators.

Table 3. Incidence of 'almost daily' pains in five office jobs.

		Incidence of 'almost daily' pains			
Groups	*n*	Neck (%)	Shoulder (%)	Right arm (%)	Right hand (%)
Data-entry terminals	53	11	15	15	6
Accounting machine operators	119	3	4	8	8
Conversational terminals	109	4	5	7	11
Typists	78	5	5	4	5
Traditional office work	55	1	1	1	0

The results reveal that serious impairments were observed in each group, but the highest figures are seen in the group operating data-entry terminals and the lowest figures in the group occupied with traditional office work.

If the answers 'occasional' pains (i.e. several times per month) are taken into consideration, the figures are higher but the relation between the five groups remains the same.

These 'almost daily' pains must be considered as relevant injuries since about 20% of all operators visited a doctor for this reason. Furthermore, painful indurations in muscles, and other medical symptoms were observed in many of these operators.

We must conclude that the constrained postures at VDUs as well as at other business machine workplaces can produce

symptoms of localized fatigue, and
in a small proportion of operators, also injuries in muscles and tendons.

An important part of the workplace is the chair. The simple observation of the sitting behaviour of office employees shows clearly that the great majority of operators adopt a very special sitting posture (see figure 2). They lean back-

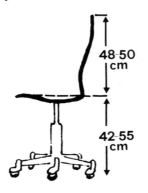

48-50 cm

42-55 cm

Figure 3. A recommended type of working chair for VDU operators. A high backrest of 48–50 cm with an adjustable inclination is needed.

wards and often extend the legs forwards. They seem to put up with a pronounced forward bending of the head, with no support of the lower part of the spine, and with lifting their arms.

We do not know the reason for this strange sitting habit of VDU operators. Is it a preferred visual angle or a preferred visual distance? Or is the operator seeking a more appropriate position for the hands? Whatever the reason may be, it is likely that VDU operators need a chair with a high backrest and adjustable inclination, as shown in figure 3.

We tried such chairs in two offices and got good reports from the operators. Nearly all operators gave a clear preference for high backrests.

10. Recommendations related to postural problems

It would certainly not be safe or wise just to extrapolate ergonomic recommendations, valuable for other workplaces, to VDU workplaces. Furthermore, it would not be wise to assess uniform guidelines for all types of VDU workplaces. In fact, there are fundamental differences between the operations at different VDU workplaces. Further research under experimental conditions is needed before we can assess workplace dimensions in centimetres and millimetres.

Nevertheless, a few general recommendations are certainly justified and can be summarized as follows:

(1) Movable keyboards are better than sunk keyboards.
(2) Special, separate devices to adjust the heights of

    desk or keyboard level
    source documents
    terminal screen

  are recommended.

(3) Forearm/hand supports are indicated, but studies to develop appropriate designs are necessary.
(4) Chairs with high backrests and adjustable inclination are recommended.

11. X-ray radiation

Another health aspect associated with the use of CRTs at VDUs must be briefly discussed: the risk of X-ray irradiation.

The visible light on the screen is generated by the interaction between electron beam and screen phosphor. However, other forms of radiant energy, of radiofrequency types of radiation and of X-ray radiation may be generated.

For the end-user of VDUs, the idea that the CRT might be a source of radiation can, of course, be a cause of anxiety. The fear is increased by the fact that the senses generally give no warning of such radiation.

Many studies show that the amounts of radio-frequency radiation as well as infrared and ultraviolet radiation are very small and confined to the immediate vicinity of the source. The ultraviolet radiation is not likely to pass through the screen glass and is, in fact, undetectable in front of VDUs.

The interaction between the bombarding electrons and some atoms in the CRT causes X-ray emissions of low energy, since most CRTs operate at a high voltage level of about 18 kV. X-ray emissions from CRTs are described in terms of the exposure rate in milliroentgens/hour (mR/h). In recent years many official institutions have measured and analysed these exposure rates. Nearly all existing VDUs show an X-ray exposure rate of less than 0·2 mR/h.

Assuming a five-day and forty-hour week, the regulations for personal occupational safety throughout Europe and the United States prescribe a permissible exposure of 2·5 mR/h to the eyes. Therefore, the VDU exposure rate is much lower than this limit. The intensity of the background radiation of natural origin is of the magnitude of 0·01 to 0·03 mR/h.

In fact, most VDUs (with a voltage of less than 20 kV) show in front of the screen an X-ray radiation of the same order as the natural background radiation, i.e. about 1 % of the safety limits.

All experts in this field conclude that jobs at VDUs present no risk of harmful X-ray radiation.

12. Psychological aspects

With the VDU, many occupational activities get a new character, associated with psychological problems. The employee, who formerly had a diversified activity, involving walking around and communicating with colleagues, is now, at the VDU, a part of a man–machine system. His personal radius of action becomes restricted. Sometimes the VDU imposes a great increase of performance, and sometimes work becomes more monotonous.

Some employees are worried: they are afraid of new technologies, of automation, and fear unemployment. This rather complex and only vaguely recognizable situation gives rise to a general negative attitude towards the VDU. But an opposite reaction can also be observed. In fact, some employees are proud to be included in the new work of modern technology, and are looking forward to the interaction with a computer.

We can assume that the psychological reactions to VDUs will differ very much depending on

the type of work,
the way the new job is organized,
the way it is introduced,
and on the various personal attitudes.

References

CAKIR, A., HART, D. J., and STEWART, T. F. M., 1979, *The VDT Manual* (Darmstadt: Inca-Fiej Research Association).

CAKIR, A., REUTER, H.-J., VON SCHMUDE, L., and ARMBRUSTER, A., 1978, Untersuchungen zur Anpassung von Bildschirmarbeitsplätzen an die physische und psychische Funktionsweise des Menschen. *Forschungsbericht Humanisierung des Arbeitslebens* (Bonn: Der Bundesminister für Arbeit und Sozialordnung).

HÖLLER, H., KUNDI, M., SCHMID, H., STIDL, H. G., THALER, A., and WINTER, N., 1975, *Arbeitsbeanspruchung und Augenbelastung an Bildschirmgeräten* (Vienna: Automationsausschuss der Gewerkschaft der Privatangestellten, Verlag des Ö.G.B.).

HULTGREN, G. V., and KNAVE, B., 1974, Discomfort glare and disturbances from light reflexions in an office landscape with CRT display terminals. *Applied Ergonomics*, **5**, 2–8.

HULTGREN, G. V., KNAVE, B., and WERNER, M., 1974, Eye discomfort when reading microfilm in different enlargers. *Applied Ergonomics*, **5**, 194–200.

HÜNTING, W., LÄUBLI, TH., and GRANDJEAN, E., 1980, Constrained postures of VDU operators. *Ergonomic Aspects of Visual Display Terminals* (this volume), p. 175.

IBM CORPORATION, 1978, *Human Factors of Workstations with Display Terminals.* Publication G 320-6102-0 (San José, California: Human Factors Center).

LÄUBLI, TH., HÜNTING, W., and GRANDJEAN, E., 1980, Visual impairments in VDU operators related to environmental conditions. *Ergonomic Aspects of Visual Display Terminals* (this volume), p. 85.

LAVILLE, A., TEIGER, C., LANTIN, G., and DESSORS, D., 1980, Quelques caractéristiques de la fatigue visuelle provoquée par le travail de détection sur microfiches. *Le Travail Humain*, **42**, 261–273.

MEYER, J. J., REY, P., KOROL, S., and GRAMONI, R., 1978, La fatigue oculaire engendrée par le travail sur écrans de visualisation. *Sozial- und Präventivmedizin*, **23**, 295–296.

NEMECEK, J., and GRANDJEAN, E., 1973, Results of an ergonomic investigation of large-space offices. *Human Factors*, **15**, 111–124.

ÖSTBERG, O., 1975, Health problems for operators working with CRT displays. *International Journal of Occupational Health and Safety*, Nov.–Dec., 24–52.

Section 1. Physical characteristics of VDTs

Electromagnetic radiations emitted by visual display units

By T. Terrana, F. Merluzzi and E. Giudici

Institute of Occupational Health, University of Milan, Milan, Italy

Non-ionizing electromagnetic radiations in the radiowave field are emitted by the oscillator circuit and the electronic components of VDU. Ionizing electromagnetic radiations are emitted by the VDU cathode ray tube. Low-energy X-rays and electric field strengths in the 10 kHz–500 MHz frequency bands were measured under normal working conditions and in a laboratory in a shielded room, where we were able to use complex instruments to measure the radio- and microwaves.

The values obtained for X-ray and radio-frequency radiation were far lower even than the most restrictive permissible exposure levels established by any agency or government.

1. Introduction

In recent years there has been increasing concern about the possible adverse effects on biological systems of electromagnetic radiations diffused into the environment by electrical and electronic equipment and systems.

Non-ionizing electromagnetic radiations in the radio- and microwave field are emitted by the oscillator circuits and the electronic components of VDUs. Ionizing electromagnetic radiations (low-energy X-rays) are emitted by the VDU cathode ray tube.

In this paper, we examine this problem with the aim both of evaluating the health risk to operators, and of classifying employees and VDU equipment in accordance with the Italian legislation concerning protection against ionizing radiations.

Measurements were made at the lower frequencies (radiowaves and microwaves as far as 1 GHz) of the electromagnetic spectrum and at higher frequencies (low-energy X-rays), as can be seen in figure 1.

We examined eight VDUs used in a photocomposition department of a well-known newspaper and five VDUs used at a commercial firm. Both sets of measurements were carried out under normal working conditions. We also thoroughly examined one VDU in a laboratory, where we were able to use complex instruments to measure the radio- and microwaves.

T. Terrana et al.

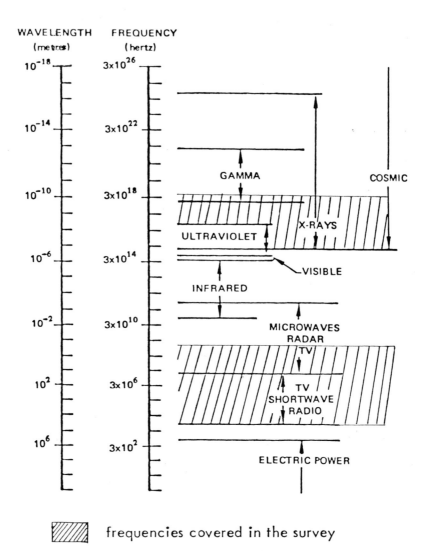

frequencies covered in the survey

Figure 1. The electromagnetic spectrum.

2. Ionizing radiations

The ionizing radiation measurements were obtained using a Victoreen model 490 Thyac III impulse counter, connected to a Geiger–Müller model 489-110 'Pancake' thin-window probe for X-ray measurements, with a minimum measurable energy of 6 keV. For measurement of the time-integrated dose we used film-badge dosimeters with a minimum measurable limit of expression more than 0·3 mR above the natural background.

The measurements were performed by slowly scanning over the display screen, which was filled with letters and symbols as in a normal operation, and over other surfaces. Five film-badges were placed against the screen and one on each of the remaining surfaces and left in place for a total of 260 h operation. The natural background of radiation was also measured with the VDU not in operation and in nearby rooms where there were no VDUs installed. Table 1 gives the results of our measurements.

Table 1. X-ray exposure levels for VDUs

VDU type	Number of units surveyed
Linoscreen 100	1
Linoscreen 300-RA	5
Linoscreen 300-RB	2
HP 2645 A	2
HP 2640 A	3
Sit-Siemens TDU 300 Cima†	60
HP 2645 A†	3
Philips EI 8009†	1
Siemens Data 8151†	1
Siemens Data 81031†	1
Siemens Data 25201†	1
Siemens ELA 64-07†	3
IBM Sistem 6†	1
IBM 3279†	1

All radiation levels found were of the order of background radiation: 0·02 mR/h. The occupational exposure standard is 2·5 mR/h.

† Data are from the survey made by CESNEF of the Milan Politecnico.

In view of the small number of VDUs we tested, we report the results of other measurements performed by similar methods by the 'Enrico Fermi' Nuclear Research Centre (CESNEF) of Milan Politecnico. Our Institute is authorized to assess protection against ionizing radiations by the Ministry of Labour, in accordance with Italian legislation.

In no case did the levels found exceed the statistical fluctuations of the background radiation. That is to say, the VDUs surveyed do not emit X-radiations.

It should, however, be remembered that low-energy X-rays can be generated in the cathode ray tube, if VDUs are operated at a sufficiently high voltage. They therefore require particular attention, both from the makers and from the operators.

3. Radio- and microwave electromagnetic radiations

Numerous epidemiological investigations carried out in the U.S.S.R. and other East European countries (Baranski and Czerski 1976) indicate that prolonged exposure to electromagnetic radiations in the radio- and microwave field, may have harmful effects on the central nervous system and behaviour, with development of symptomatology consisting of general fatigue, nausea,

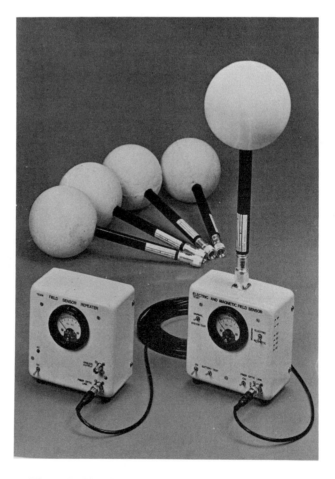

Figure 2. Electric and magnetic field sensor system.

headache, irritability, dizziness, loss of appetite, sleepiness, difficulty in concentration, poor memory, depression, etc., which are frequent among VDU
operators. Measurements at workplaces were performed with an electric and
magnetic field strength measuring system (SBO8) produced by Aeritalia of
Turin (figure 2). The SBO8 is a portable system for direct and isotropic measurements of electric and/or magnetic field strength in the 100 kHz–500 MHz
frequency bands, under near or far field conditions. All sensors used were of the
isotropic and balanced type: this permits measurements to be made of electromagnetic fields with different orientation and polarization.

The measurements were performed with a completely illuminated screen
and in the following positions: in contact with the screen, on the top, right and
left side, bottom and back surfaces, at keyboard level and at operator position.
We also measured the background with VDU not in operation and in nearby
rooms where there were no VDUs.

Table 2 gives the electric field strength measurements, expressed in V/m;
the magnetic field was practically zero. Our values ranged from 0·2 V/m to
3·5–3·6 V/m. The latter values were found only in a limited area in contact
with the top surface of the HP VDUs and probably they originated from the
high voltage circuit. In any case, if the sensor was moved a few centimetres
away from the VDU surface, the values fell to the background level.

Table 2. Electric field strength measurements for VDUs.

VDU type	Measurements location and readings in units of V/m						
	Screen	Over	Below	Rear	Right and left side	Operator position	Keyboard
Linoscreen 300-RA	0·9–1·7	0·5	0·2	0·4	0·6–0·7	0·5	0·6
Linoscreen 100	0·9–1·1	0·2–0·3	0·1–0·2	0·2–0·3	0·9–1·1	0·2	0·2
Linoscreen 300-RB	0·9–2·0	0·4–0·6	0·4	0·3	0·2–0·5	0·2	0·5
2645 A HP	1·5–2·2	0·9–3·5	0·3–0·4	0·3	0·5–1	0·2–0·3	0·3
2640 A HP	1·5–1·7	0·2–3·6	2·0	0·3	0·2–0·6	0·3	0·3

Background = 0·2–0·3 V/m.

At the operator position level we measured values of 0·2–0·5 V/m, which
correspond to the environmental background of electromagnetic and radio-
frequency radiations. Measurements were also made on an HP 2640 A VDU
in the laboratory in a room shielded for the suppression of external interference,

using an automatic measuring system (figure 3). This system has the advantage of reducing the testing time and of achieving a higher accuracy in frequency and amplitude measurements.

Figure 3. Emission measurement automatic system. Avionics Sector of Aeritalia, Turin.

The following instruments were used: a Singer Stoddard (S.S.) Model 17/27 Field Intensity Meter (FIM) with a 41 in. rod antenna and programmable antenna coupler for frequencies between 10 kHz and 32 MHz; and S.S. Model 37/57 FIM equipped with a biconical antenna and conical log spiral antenna for frequencies between 30 and 200 MHz and between 200 MHz and 1 GHz respectively. Each of the above antennas was calibrated by the manufacturer and the data from the individual calibration curves were used to complete the electric field strengths. Each system was placed approximately 1 m in front of the VDU. Figure 4 shows the graph recorded by the instrument, automatically scanning each frequency; and figure 5 gives the levels in μV/m measured in the 10 kHz–500 MHz frequency band. The line underneath refers to the background value of the shielded room.

The levels thus measured varied from 400 to 600 μV/m in the 10–100 kHz and 25–225 MHz frequency bands respectively. No significant levels were

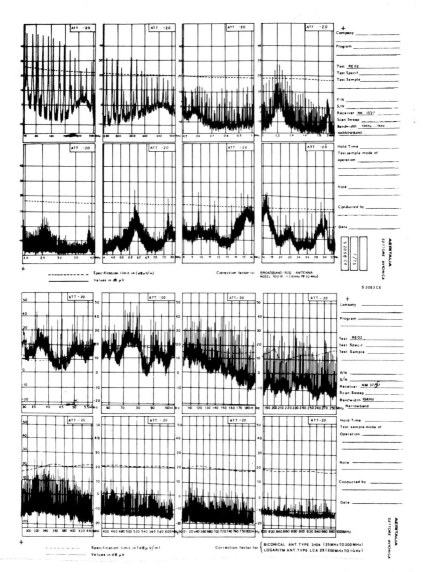

Figure 4. Electric field strength measurements. Values in dB μV recorded automatically scanning each frequency from 10 kHz to 1 GHz.

measured at microwave frequencies (above 300 MHz and up to 1 GHz). However, our equipment was limited as far as 1 GHz. These laboratory measurements, carried out in a shielded room, with a background value near zero, show that VDUs produce an electric field, though of very low intensity.

Table 3 lists the maximum permissible exposure levels in the U.S.A. and in the U.S.S.R., for eight working hours at the various frequencies (Tell 1972).

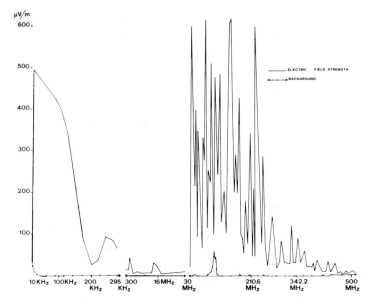

Figure 5. Electric field strength measurements. Values in μV/m in the 10 kHz–500 MHz frequency band.

Table 3. Radiofrequencies and occupational exposure standards.

Reference	Frequencies	Occupational exposure standards
U.S.A. ANSI† (1974) ACGIH‡ (1978)	< 10 MHz	10 mW/cm² power density which for a plane wave corresponds to an electric field strength of 200 V/m
U.S.S.R. (1965)	100 kHz–30 MHz 30 MHz–300 MHz	20 V/m 5 V/m

† American National Standards.
‡ American Conference of Governmental Industrial Hygienists.

The American limit of 10 mW/cm², for a continuous occupational exposure, was fixed for frequencies between 10 MHz and 100 GHz and is expressed in terms of power density. In plane wave conditions, this value corresponds to an electric field intensity of 200 V/m.

The U.S.S.R. limit is 20 V/m for frequencies between 100 kHz and 30 MHz and 5 V/m between 30 MHz and 300 MHz. Our values are lower by far even than the most rigid levels fixed in the U.S.S.R. No experimental or epidemiological data are available at present to prove that such radio-frequency radiation levels can produce any harmful effect on the human organism.

We believe that the disorders reported by VDU operators are not attributable to exposure to electromagnetic waves in the radio-frequency field, but to other factors discussed in this volume. To conclude, the problem of electromagnetic radiations emitted by VDUs was examined in a report by Moss *et al.* (1977) and in a very recent article by Weiss and Petersen (1979). Our conclusions agree with those of these studies.

References

BARANSKI, S., and CZERSKI, P., 1976, *Biological Effects of Microwaves* (Stroudsburg, Pennsylvania: Dowden, Hutchinson & Ross).

MOSS, C. E., MURRAY, W. E., PARR, W. H., MESSITE, J., and KARCHES, G. J., 1977, *An Electromagnetic Radiation Survey of Selected Video Display Terminals,* DHEW Publication No. (NIOSH), pp. 78–129.

TELL, R. A., 1972, Broadcast radiation: how safe is safe? *I.E.E.E. Spectrum,* **9,** 43–51.

WEISS, M. M., and PETERSEN, R. C., 1979, Electromagnetic radiation emitted from video computer terminals. *American Industrial Hygiene Association Journal,* **40,** 300–309.

The concept of contrast. A short note and a proposal

By Hans-Henrik Bjørset and Bjørn Brekke

Lysteknisk Laboratorium EFI/NTH, Universitetet i Trondheim,
N-7034 Trondheim-NTH, Norway

Due to the existence of various definitions of contrast and the somewhat confusing use of these and related concepts among the speakers of this conference, we have thought it useful to present a short note to clarify the proper use of the different expressions.

1. Contrast

The definition of contrast adopted by the CIE (The International Lighting Commission) relates to the luminance contrast between an object and its background:

$$C = \frac{L_o - L_B}{L_B}$$

where L_o is the object luminance, and L_B the background luminance. The definition implies that when viewing a dark character against a light background, as in an ordinary typed manuscript or a newspaper, the contrast is *negative* (because then $L_o < L_B$). Accordingly, the ordinary type of VDU screen with dark screen background and light letters must be said to have a *positive* contrast. The definition

$$C' = \frac{L_o}{L_B},$$

known especially from photography in former days, should not be called a *contrast*, but rather a *luminance ratio*.

2. Modulation

The concept of modulation is widely used in optics, and is adopted from electrical signal theory. According to its definition, it is valid only for a regular sine-wave test pattern, i.e. a pattern of parallel lines where the luminance along the direction at a right angle to the direction of the pattern lines varies sinusoidally between a minimum L_{min} and a maximum L_{max}. The modulation of such a regular pattern is defined as

$$M = \frac{L_{max} - L_{min}}{L_{max} + L_{min}}.$$

If the definition is strictly followed, in the case of a character viewed against a background, the concept of modulation should not be used for the character itself, but rather for its Fourier transform, or sine-wave spectrum. However, modulation is frequently used in connection with other regular patterns, for example square-wave patterns, and one then sometimes speaks about *equivalent modulation*.

3. Proposal

The Norwegian participants in this conference wish to propose that the Workshop on 'Ergonomic Aspects of Visual Display Units' in Milan, 17–19 March 1980, make a decision on using just one formula for the calculation of the contrast, to prevent future confusion in research work, and on what is to be called positive or negative contrast. The proposal is that the most common formula should be used, namely

$$C = \frac{L_o - L_B}{L_B}.$$

As already mentioned, this formula is adopted by the CIE. The work within several of the CIE Technical Committees will, no doubt, be of great interest to this association.

Using the same general formula for the calculation of the luminous contrast as the CIE, all the research work that is based on that formula, concerning contrast vision, contrast sensitivity, visual level, visual performance and so on, can be used directly.

It may be useful to have a liaison between the CIE and this association for the future.

Resolution model for a VDU-based person/machine interface: an overview

By N. D. LUBART

IBM Corporation, Austin, Texas, U.S.A.

Until the development of the VDU resolution model by Geise *et al.* (1978), there was no direct, simple way to relate the physical parameters of the VDU to the ergonomic parameters of the human being and workplace. Here, an overview is given of how the model works, including an examination of the assumptions upon which the model is based.

1. Introduction

Models based on known physical principles can be used to determine the physical parameters of the VDU (see Sherr 1970). However, the complete design of a display system requires the specification of the person/machine interface in terms of ergonomic parameters of the human being and work place. This important relationship has until now been treated in an *a posteriori* manner through essentially empirically derived 'rules of thumb' (see Buckler 1977). The empirical results were often dependent on the particular display system used, and a general model was lacking. This is not acceptable to a display system designer where design cycles are long and mistakes costly—to industry and the human being using the system. This model is meant to give such guidance to the display designer.

2. Method

The VDU resolution model proposed by Geise *et al.* (1978) rests on the observation that the threshold visibility limits for a VDU with simple images, such as text, involves essentially only the high-resolution elements of the eye, the cones. Figure 1 shows some typical alphanumeric Roman characters. The information contained in the recognition of the text is highly localized and essentially involves the detection of a dark region between two bright regions for a (so-called) negative image. In high-resolution displays, such angular distances can be as small as 0·5 to 1 minute of arc. The double-headed arrows show such a typical pattern of bright and dark regions. Such a luminance distribution, shown in figure 2, is generated by a closely spaced pair of scanning lines, where the luminance distribution is taken along the double-headed arrow

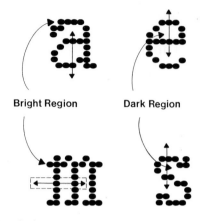

Figure 1. Resolution elements in typical alphanumeric characters.

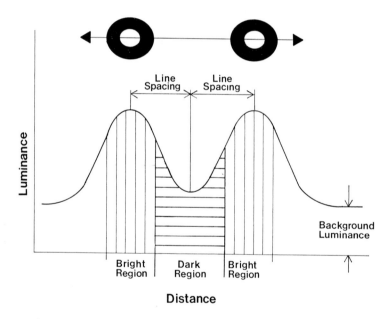

Figure 2. Luminance distribution of closely spaced scanning lines.

in figure 1. On a VDU, the luminance distribution is non-uniform and has no definite boundaries between dark and bright regions. An extensive body of experimental literature exists which measures the threshold detection of dark regions contrasted with a surrounding bright region (and bright regions with a surrounding dark region), but the regions have definitive boundaries. The luminance cross-section of a VDU spot is generally Gaussian with a shape parameter called the standard deviation. Other parameters are the peak lumi-nance of the spot (a VDU parameter, possibly adjustable) and background luminance (a VDU and workplace parameter). Contrast ratio is difficult to define and the effective contrast ratio between Gaussian spots is much less than the ratio usually calculated between spot and background luminances.

A first approach to the problem of treating a non-uniform luminance dis-tribution without definitive boundaries can be found by considering the physio-logical nature of the eye (Cobb 1915, Ganong 1971, Graham 1965).

"Under threshold visibility conditions the observer perceives an average spatial luminance in the regions to be detected. If this were not true, then shades of grey would be detected within the target regions. However, the detection of shades of grey also implies the detection of still smaller region; for example, if the centre of the dark region is detected as different from its edge. Obviously this is a contradiction of the original assumption of threshold visibility which implies that the size of the target is already equal to the liminal value required for visibility and any smaller region cannot be detectable." (Geise *et al.* 1978.)

The resulting spatial luminance distribution perceived by the observer is shown in figure 3 superimposed over the actual luminance distribution. Now, contrast ratio can be determined if the perceived boundaries can be determined. The locations of the boundaries are determined by comparisons to the classical threshold visibility data, such as shown in figure 4, taken from Luckiesh and Moss (1937) and Blackwell (1946), which were compiled using observers of a given visual acuity. Any other threshold visibility data can be used of the form shown in this figure. The threshold angular size is shown for a target of a given luminance contrasted to an adjacent region of higher or lower luminance, the contrast ratio being the ratio of target luminance to adjacent region luminance,

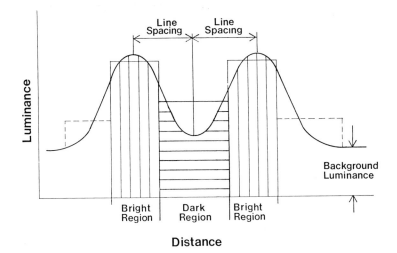

Figure 3. Luminance distribution perceived by an observer.

when the target is brighter than the adjacent region, or the reciprocal, when the target is darker. For example, consider the solid lines—representing a dark target on a bright background—for a contrast ratio of 2. If the background is $30 \, cd/m^2$, the threshold angular size of the target for these observers is about 1 minute of arc, so that the target must exceed 1 minute of arc to be visible. Likewise, for a contrast ratio of 1·03, the target must exceed 10 minutes of arc to be visible. The physical dimensions on the VDU are converted to angular

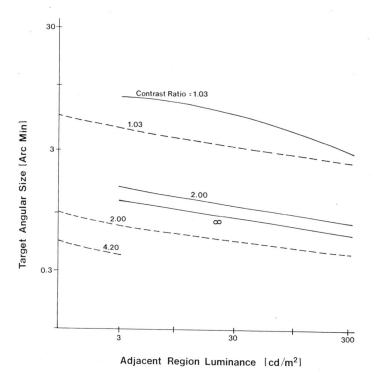

Figure 4. Classical threshold visibility data from Luckiesh and Moss (solid curves) with an adjacent region brighter than target, and Blackwell (dashed curves) with target brighter than adjacent region.

sizes using the observer viewing distance. For any assumed boundaries, the luminance of the bright and dark regions and the resultant contrast ratio can be computed. If the angular size of both the bright region contrasted to the dark region and dark region contrasted to the bright region exceed their respective liminal angular sizes determined from the threshold visibility data, then the dark region between the two bright regions is detected and the information to be detected is resolved. A computer program is used to examine all possible combinations of dark and bright region sizes.

3. Results

Typical results of these calculations are shown in figure 5. In this calculation, to reduce the result to a two-dimensional figure, four of the six possible variables considered in this model were fixed—peak luminance of the VDU spot, background luminance of the unilluminated screen, observer visual acuity, and observer viewing distance. Then, the required VDU beam spot size (a physical parameter of the VDU characterized by the standard deviation of the Gaussian luminance distribution) can be determined as a function of the minimum scanning line spacing (a design parameter of the VDU). For example, if the VDU spot size is specified, the ergonomically acceptable and unacceptable choices of line spacings can be determined. If the minimum acceptable scanning line spacing is known, the maximum total number of scan lines which fit in an ergonomically acceptable manner on the VDU can be calculated from the size of the screen.

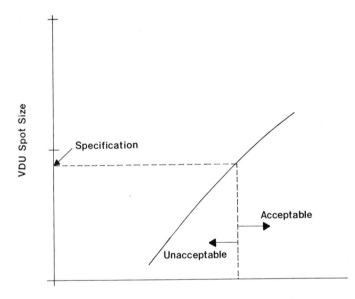

Figure 5. Typical results of model calculations.

4. Discussion

Based on this quantitative model, the selection of the VDU characteristics can be made with confidence as to the ergonomic acceptability of the final design before the display system itself becomes available.

References

BLACKWELL, H. R., 1946, Contrast thresholds of the human eye. *Journal of the Optical Society of America*, **36**, 624–643.

BUCKLER, A. T., 1977, A review of the literature of the legibility of alphanumerics on electronic displays (Aberdeen Proving Ground, Maryland: U.S. Army Human Engineering Laboratory).

COBB, P. W., 1915, The influence of pupillary diameter on visual acuity. *American Journal of Physiology*, **36**, 335.

GANONG, W. F., 1971, *Review of Medical Physiology* (Los Altos, California: Lang Medical Publications).

GEISE, D. M., LUBART, N. D., and CHANG, I. F., 1978, Resolution model for a CRT based person/machine interface. *Proceedings of the Society for Information Display*, **19**, 105–111.

LUCKIESH, M., and MOSS, F. K., 1937, *The Science of Seeing* (New York: D. Van Nostrand).

SHERR, S., 1970, *Fundamentals of Display System Design* (New York: John Wiley).

Section 2. Visual functions

Ophthalmological aspects of work with display workstations

Institut für Arbeitsphysiologie der Technischen Hochschule München,
Barbarastr. 16, 8 München 40, F.R. Germany

The visual display unit (VDU) is only one of the pieces of equipment at
workplaces which differ from one another in the contents and the process
of the work involved. However, the VDU brings some specific changes
which may increase strain on workers, if no attention is paid to it. Alphanumerics are often unusual. The image can flicker, adaptation is stressed,
the shining surface of the screen can deteriorate vision, and the VDU
cannot be moved. This means special demands for visual acuity and
accommodation.

1. Introduction

Although there have recently been many agreements in the Federal Republic
of Germany between employers and employees concerning the display work-
station, we must say that *the* display work-station does not exist.

There are many different workplaces with a display screen. These differ
from one another in the contents and the process of the work involved. Display
work-stations generally possess a keyboard, papers, and the screen. The following study confines itself to the screen, even if this restriction to one object
means unauthorized interference with the complex workplace. Bad seeing
conditions can lead to bad carriage: the muscular system gets overstressed and
discomfort appears.

In the future the cathode-ray-tube display will be introduced into more and
more offices. This means that visual conditions in the office must be so good
that even employees with limited vision could work with the display. One
employee may have limited visual acuity, another may have poor binocular
vision, while still another may be colour-blind. Therefore it is worth investi-
gating the single factors.

2. Characteristics of the visual display unit

What particular changes has the display screen brought about, apart from
changes to the contents and the process of work?

(a) The representation of the alphanumerics is unusual. The size of the
characters, the form of the characters and the contrast must be mentioned. A

further point concerns the flickering of the image and the demand for eye adaptability.

(*b*) The surface of the screen shines, so there are reflections and veiling reflections, with possible glare and dazzling and binocular competition.

(*c*) The usual screen is an additional piece of work equipment of great dimension. Besides, the screen is practically immovable because of its weight. Because of this, there is no possibility of changing the distance between the equipment and the eye by moving the display.

3. Presentation of visual information

Alphanumerics cannot be reduced or increased in size without limit. The capability of resolving power of the eye determines the lower limit. The higher limit is determined by the extension of the foveal field of the sharpest vision. In the former case the limit is reached when a text must be read letter by letter. In the latter case the limit is reached when a text can no longer be read syllable by syllable. It leads to a kind of tubular vision. In between there is a field of optimal legibility. Figure 1 shows the result of an investigation with 40 persons. They had to read a meaningless artificial text. After every attempt the readability had to be judged. The environmental conditions were: 500 lux horizontal illumination, 20 cd/m² luminance of surrounding area. The usual negative representation of letters with 100 cd/m² had been chosen. An exterior height of characters between 20 and 28 minutes of arc of sight proved to be a good value. The differences in the psychological values, as there were in speed of reading and number of mistakes, were not significant. The optimal character height for people with normal vision therefore requires a visus of at least about 0·2. The

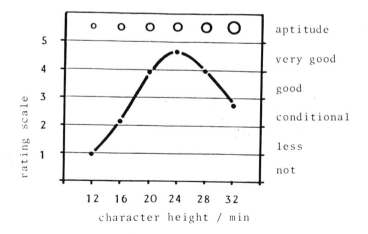

Figure 1. Readability of artificial texts with letters of different size.

size chosen for single characters should not be reduced, even if the number of character areas on a normal-sized screen becomes severely limited. The above-mentioned values were received for emmetropics with normal visual acuity. We should not forget that every correction of short-sightedness with glasses leads to a diminution of visual acuity because of the distance between the glasses and the corneal vertex (figure 2). So the curve for height of characters must be shifted to higher values.

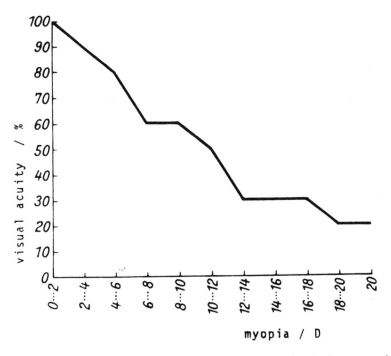

Figure 2. Loss of visual acuity for corrected myopic eyes (after Sachsenweger 1962).

Figure 1 was raised for very legible characters. Reading performance is determined to a great extent by the quality of the characters, where 'quality' concerns itself with contrast, form, and number of points of characters. Let us point out this complex situation with an example of a legible meaningless artificial text. The readability of such a text should not be confused with the perceptibility of a single character. In the first case (figure 3(*a*)), a text with well contrasting characters and with usual height–width proportions was read. The maximum reading speed reached was 6·8 lines/min with 56 characters/line. The number of mistakes remains low and constant up to the highest reading speed. Remaining time at lower speeds is not used for correction. The number of eye movements too is low. We have different results in the second

ERRORS / LINE OO   –   OMISSIONS / LINE x x
NUMBER OF EYE MOVEMENTS / LINE ⸺⸺ (x 10)

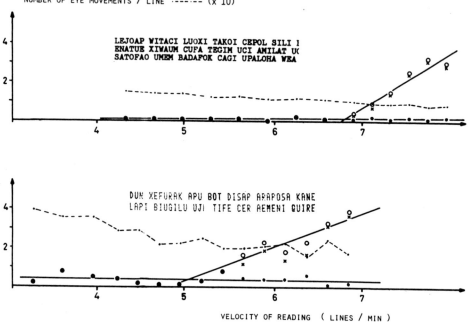

VELOCITY OF READING (LINES / MIN)

Figure 3. Errors, omissions and eye movements for reading texts with different quality of letters.

example with characters of less contrast and less width. Not only is the highest possible velocity of reading reduced to 4·9 lines/min, but the number of mistakes increases both at lower and at higher speeds of reading. The number of eye movements increases as well. The reader spells instead of reading.

In the border area of the resolving power of the human eye the maximum intensity of a point sinks more markedly than that of a line by the 'blurring' of the retinal image. In some forms of representation of alphanumerics the effect is further supported by a differential resolution of dot-scanning horizontally and vertically.

Eye movements proceed in two or more stages. A corrective saccade which follows a large one is in preparation during the performance of the first saccade (Kornhuber 1978). Therefore it is important to lead the eye. Routine information should appear clearly in a predictable place. Screens which are written without an overall plan increase the strain on the eyes. There is no knowledge about how much distortions and little movements of characters change the readability of characters. In this connection a comment should be made concerning the processing of visual information in cortical centres, though it is not intended to deal with the problem thoroughly. In lines of meaningless alphanumerics, the time of visual–mental response or processing time increases with the number of characters perceived at once. The number of mistakes increases strongly to more than three alpha-characters. Further there is an information rate that guarantees an optimum, i.e. a minimum, processing time. Therefore the device should run so speedily that the user can choose in advance the speed best for him—the speed which is determined by his own nervous system. The example of velocity reading has pointed out that a slow-down cannot be applied.

An unsolved problem concerns the periodically necessary refresh rate of the scope. In many displays today, the flicker fusion frequency falls short. Flicker fusion frequency changes with many parameters. It is peripherally higher than central in the luminance range of the displays. It rises with the middle luminance of the screen. Besides, it is basically determined by the modulation factor, i.e. determined by the time-constant of the phosphor used, which goes from fractions of milliseconds (P4) to several hundred milliseconds (P39). It must be added that the effective frequency can go up by means of eye movements. There are additional differences in the generation of the image. All the lines can be written one after another or, as with television, first the odd lines and then the even ones. This method gives an effective frequency twice that of the full image. As long as the lines are close to one another, this process functions well. But if the angle of vision becomes too big, it can lead to a visible low-frequency noise of the point luminance. Under unfavourable marginal conditions, interferences with neon lights might appear and lead to a surge of luminance. Because of the multitude of parameters and the relatively unknown functional coherence, the only test that we could recommend is the test of practical research with the following marginal conditions: screen with maximal luminance—this means with maximal modulation of luminance—completely written on the side field of vision. A specification of 50 Hz is of no value at all.

4. Surface of the visual display unit

A fundamental problem of the present screen and of coming ones is the reflections which disturb not only by means of the diminution of the character contrast, but equally strongly by means of the related glare, which might lead to binocular discomfort and conflict. We must set up the cathode ray tubes in such a way that these effects do not appear with normal sitting posture.

5. Dimensions of the visual display unit

A significant change for usual workplaces results from the size and weight and therefore permanent position of the screen. In principle the eye can sharply adjust itself to different distances. This process of accommodation is well developed in youth, while the range of accommodation decreases constantly

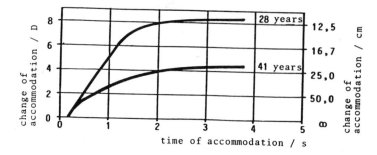

Figure 4. Time of accommodation required to accommodate from far (resting point of accommodation) to near for two persons of different age.

with advancing age. The adjustment of the eye to a new distance takes time. This time can take considerable values even for young persons. In figure 4 various changes in the distance of vision are put together, taken from the resting point to a near point for two persons of different age. As we see, the time for an older person is larger than that for a younger person, where the lapse, referred to as the maximum value of accommodation, is the same. This fact would correspond to the observation of Fincham (1954), that the effort of accommodation/dioptre increases with decreasing range of accommodation.

The demand for an equal distance of vision of the three pieces of equipment—display, keyboard, paper—derives from this reaction time. At the same time, however, such a demand means uneconomical static muscular work for the

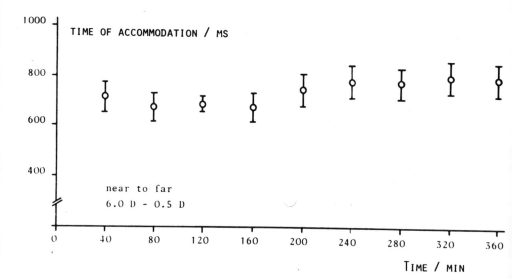

Figure 5. Time of accommodation during a long session. The person accommodated about 15 times per minute from far (0·5 D) to near (6·0 D).

ciliary muscle. Figure 5 shows fatigue even with strong constant change of distance between 2 m and 0·17 m (6 D) begins only after 2·5 hours. With a constant distance of vision, such a deterioration of efficiency can already be observed monocularly after some 10 min. As figure 4 further demonstrates, a reaction time is needed even without any change of the distance if optotypes near the limit of visual resolution are used. Also, the reaction time does not substantially increase even with a one-dioptre change in distance of vision. Therefore the demand for equal distance of objects can be made relative.

A young person will not be handicapped in his visual efficiency by the various necessary changes between front, middle and back sitting posture. A sufficient size of characters is of course required. An older employee is, however, considerably limited in his efficiency of accommodation. He needs glasses for objects close to him as a substitute for the dioptric power of his lenses. With the glasses the range of accommodation does not improve but rather the far point gets shifted to a near distance. This means that with advancing age the distance of vision conditioned or not by glasses must be adhered to more and more strictly. There was hardly any limit at work as long as only papers were used. With a change in the sitting posture, the papers could be moved around without any difficulties. In this way the visual distance could be held constant. It is different, however, in workplaces with a screen or heaps of computer paper. Because of their weight these materials cannot be moved. The user is tied to the work materials by means of the distance of vision. That leads to the all-too-familiar poor posture and in the long run to orthopaedic injuries. It is our serious task then, to create work glasses in such a way that the employee is physically confined by the screen as little as possible. There are two possibilities: (*a*) choice of an appropriate distance of vision, where the glasses are adjusted to this distance of vision; (*b*) choice of sufficient illumination level in the office.

There are two demands as far as the distance of vision is concerned. First it must be in an accessible area, so that we can work with the work materials. Secondly the remaining part of the accommodation must be thoroughly exploited. Figure 6 demonstrates the conditions. The far point with reading glasses lies on the abscissa. The related near points for different available accommodations lie on the ordinate. The range of sharp vision with glasses belonging to every far point can be read as the difference between the curve for 0 D and *x* D. For a far point of 0·67 m and an effective range of accommodation of 1 D, the near point would lie at 0·40 m, so that an appropriate range of working area of 0·27 m could be sharply seen. According to figure 6 it becomes evident that the size of the range of focusing decreases as the far point moves increasingly nearer. When the far point is at 0·50 m, the near point is at 0·33 m. The acute field of sight is reduced from 0·27 m to only 0·17 m. It is understandable that glasses cannot be fitted without some knowledge of the working place. Therefore cases of insufficient correction are often observed in spite of glasses (Schmidtke and Schober 1967). Moreover, it is clear that the

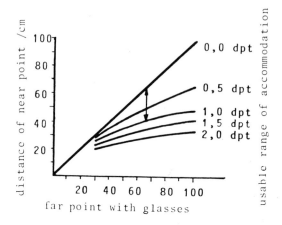

Figure 6. Decreasing of the range of vision with increasing optic power of the glasses.

right glasses at work, particularly when work is done with a display unit, are of greater importance than glasses in a conventional office.

Glasses of 1 to 1·5 D allow the user sufficient space of movement, while 2 D means a strong distance limitation to the device.

The effort to compensate the shrinking range of accommodation with optical media has led to bifocal and multifocal glasses. These work on the assumption that every distance of vision has a corresponding angle of inclination. This may be realized to a first order for vision in free space, but not in an office where equipment is arranged rather arbitrarily. That is why such glasses lead to a corresponding forced head posture, as has often been observed (Cakir *et al.* 1978).

Secondly the level of illumination of the office has been mentioned. If we see workplaces today with display units, we often find them in practically dark areas. The reason is that ceiling lighting and light-coloured walls lead to dazzling through reflections. Is this wise?

The visual acuity of the human eye is a function of the retinal luminance. Visual acuity rises with increasing values. In a range of middle illumination between 100 and 1000 cd/m² it reaches a maximum. This effect is partly based on the decrease of the diameter of the pupil and on the elimination of the spherical aberration of the eye. The decreasing diameter of the pupil brings with it a further advantage which is often overlooked. The depth of focus of the eye increases. The influence of the diameter of the pupil on the depth of focus is shown in figure 7 which is a composite of several single curves. We shall not go into more detail at this point. In any case there is a deviation from the desired value in the direction of a weaker power of refraction, i.e. less effort of accommodation. This deviation apparently is a function of the diameter of the pupil. A diameter of 1 mm means simultaneously greater depth of focus and less effort of accommodation. The depth of focus in the form applied here as a rate of recognition for optotypes is a function of the size of the characters. The stated values refer to a Landolt's ring, which lies about 20% above visual acuity 1·0. For larger optotypes the effect is intensified.

Older employees can compensate for a part of the loss of the breadth of the accommodation by means of depth of focus if the illumination level is high, so we should beware of decrease in the intensity of illumination for the above-mentioned reason of dazzling.

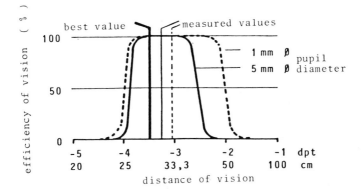

Figure 7. Depth of focus of the eye for different diameters of the pupil.

The relationship between visual distance and colour of display is currently being discussed. According to previous investigations the eye focuses on a green of middle wavelength. It is far-sighted for light of greater wavelength and short-sighted for light of shorter wavelength. Therefore light in a red wavelength is not as favourable under the same luminance as light in green wavelength. To what extent this statement is also quantitatively valid for colours within the colour triangle is still undecided. Current experiments with colours of mixed wavelength on the value of accommodation have not shown any conclusive results as yet.

Recent experiments in our laboratory lead to the surprising result that 30% of people with inconspicuous binocular vision are not able to follow mono-cularly a small optotype through sudden changes of distance. They often come to a standstill at short distance with a kind of accommodation spasm that they cannot relax. This points out, as has already been shown, the leading role which the vergence of the axes of the eye plays with dynamic phenomena in a regulation circle of accommodation and vergence. Further, vergence takes place more rapidly than accommodation. This shows that good binocular vision is important.

6. Conclusions

No damage to the eye from work on the screen of the cathode ray tube has yet been reported. On the contrary chronic or acute restrictions of vision which already exist may cause discomfort earlier, due to the particular conditions of the CRT work-station, and consequently the problems must be dealt with at an early stage. Since the CRT work-station is the office workplace of the future, work conditions should be set up in such a way that even employees with impairments of vision which cannot be corrected would be able to use the screen.

References

CAKIR, A., REUTER, H.-J., V. SCHMUDE, L., and ARMBRUSTER, A., 1978, Untersuchungen zur Anpassung von Bildschirmarbeitsplätzen an die physische Funktionsweise des Menschen. *Forschungsberichte Humanisierung des Arbeitslebens.* (Bonn: Der Bundesminister für Arbeit und Sozialordnung).

FINCHAM, E. F., 1954, The proportion of ciliary muscular force required for accommodation. *Journal of Physiology*, **128**, 99–112.

KORNHUBER, H. H., 1978, Blickmotorik. *Physiologie des Menschen*, edited by O. H. Gauer, K. Kramer and R. Jung (Munich, Vienna, Baltimore: Urban & Schwarzenberg), Bd. 13.

KRUEGER, H., and MÜLLER-LIMMROTH, W., 1979, *Arbeiten mit dem Bildschirm—aber richtig!* (Munich: Bayerisches Staatsministerium für Arbeit und Sozialordnung).

SACHSENWEGER, R., 1962, *Ophthalmologische Optik und Brillenlehre* (Berlin: VEB Verlag Volk und Gesundheit).

SCHMIDTKE, H., and SCHOBER, H., 1967, *Sehanforderung bei der Arbeit* (Stuttgart: A. W. Gentner).

Accommodation and visual fatigue in display work

By O. Östberg

Department of Human Work Sciences, University of Luleå,
S-95187 Luleå, Sweden

We are in the midst of the evolution of the species *Homo Termino-Videns*. Demands for (eye) rest-time allowances are commonplace among VDU operators the world over. Today some 13 % of Swedish salaried employees daily sit at a VDU and Sweden is the first country to have issued National Safety and Health Directives on VDU work. Experiments using a laser optometer have now shown that visual tasks in VDU work may induce temporary effects in the visual accommodation system; increased refractive power in darkness ('night myopia') and levelling-out of accommodation responses in good lighting ('distance myopia' and 'near hyperopia'). It is believed that laser optometry will eventually make possible the formulation of objective criteria of visual fatigue and its prevention.

1. Swedish safety and health directives on VDU work

Today some 13 % of Swedish salaried employees daily sit at a VDU, and more than 25 % of the total Swedish active workforce work daily with computerized information (Zetterberg 1979). By way of comparison ,the Federal Republic of Germany has eight times more workers than Sweden, but fewer VDUs.

We are in the midst of a rapid evolution of the species *Homo Termino-Videns* (the VDU-viewing man). This has alerted trade unions all over the world, which in turn has alerted the safety and health authorities. By the publication of Reading of Display Screens (1978), Sweden was the first country to adopt national directives on VDU work, but similar regulations are being announced in other countries (Krueger and Müller-Limmroth 1979). The main points of the Swedish VDU directives are as follows.

(1) Ambient lighting must be suitably adapted. Special importance must be attached to lighting conditions at workplaces where reading of display screens occurs regularly. Generally the illumination required is lower than in ordinary office work. In workplaces where work is continuously conducted at display screens, an illumination of between 200 and 300 lux may be suitable.

Note: Lower illumination levels may be appropriate in certain working environments of a special nature (e.g. in monitoring and traffic control).

(2) When ambient lighting is subdued as per point (1), supplementary lighting must be provided for other working areas near the display screens. Supplementary lighting must be adjustable and fitted with glare control arrangements.

(3) Excessive differences of luminance in the field of vision produce what is termed contrast glare. The workplace should therefore be organized in such a way that the background of the display screen is of suitable luminance and the employee's field of vision does not include a window or any other glaring luminances. Bright reflections in the display screen are to be avoided.

(4) The visual distance to the display screen and the angle of inclination of the display screen should be individually adjustable with due regard being paid to other ergonomic requirements. In the case of employees who wear spectacles, it is important that the optical correction is well adapted to the visual distance, and vice versa.

Note: Ordinary spectacles for private use are often unadapted to the visual distance occurring in display screen work. Traditional bifocal lenses are unsuitable in many cases, because they often entail a strenuous work posture when used for display screen reading.

(5) If an employee has a refractive error and incurs visual discomfort in connection with display screen work when using spectacles intended for normal purposes, the display screen must be moved to a position where the discomfort is eliminated. If this is not possible, the employer is to provide the employee with special spectacles which have been tested for display screen work.

(6) If eye fatigue or visual discomfort tends to develop, the work must be organized in such a way that the employee can intermittently be given periods of rest or work involving more conventional visual requirements.

2. Demands for VDU rest-time allowances

Traditional office tasks can be carried out in a great many ways and usually an office worker is free to choose his preferred way. This freedom is often drastically reduced when the job becomes computerized. Herein lies the need for increased ergonomic efforts to improve VDU workplaces and work routines, and also the reasons behind operators' demands for "teabreaks every hour" (Östberg 1979). The demands for rest-time allowances originate from the operators' knowledge that intense VDU viewing is concomitant to eye fatigue or visual discomfort, and their apprehension of long-time effects of these ailments. Accordingly, the Swedish Board of Occupational Safety and Health put some stress on the visual hygiene aspects of VDU work, and in particular point (6) in the above-quoted regulations acknowledges the need for periods

Figure 1. Trade unions are making a case for improved VDU working conditions (top). Employers may not share the unions' views and may think of rest pauses as unproductive (bottom). The researchers, in delineating the problem areas, may feel squeezed between the bargaining parties (middle).

of rest. It remains to be clarified, however, how and by whom it shall be decided that eye fatigue or visual discomfort is at hand, and also on the frequency and the duration of the breaks.

In a VDT-Health Collective Bargaining Kit (1977), newspaper guilds are recommended to make rest-time allowances the number one demand. But when the Australian Journalists Association demanded that "members who operate VDTs be given a break of 15 minutes after every two hours", the Australian Arbitration Court decided that the need for break was not properly founded (C No. 5016 of 1978). The demand of '15 minutes off after two hours on' on the other hand seems very modest compared to 'one hour off after one hour on', which is the present action programme of the Austrian Federation of Salaried Employees in the Private Business Sector (Höller *et al.* 1975). The great need for objective criteria of visual fatigue is illustrated in figure 1.

3. Laser optometry in assessment of visual fatigue

As reviewed by Östberg (1976), many attempts have been made to find objective criteria of visual fatigue employing for example measures of reading rate and comprehension, eye fixations and regressions, pupil diameter, blink rate, glare sensitivity, dark adaptation time, flicker fusion frequency, and temporary 'myopization' and 'esophorization'. In a follow-up review (Östberg 1978) it was concluded that one of the most promising lines of research was employing measures of the refractive power of the eye. In the present paper it is shown that with the advent of the laser optometer technique the promises seem to have come true, promises that were seen 45 years ago:

> Apparently, the interruptions (rest pauses of ten minutes) in close visual work throughout the day were sufficient to prevent an accumulation of the tonus of the ocular muscles. It is conceivable that the time required to dissipate muscular fatigue may eventually prove to be an important datum in the field of ocular hygiene for determining the duration of rest periods. (Luckiesh and Moss 1935.)

The principles of laser optometry are as follows. When the beam from a low-powered laser is reflected from the surface of a slowly rotating drum, and then by means of a shutter and a look-through mirror is projected onto the subject's retina, the subject sees a speckled laser light patch superimposed on the image of the focused view. The speckles appear to stream with or against the direction of rotation of the drum, depending on whether the eye is focused closer or farther than the drum surface. The drum's position can be adjusted until the streaming of the speckles stops or changes direction, thus revealing the conjugate focus of the eye. The speckles are not stimuli in the sense that they really exist, but are merely the result of constructive and destructive interference at the retinal level of the coherent laser light. The important characteristics are (i) that the direction of the speckle motion depends on the refractive state of the eye, and (ii) that the refraction can take place whatever the subject is focusing, or even in the absence of visual objects.

Laser optometry makes it possible to test the hypothesis of a temporary work-induced myopia, i.e. that after a period of taxing visual near work the emmetropic eye would exhibit too much refractive power for distant visual objects. For very close objects, the temporary after-effects could well be the reverse, i.e. that the refractive power has decreased in accordance with the notion of a temporary moving out of the focusing nearpoint after a period of taxing visual near work (Stone 1980).

To some extent the normal eye even in normal conditions shows 'myopia' in distance viewing and 'hyperopia' in near viewing, a levelling-out effect that becomes more pronounced the more unstructured the visual stimulus is and the fewer depth cues it contains. In the dark the focus of the eye adopts an intermediate position, which in one laser optometer study on 220 college students was found to have a mean value of 1·52 diopters equivalent to a focusing distance of 0·66 m (Leibowitz and Owens 1978). The physiological mechanisms and the significance of this 'night myopia' are still under debate even though its existence was reported long ago (Maskelyne 1789, Rayleigh 1883).

4. Accommodation before and after VDU work

The aim of the investigations reported here was to explore the possibilities of using laser optometry in the search for objective criteria of visual fatigue.

4.1. *Methods*

The laser optometer, its construction, calibration and handling, and some of the investigation results, are fully described elsewhere (Östberg and Hedman 1979, Östberg *et al.* 1980). In order to investigate the effects of VDU work on visual accommodation for various stimulus distances as well as in dark conditions, the experimental set-up was as shown in figure 2.

The subject was comfortably seated to allow an unobscured view of the test targets with the right eye at the laser optometer eyepiece. The test targets consisted of well-lit high-quality graphics resolution test charts located at the distances 0·25, 0·33, 0·50, and 1·00 m respectively, but all subtending the same viewing angle as seen from the eyepiece. At 6 m was a test target made up of a large encircled cross. In its centre was an almost invisible small red pilot lamp serving as a sight aligner during the dark focus measurements.

The subject was requested to attempt to discern the finest details of the test target put in the line of sight by the experimenter. By operating a switch the experimenter intermittently superimposed the laser speckles on the subject's retinal image of the test target, whereupon the subject by means of a response box indicated the perceived motion of the speckles: up, down or still. The experimenter could after a few exposures of 0·5–1·0 s each, via a bracketing

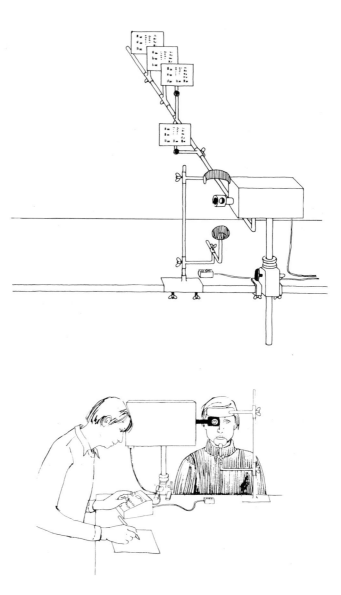

Figure 2. The laser optometer set-up used in the experiments. While the subject is looking at a specified target (top) the experimenter operates the control panel to expose the subject intermittently to brief glimpses of the laser speckles (bottom).

Figure 3. Groups of subjects taking part in the experiment. The ATC group (top) consisted of nine air traffic controllers. The TELE group consisted of 11 sales department clerks (middle) and nine telephone directory operators (bottom).

technique, accurately assess the accommodation adopted by the subject while viewing the test target. Two assessments were made for each target, and the order of presentation of the targets was randomized between and within subjects. A complete test session lasted 15–20 min. Two groups of subjects took part in the experiments (see figure 3).

The *ATC group* consisted of nine subjects (three females and six males) working as air traffic controllers at Luleå Airport. They were between 25 and 40 years old and were highly motivated to take part in the experiments. Each subject was tested immediately before and after two hours of work at a radar screen. One week before the tests, each subject was familiarized with the testing procedure.

The *TELE group* was made up of two subgroups. One subgroup consisted of 11 women performing a mixture of traditional office work and VDU work at a sales department of the Swedish Telecommunications Services. They were between 18 and 32 years old. The second subgroup consisted of nine women working in a pool for telephone directory service. Their ages were between 19 and 50 years. Both subgroups were tested during the first hour at work in the morning and during the last hour at work in the afternoon.

The intention was that the tests on the TELE group should be made during one day with 'less than normal' VDU viewing, and during one day with 'more than normal' VDU viewing. This proved difficult as the work load was dependent on the customers, which in particular meant that on a 'more than normal' day the subjects could have spent very little time viewing the VDU during the half-hour preceding the afternoon tests, and vice versa on a 'less than normal' day. Compared to the ATC group, the two TELE subgroups had far less visually taxing VDU tasks even during busy times.

4.2. Results

The results are presented in separate diagrams for the ATC group and the TELE group (figures 4 and 5). Along the horizontal axis are the stimulus values expressed as the distance from the subject's eye to the test chart, where the diopter value is equal to the inverse value of the distance in metres. Along the vertical axis are the response values as measured by the laser optometer.

A stimulus–response regression line was first calculated for each measurement occasion for each subject. The regression lines shown in the diagrams are the means of such individual regression lines. For perfect accommodation (the identity line) a stimulus distance of 2 dioptres, equal to 0·5 m, should result in a response of 2 dioptres, and so on. A dark focus value is the accommodative response to darkness, which in the diagrams are represented by a stimulus of zero dioptres. Tests for before/after effects were performed with the paired *t*-test; two-tailed for the dark focus values and one-tailed for the regression lines.

The *ATC group* (figure 4) very clearly showed the expected levelling-out effect after the two hours' uninterrupted work spell at the radar screen. For

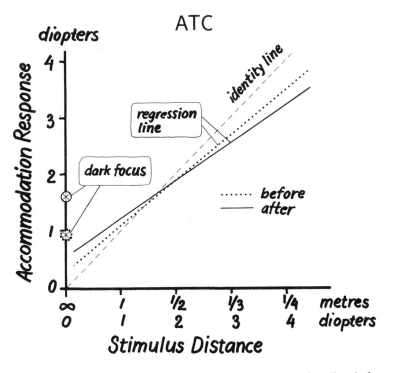

Figure 4. Mean dark focus and mean accommodation regression line before and after two hours' uninterrupted radar screen work for the ATC group. The changes in dark focus and regression line slope are statistically significant.

each single subject the accommodation became more 'myopic' for distant stimuli and more 'hyperopic' for near stimuli, and the difference in slope of the regression lines is highly significant ($p < 0.001$). The changes towards a more 'myopic' dark focus was also safely significant ($p < 0.01$).

The *TELE group* (figure 5) exhibited slope and dark focus changes in the same directions as those of the ATC group, but the changes were less marked and statistically not significant, either for the pooled data of figure 5 or for the two subgroups during the two measurement days. Save for the fact that the TELE group did not have as visually taxing a VDU task as that of the ATC group, it is believed that a contributing factor to the non-significant results is the large variance. The large variance can in turn be explained by (i) lack of pre-tests to make the subjects familiar with the laser optometer, (ii) disturbed and temporarily interrupted measurements due to an instrument breakdown, and (iii) uncorrected astigmatism in some of the subjects, which made the accommodation assessments imprecise. A measure of the total variance is shown by the 95% confidence interval around the mean of the morning regression lines.

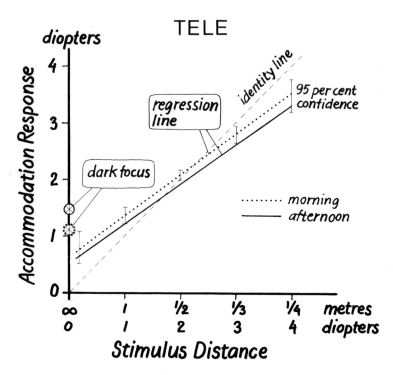

Figure 5. Mean dark focus and mean accommodation regression line before and after a workday involving VDU viewing for the TELE group. Note that the changes in dark focus and regression line slope are similar to those of the ATC group but without being statistically significant.

4.3. *Discussion*

The results confirmed the belief that the laser optometer technique can be used to assess fatigue in the visual accommodation system. In particular it was shown that accommodation levelling-out ('distance myopia' and 'near hyperopia') resulted from a period of work at a visually taxing VDU task, and to some extent also at less taxing VDU tasks.

From the regression lines it can be concluded that a subject's accommodation response is usually correct (no 'distance myopia' and no 'near hyperopia') for a viewing distance of about 0·5–1·0 m, which is a range that also covers the dark focus values. These results were expected and are in line with those of for example Johnson (1976). However, as a result of the visual tasks, the dark focus values changed from 0·94 to 1·62 dioptres (ATC) and from 1·11 to 1·38 dioptres (TELE). Dark focus changes have not been reported in the literature before, and do not quite fit in with the hypothesis of dark focus as a stable "individually characteristic intermediate resting position" (Leibowitz and Owens 1978). At this point it must be stressed that it is not known whether the dark focus and/or point of correct accommodation represents an optimal viewing distance in terms of accommodation strain.

Östberg and Hedman (1979) found no time-of-day effects on accommodation, and Östberg *et al.* (1980) found no effects on accommodation after two busy hours with traditional office work. Both these studies employed very few subjects. Further experiments with a sufficiently large number of subjects of various ages and visual status are obviously needed.

5. Concluding remarks

Trade unions have argued that VDU viewing tasks impose undue strain on the operator's eyes, but employers naturally have been reluctant in signing agreements granting the operators rest-time allowances. In response to the rapid increase in the number of VDU workers, national safety and health bodies are gradually producing information material, recommendations, and, in the case of Sweden, directives.

Research using laser optometry has now shown that there are detectable temporary after-effects from tasks involving VDU-viewing. Laser optometry for measurement of the refractive state of the eye will perhaps become a flourishing research field and will perhaps take over or vitalize the eye movement research domain, a field in which 'The Last Whole Earth Eye Movement Conference' was held in February 1980.

The findings of temporary accommodation after-effects induced by VDU work show that visual fatigue may result from VDU work and that laser optometry is *one* way of objectifying visual fatigue. The visual problems of microscope work and automobile driving are other areas where laser optometry has proved useful. It could well be that temporary after-effects can also be demonstrated after intense book reading (Pheiffer 1955), but such findings do not invalidate the findings of after-effects from VDU reading, rather they indicate that closer attention should be paid to visual fatigue in general (Östberg 1978).

In the view of the present author, we have not advanced very much further from the days of Ramazzini, who 280 years ago wrote on the diseases of printers, sedentary workers, learned men, and those who do fine work:

In printers the tonus of the membranes and fibres of the eye is seriously weakened. Those who sit at the forms and compose may do well to wear spectacles, and now and again they should rub their eyes gently; also bathe them. The affliction in store for those who do fine work, as a result of their craft, is myopia. But it would help such workers very much if besides wearing spectacles they would give up the habit of keeping the head constantly bent and the eyes fixed on what they are making; if they would now and again drop their work and turn their eyes elsewhere or snatch a respite of several hours from their task and rest the eyes by looking at a number of different things. And we know what Plautus says: 'Sitting hurts your loins; staring, your eyes'. (Adapted from Ramazzini 1700.)

Acknowledgment

Financial support was given by the Swedish Work Environment Fund.

References

HÖLLER, H., KUNDI, M., SCHMID, H., STIDL, H. G., THALER, A., and WINTER, N., 1975, *Arbeitsbeanspruchung und Augenbelastung an Bildschirmgeräten* (Vienna: Automationsausschuss der Gewerkschaft der Privatangestellten).

JOHNSON, C. A., 1976, Effects of luminances and stimulus distance on accommodation and visual resolution. *Journal of the Optical Society of America*, **66**, 138–142.

KRUEGER, H., and MÜLLER-LIMMROTH, W., 1979, *Arbeiten mit dem Bildschirm—aber richtig!* (Munich: Bayerischen Staatsministerium für Arbeit und Sozialordnung).

LEIBOWITZ, H. W., and OWENS, D. A., 1978, New evidence for the intermediate position of relaxed accommodation. *Documenta Ophthalmologica*, **46**, 133–147.

LUCKIESH, M., and MOSS, F. K., 1935, Fatigue of convergence induced by reading as a function of illumination. *American Journal of Ophthalmology*, **18**, 319–323.

MASKELYNE, N., 1789, An attempt to explain a difficulty in the theory of vision, depending on the different refrangibility of light. *Philosophical Transactions of the Royal Society of London*, **79**, 256–264.

ÖSTBERG, O., 1976, Review of visual strain, with special reference to microimage reading. Paper read at the International Micrographics Congress, Stockholm, 28–31 September 1976.

ÖSTBERG, O., 1978, Towards standards and threshold limit values for visual work. In *Current Concepts of Ergophthalmology*, edited by B. Tengroth and D. Epstein (Stockholm: Societas Ergophthalmologica Internationalis).

ÖSTBERG, O., 1979, The health debate. *Reprographics Quarterly*, **12**, 80–83.

ÖSTBERG, O., and HEDMAN, L., 1979, *A Field Laser Optometer for Ergonomics of Vision Investigations*, University of Luleå (Sweden) Technical Report, No. 1979: 52T.

ÖSTBERG, O., POWELL, J., and BLOMKVIST, A. C., 1980, *Laser Optometry in Assessment of Visual Fatigue*, University of Luleå (Sweden) Technical Report, No. 1980: 1T.

PHEIFFER, C. H., 1955, Book retinoscopy. *American Journal of Optometry and Archives of American Academy of Optometry*, **32**, 540–545.

RAMAZZINI, B., 1700, *De Morbis Artificum* (*Diseases of Workers*, English edition, New York: Hafner Publishing, 1964).

RAYLEIGH, LORD, 1883. On the visibility of small objects in a bad light. *Proceedings of Cambridge Philological Society*, **4**, 324.

Reading of Display Screens, 1978, Directives No. 136 (In Swedish) (Stockholm: Arbetarskyddsstyrelsen).

STONE, P. T., 1980, Light and the eye at work. *The Ophthalmic Optician*, January 5, 8–13.

VDT-Health Collective Bargaining Kit, 1977 (Washington: The Newspaper Guild).

ZETTERBERG, H. L., 1979, *The Working Life End-users of Computerized Information* (In Swedish) (Stockholm: IBM Svenska AB).

Worker strain related to VDUs with differently coloured characters

By M. HAIDER, M. KUNDI and M. WEIßENBÖCK

Institute of Environmental Hygiene, University of Vienna, Austria

In an experimental setting the differential strain of work on three different VDUs with green and yellow characters has been studied on 13 trained VDU workers; nine office workers served as controls. The usefulness of certain physiological and psychological indicators to characterize the strain on VDU workers is demonstrated. Concerning work with VDUs with green and yellow characters, we found in some indicators no differences at all, while some showed beneficial effects of yellow, and some of green, characters.

Performance showed improvements over the three-hour working period, with a higher rate of improvement for work with yellow characters. Heart rates declined over the working period, but less so for work with yellow characters. The decrease of visual acuity during work (temporary myopization) correlated well with different lengths of working spells and the occurrence of breaks. Furthermore, less temporary myopization occurred for work with yellow characters. Significant differences of colour-contingent after-effects (colour adaptations) betwen VDU workers and controls have been measured by anomaloscope readings for both colours of character. The Müller–Lyer optical illusion was higher after work. This higher amount of illusion persisted longer for VDUs with yellow characters. Gross changes in subjective state and high rates of asthenopic and other symptoms could be observed with no significant differences between VDU work with green and yellow characters.

Sustained VDU work doesn't change visual receptor functions but leads, according to our results, to functional changes in accommodation mechanisms (temporary myopization) and selective colour adaptation processes. Furthermore, prominent changes in the state of well-being could be demonstrated.

1. Introduction

During recent years some field studies of worker strain related to VDUs have appeared (Cakir *et al.* 1978, Haider *et al.* 1975, Hultgren and Knave 1974, Human Factors Center of IBM 1978, Läubli *et al.* 1980, Meyer *et al.* 1978, Östberg 1975, Siemens A G. 1979). Only a few reports included physiological measurements (Laville *et al.* 1980, Östberg 1976). In the first research study of our group (Haider *et al.* 1975) we found clearly demonstrable functional changes of the visual system with experimentally controlled work on VDUs lasting two or four hours. Very characteristic functional changes proved to be a kind of 'temporary myopization' and some colour-contingent after-effects. In the study reported here we include these as well as other physiological and psychological parameters to characterize the worker strain related to VDUs with coloured characters.

2. Methods

In four experimental settings subjects worked during three hours (8.30–11.30 a.m.) on VDUs. Three different CRT terminals were used; two of them had fixed colour of characters (green and yellow respectively) while the third had the possibility of displaying up to 64 different colours, although only two (green and yellow) were used at any one time (see table 1). Thus the experimental design could be viewed as an incomplete 3×2 design with a factor 'colour' having two levels and a factor 'unit type' having three levels. The colours green and yellow were chosen for practical reasons since most VDUs use one of these colours (white was excluded for now from consideration; it will serve in a further stage of experimentation as control setting).

Each subject was tested individually on four days; consecutive sessions were separated by at least one week. The sequence of experimental conditions was balanced with respect to 'colour'. The four working programmes were equal in their structure and no difference in difficulty could be expected; nevertheless, their sequence was rotated so that each programme was presented approximately equally often in each position. The total working time on a VDU for each experimental condition was held constant. It was paced by computer

Table 1†.

VDU number colour	Phosphor	Mean adjusted contrast character– background	Mean adjusted horizontal illumination at working place	Refreshing rate
1 green	P 39	4·2 : 1	342 lx	25 Hz interlaced scan
1 yellow	Mixture of P 39 and a long persistence red	4 : 1	350 lx	25 Hz interlaced scan
2 green	Not specified	4 : 1	352 lx	50 Hz
3 yellow	Mixture of P 4Y and P 22R	3·9 : 1	345 lx	50 Hz

† We wish to express our gratitude to the following companies for their willingness to put a VDU terminal at our disposal: IBM-Austria, Nixdorf Computers, Olivetti, Philips Data Systems, and RS-Tektronix.

(time for instruction and data transfer-time were excluded from calculation of working time). The working time was subdivided into blocks of one hour each. All blocks had the same structure.

Each one-hour block consisted of tasks which had to be solved with or without a source document (referred to as 'screen–screen' and 'copy–screen' tasks). Copy–screen and screen–screen tasks were presented alternately; total working time for these tasks was 25 and 35 min respectively (for a complete description of time arrangement refer to table 2).

Since the main interest of the present study lies in the effects of VDU work on the visual system, activation variables and subjective state, several measurements were taken before, during and after the working periods as follows.

(a) 'Subjective state scaling': we used a questionnaire constructed by Nitsch (1976), which was analysed by means of a hierarchical factor-analysis method (BISTRAN-analysis). The eight factors of the last (third) step are: 'strain', 'social contact', 'social appreciation', 'self-confidence', 'state of mood', 'tension', 'recreation' and 'wakefulness'.

(b) Visual acuity (visus): we used visus-tables with optotypes (numbers, letter E). The reading distance was 4 m. Each eye was tested separately.

(c) Colour-contingent after-effects (chromatic adaptation): we used the anomaloscope to test colour-contingent after-effects. Subjects had to adjust the yellow–blue ratio until subjective equality with the standard yellow was reached, while green and red were fixed at the values of the Rayleigh equation (671 and 546 nm).

(d) Organization of perception: as indicator the amount of optical illusion (Müller–Lyer) was used. The total length of the figure was fixed at 50 cm. The subject could differentially adjust the relation of the two parts until subjective equality was reached.

(e) Subjective scaling of colour perception and vision: subjects were asked to mark their present visual acuity on a continuous scale ranging from 'very good' to 'very poor' and their colour vision on a scale ranging from 'same as always' to 'quite different from usual'.

(f) Activation: during the whole experimental session the ECG was recorded. The heart rate was used as a measure of activation and work strain.

At the end of the session the subjects had to answer a questionnaire with items about asthenopic and other symptoms. The time arrangement of all measurements is demonstrated in table 2.

2.1. *Working room and working place*

A room at the Institute of Environmental Hygiene was adapted for the purpose of this study. Daylight was excluded, and artificial light could be adjusted by the subject between 250 and 500 lx. Before the working programme, work surface and chair were adjusted. The contrast character–background was

Table 2. Experimental procedure.

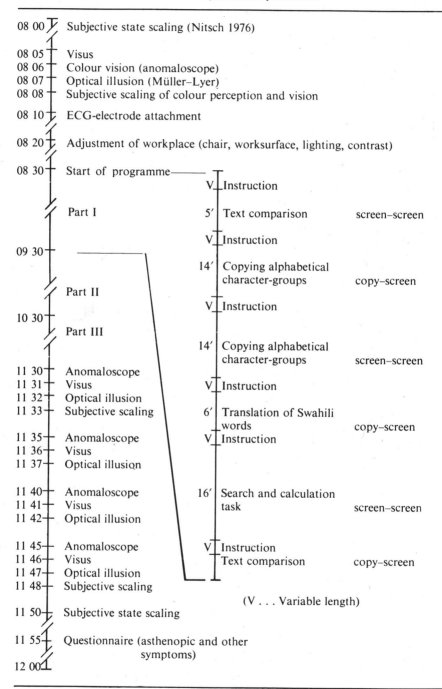

08 00	Subjective state scaling (Nitsch 1976)			
08 05	Visus			
08 06	Colour vision (anomaloscope)			
08 07	Optical illusion (Müller–Lyer)			
08 08	Subjective scaling of colour perception and vision			
08 10	ECG-electrode attachment			
08 20	Adjustment of workplace (chair, worksurface, lighting, contrast)			
08 30	Start of programme	V Instruction		
	Part I	5′ Text comparison	screen–screen	
		V Instruction		
09 30		14′ Copying alphabetical character-groups	copy–screen	
	Part II	V Instruction		
10 30	Part III	14′ Copying alphabetical character-groups	screen–screen	
11 30	Anomaloscope	V Instruction		
11 31	Visus			
11 32	Optical illusion	6′ Translation of Swahili words	copy–screen	
11 33	Subjective scaling	V Instruction		
11 35	Anomaloscope			
11 36	Visus			
11 37	Optical illusion			
11 40	Anomaloscope	16′ Search and calculation task	screen–screen	
11 41	Visus			
11 42	Optical illusion			
11 45	Anomaloscope	V Instruction		
11 46	Visus	Text comparison	copy–screen	
11 47	Optical illusion			
11 48	Subjective scaling			
		(V . . . Variable length)		
11 50	Subjective state scaling			
11 55	Questionnaire (asthenopic and other symptoms)			
12 00				

adjusted too. The subjects performed all adjustments themselves, according to their personal preference.

The mean contrast character–background was 4 : 1 (range : 3 : 1 − 7 : 1) and was nearly the same for all VDUs and character colours. The mean illumination was 350 lx.

2.2. *Subjects*

The experimental group consisted of 13 female volunteers who normally work with VDUs at their factory. The median age was 32 years (range 21–41); six wore spectacles. All subjects had been tested before at the second ophthalmological clinic of the Vienna University (head: Professor H. Slezak) to exclude uncorrected deficiencies. The control group consisted of nine female office workers. The median age was 29 years (range: 23–45); three wore spectacles. Between the measurement periods in the morning (8 a.m.) and noon (11.30 a.m.) they had performed normal office work (mainly typing).

3. Results

3.1. *Performance and activation*

A clear improvement of performance occurs over the three hours of work. As shown in figure 1, there is no overall difference between performance values for green and yellow characters, but an interesting differential effect appears. The values for work with yellow characters are lower at the beginning but higher at the end of the working period than the values for work with green characters. In other words, performance with yellow characters is worse at the beginning but shows a stronger improvement than work with green signs. This interaction is statistically significant, as well as a similar interaction of heart rates. The values for heart rates at corresponding times may be seen in figure 2. Here a similar differential effect appears: heart rates for yellow signs are lower during the first hour of work, but they show less decline during the second and third hour for work with green characters.

3.2. *Changes of visual acuity (temporary myopization)*

We could replicate the results of our first study, that a temporary reduction of visual acuity occurs during sustained work with VDUs. It takes about 10 to 15 min to regain good distant vision after the task of focusing continuously on the nearby screen or copy. There exist statistically significant differences between the two experimental sessions and the controls, who showed practically no change at all. But there are also statistically significant differences between work with green and yellow signs. These differences are demonstrated in figure 3. Yellow characters produce less reduction in visual ability than green ones.

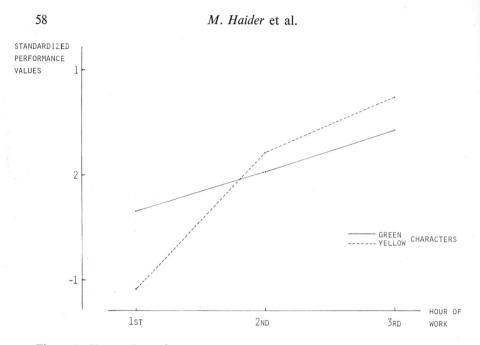

Figure 1. Changes in performance (one-hour means) over the three-hour VDU work
period with green or yellow characters.

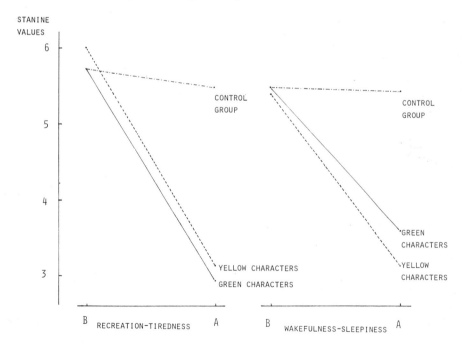

Figure 2. Mean heart-rate changes (one-hour means) over the three-hour VDU work
period with green or yellow characters.

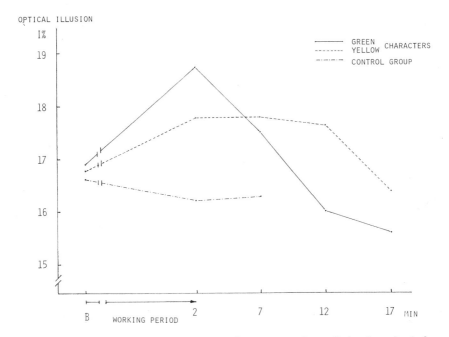

Figure 3. Temporary myopization, expressed as mean values of visual acuity before and after a three-hour working period.

In figure 4 we have combined the results of all our studies for work on different VDUs with green characters. This clearly demonstrates a trend for shorter work periods as well as for periods with breaks to produce less change in visual ability than longer, continuous spells of work. The first one-hour period shows little decline, the second one-hour period, performed after a break, leads to a similar result. A four-hour work period with breaks produces a clear and longer lasting temporary myopization, having a magnitude of about 1/4 diopter. The three-hour continuous work period without breaks (same curve for green characters as in figure 3) shows the strongest effect.

3.3. *Colour-contingent after-effects* (*colour adaptation*)

The anomaloscope values for the two experimental sessions and the control group are shown in figure 5. There are again statistically significant differences between all three situations. Similar to the results for temporary myopization there is slightly less displacement for work with yellow characters than for work with green ones. The values used are the differences between the adjustment to 'subjective equality' before and after work. The values after work show a monotonic return to the baseline, but even 15 min after work the baseline values are not completely restored.

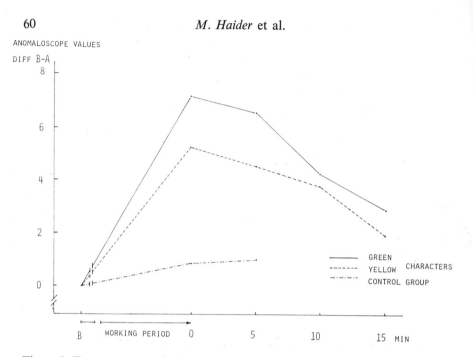

Figure 4. Temporary myopization, expressed as mean values of visual acuity before and after working periods of different length, with and without breaks.

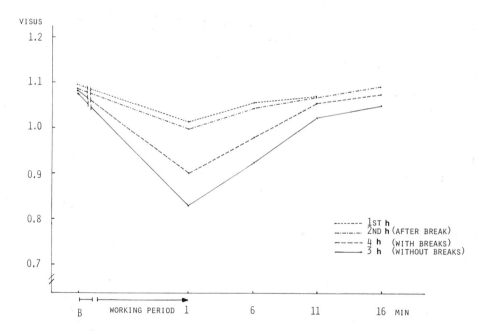

Figure 5. Colour adaptation, expressed as difference of micrometer readings on the anomaloscope before and after a three-hour working period.

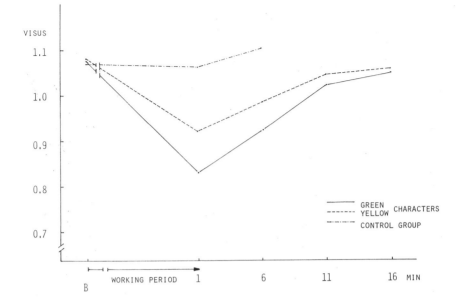

Figure 6. Changes of mean percentáge in optical illusion before and after a three-hour working period.

3.4. *Changes in the Müller–Lyer optical illusion*

The amount of the optical illusion has been expressed as a percentage between 'subjective' and 'objective' equality of the two parts of the line. The changes in this percentage of illusions are seen in figure 6. There is a significantly higher amount of illusion after VDU work, but no significant difference in the overall values for work with green and yellow characters. But the interaction is statistically significant. Work with yellow signs produces at first less change in illusion magnitude than work with green characters. But the change lasts longer after work with yellow signs.

3.5. *Subjective state and symptoms*

From the eight factors of the Nitsch questionnaire on 'subjective state', five factors showed significant changes. Two of them are depicted in figure 7. According to this result the subjects were considerably more tired and sleepy at the end of the continuous three-hour work period with VDUs. This was very clear if compared to the same time period of normal office work, which showed little change. But there was no significant difference between work with green and yellow signs. This statement is also true for the different symptoms, summed up in table 3. It appears in this table that work with yellow characters results in somewhat fewer 'eye symptoms' and somewhat more

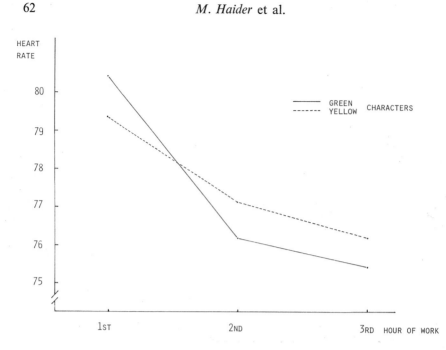

Figure 7. Stanine values of two factors from the Nitsch-questionnaire before (B) and after (A) a three-hour working period.

Table 3. Asthenopic and other symptoms.

	Green %	Yellow %
Eye-twitching	85	69
Sore eyes	69	62
Headache	62	77
Neck-ache	69	62
Backache	69	69
Arm-ache	54	54

complaints about headache, but these results are not statistically significant. The percentage of asthenopic and other symptoms is rather high, showing that our experimentally produced work on the VDU was obviously strenuous.

4. Discussion

The differential strain of work on VDUs with differently coloured signs may be expressed by changes of general performance and physiological parameters, by parameters characterizing strain of the visual system, or by changes in subjective state scaling and the appearance of asthenopic and other systems.

In many of these parameters we found differential changes, but most of them are small and some changes are difficult to interpret.

We used green and yellow characters because the deficiencies of the optic system (chromatic aberrations, etc.) do not play an important role for these colours and they are therefore most likely to be used in VDU work. Performance and heart rate showed some characteristic differential effects: performance with yellow VDU-signs was more improved during the second and third hour of work, and at the same times the heart rate showed less decline. It has to be mentioned that so far all subjects had worked on VDUs in industry with green characters. Therefore green signs were familiar to them and yellow signs unfamiliar. This may explain the rather bad performance with yellow signs at the beginning. The improvement during the second and third hour corresponds to 'higher activation', characterized by higher heart rates. Whether this has to do with yellow colour as 'activating' as opposed to green as 'relaxing', or again with 'novelty' of yellow or with changes in strain and sitting position, has yet to be clarified.

The changes in visual acuity which we found in all our studies signify a 'temporary myopization', probably due to the accommodation strain. This interpretation is supported by results of Östberg (1980) demonstrating changes in the direction of myopization for far vision. Such methods are obviously quite reliable to show differences in the strain of VDU workers with different lengths of work and with the occurrence of breaks. It could be used as one of the leading parameters in planning and evaluation of different length of work periods with VDUs and of optimal work–rest schedules. Work with yellow characters produced less change in visual ability, that is, less temporary myopization. This may be one reason to recommend a more widespread use of yellow characters in future work with VDUs. Generally it may be stated that both colours are recommendable from a psychophysiological point of view.

The colour-contingent after-effects may be interpreted as some kind of 'chromatic adaptation'. But obviously it is a complex phenomenon, because the time course of such contingent adaptations may be of the order of many minutes (as our mean values) but may also be of the order of hours or even days, as some complaints of workers show. Obviously these phenomena are an expression of the complex neural system, including lateral geniculate and visual cortex, which extracts and evaluates the 'colour specific information'. It may even be that these 'contingent after-effects' have more in common with perceptual learning or conditioning than with simple neural adaptations. There is no question that longer lasting specific colour adaptations occur after prolonged work with coloured VDU signs. We have seen it with different kinds of VDUs, with two different measuring devices (Helmholtz apparatus and anomaloscope) and with two different colours of characters (green and yellow).

Optical illusions were sometimes used as a criterion measure for general fatigue. It was hypothesized that fatigue is accompanied by an impairment of perceptional organization. However, the results were contradictory. Our results seem to show that there may still be a relation between 'visual fatigue' and amount of optical illusion, even if no clear relation between 'general fatigue' and amount of illusion could be established.

That the changes in subjective state and the amount of asthenopic and other symptoms is rather high has also been found in field studies with larger populations (Läubli *et al.* 1980). This demonstrates that besides functional changes in the visual system and other physiological parameters there are important changes in the whole state of well-being after intense prolonged work with VDUs.

Acknowledgments

This study was financially supported by the Austrian Gewerkschaft der Privatangestellten.

We thank Dipl. Ing. Fred Margulies for his valuable help.

References

CAKIR, A., REUTER, H.-J., VON SCHMUDE, L., and ARMBRUSTER, A., 1978, Untersuchungen zur Anpassung von Bildschirmarbeitsplätzen an die physische und psychische Funktionsweise des Menschen. *Forschungsbericht der Humanisierung des Arbeitslebens*. (Bonn: Der Bundesminister für Arbeit und Sozialordnung).

HAIDER, M., SLEZAK, H., HÖLLER, H., KUNDI, M., SCHMID, H., STIDL, H. G., THALER, A., and WINTER, N., 1975, *Arbeitsbeanspruchung und Augenbelastung an Bildschirmgeräten* (Wien: Vlg. des Ö.G.B., Automatisationsausschuß der Gewerkschaft der Privatangestellten).

HULTGREN, G. V., and KNAVE, B., 1974, Discomfort glare and disturbances from light reflections in an office landscape with CRT display terminals. *Applied Ergonomics*, **5**, 2–8.

HUMAN FACTORS CENTER OF IBM CORPORATION (U.S.A.), 1978, Ergonomische Faktoren der Bildschirmarbeit. Übersetzung der IBM Form G 320-6102-0, IBM Deutschland GmbH.

LÄUBLI, TH., HÜNTING, W., and GRANDJEAN, E., 1980, Visual impairments in VDU operators related to environmental conditions. *Ergonomic Aspects of Visual Display Terminals* (this volume), p. 85.

LAVILLE, A., TEIGER, C., LANTIN, G., and DESSORS, D., 1980, Quelques caractéristiques de la fatigue visuelle provoquée par le travailde détection sur microfiches. *Travail Humain* (in the press).

MEYER, J. J., REY, P., KOROL, S., and GRAMONI, R., 1978, La fatigue oculaire engendrée par travail sur écrans de visualisation, *Sozial- und Präventiv-medizin*, **23**, 295–296.

NITSCH, J. R., 1976, Die Eigenzustandsskala (EZ-Skala).—Ein Verfahren zur hierarchisch-mehrdimensionalen Befindlichkeitsskalierung. In *Training und Beanspruchung*, edited by J. R. Nitsch and I. Udris (Bad Homburg: Limpert).

ÖSTBERG, O., 1975, Health problems for operators working with CRT displays. *International Journal of Occupational Health and Safety*, Nov./Dec. 24–52.

ÖSTBERG, O., 1976, Review of visual strain, with special reference to microimage reading. *Transactions of the International Micrographics Congress*, Stockholm 28–30 Sept.

ÖSTBERG, O., 1980, *Laser Optometry in Assessment of Visual Fatigue*. Technical report 1T (Department of Human Work Sciences, University of Luleå).

SIEMENS A. G. (Berlin und München), 1979, *Ergonomie am Bildschirmarbeitsplatz*. ZT-ZFO-FWO (Erlangen: Ang. Arbeitswissenschaften).

Dioptric problems in connection with
luminance–brightness relationship on VDUs

By Lucia R. Ronchi

National Institute of Optics, 6, Largo Fermi, 50125 Florence, Italy

and

G. Cicchella

Department of Preventive Medicine of Occupational Disease,
University of Florence, Largo Palagi, 1, 50139 Florence, Italy

The luminance–brightness discrepancy is estimated by comparing the target appearing on a green display to a white reference target lit by A-illuminant. The dependence on target size is investigated. Variability between individuals is also reported. Some practical implications are suggested.

1. Basis of the problem

The photometric assessment of visual displays relies upon data gathered by means of non-visual or visual photometers. Data recorded in the former case are free from peculiar problems, provided the kind of instrument used is adequately specified. This is also the case for visual flicker photometry. On the other hand, the data recorded by a visual instrument based on simultaneous brightness match suffer from the so-called luminance–brightness discrepancy (Kaiser 1971, Kaiser et al. 1971, Padgham 1971, Wagner and Boynton 1972). Luminance (L), the photometric analogy of radiance (L_e) is defined by the equation:

$$L = K_m \int V_\lambda L_e \, d\lambda$$

where K_m is a constant depending on the units in which L and L_e are measured, λ is the wavelength and V_λ is the standard relative photopic luminous efficiency function. Classically speaking, the task of a photometrist consists in equating the brightness of two half-fields. One of these, lit by the calibrated source within the instrument, is 'white'. The test half-field hue depends on the phosphor used on the display. In general, two heterochromatic fields matched in brightness differ in luminance. If they are equated in luminance, they differ in brightness, since monochromatic stimuli look brighter than white ones of matched luminance. The amount of the discrepancy depends on several factors, such as dominant wavelength, saturation and size of the test field. The discrepancy is the smaller, the more unsaturated is the stimulus (Kaiser *et al.* 1971), irrespective of whether desaturation is due to the relative white content or to the peculiar test field size (so reduced that small field desaturation takes place, or so large that rod intrusion occurs).

In order to have an idea of the amount of the luminance–brightness discrepancy in the case of visual display units, we performed the experiment described in this paper.

2. Materials and method

The observer was requested to match the brightness of a green target on the display of an Interactive Display System (Olivetti TCV 270) to that of a white field lit by an A-illuminant. The luminance of the latter was varied in small steps (0·1 log units) across a pre-established range. The equi-brightness condition was estimated (in terms of liminal density of neutral Wratten filters attenuating the white beam), through the constant stimuli method, by applying probit analysis (Finney 1962). Next, the luminance of either stimulus was measured by means of an EG.G Photometer–Radiometer System (Mod. 450).

Some sessions were devoted to a point-like target subtending 2·5 min of arc at the eye. For this, an opaque screen, in which a pinhole was pierced, was applied on the display. The white source was of the same size. The observer saw two bright points, 40 min of arc far apart from one another, on a dark background, surrounded by a white extended field, 1 cd/m² luminance. The viewing distance was 1 m.

Other sessions were devoted to a streak-like target (capital I). By varying the viewing distance from 1·8 m to 1·0 m, the visual angle subtended by either side of the target passes from 1·8 by 7·4 to 3·3 by 13·3 min of arc. The white target of variable luminance was of the same size, the distance between the two targets being 40 min of arc in every case.

To obtain targets larger than those above, a grating-like full display signal was switched on; next it was suitably defocused to destroy the bright–dark transitions, and to render the test field as uniform as possible. The green and the white stimuli to be matched in brightness were now contiguous, in the form of a bipartite photometric field, subtending at the eye 3·5 degrees in some sessions, 7 degrees in others.

Twelve highly experienced normal observers, with good colour discrimination (as revealed by F-M 100-Hue Test), took part in ten sessions each. Some of them had recently been taking part in an experiment on brightness–luminance discrepancy for LED sources (Ronchi *et al.* 1980). Their ages ranged from 26 to 52 years.

3. Experimental findings

We assume as a measure of luminance–brightness discrepancy the ratio of white to green target luminances (w/g) at the brightness match. Quantity w/g is then plotted versus stimulus size, as shown in figures 1(*a*) to (*c*). In agreement with expectation, w/g is found to be relatively low for both small and large targets. For the sake of reference, we produce in table 1 the luminance–brightness discrepancies computed by the use of Sanders and Wyszecki's (1958) formula for large (10°) fields.

Observers to whom figure 1(*a*) refers exhibit the smaller luminance–brightness discrepancy, and their responses seem to be reasonably acceptable. Figure 1(*b*) shows the responses of the observer who exhibits the largest luminance–brightness discrepancy. By manipulating her dioptric correction, within a range of 2 dioptres, the w/g ratio is found to vary across the displayed bars. Figure 1(*c*) shows the w/g average and standard deviation estimated across the whole sample of twelve observers.

Lastly, let us report a simple situation which can be frequently met in everyday practice.

We measured the luminance of our green display, at a fixed setting of the knob controlling the luminance, by means of three different tools: a photoelectric photometer (Autospot 1°, Minolta) gave 10 ft L (hence, 34·26 cd/m^2). Similarly, the EG.G power meter gave 34·0 cd/m^2. When using a visual photometer (Schmidt and Haensch P 638), where the observer has to match the brightnesses of the two halves of a bipartite 7 degree diameter field of different hues (white and green, respectively), strong individual differences are noticed,

Table 1.

Screen type	Colour		Luminance–brightness discrepancy, calculated for a 10 degree field
	Fluorescence	Phosphorescence	
BA	purplish-blue	—	1·74
BE	blue	id.	1·41
BF	purplish-blue	—	1·45
GH	green	id.	1·39–1·41
GJ	yellowish-green	id.	2·57
GM	purplish-blue	yellowish-green	1·67–0·87
GP	bluish-green	green	1·33
GR	green	id.	2·75
GU	white	id.	1·02
LA	orange	id.	1·42
LB	orange	id.	1·43
LC	orange	id.	1·58
W	white	—	1·099
W	white	—	1·04
YA	yellowish-orange	id.	1·28

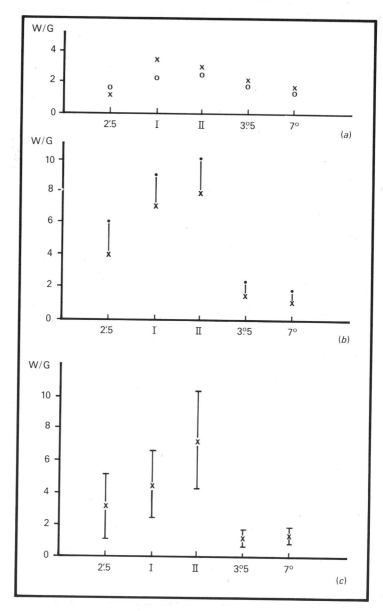

Figure 1. Ordinates: luminance–brightness discrepancy, as defined in the text. Abscissae: the target used, on an arbitrary scale; 2·5 min of arc pinhole; capital I viewed from different distances (I, 1·8 m; II, 1·0 m); bipartite fields subtending 3·5° and 7° of visual angle. (*a*) Data from two observers showing the minimum discrepancy; (*b*) data from the observer showing the maximum discrepancy; bars denote the range of variability by manipulating her dioptric correction; (*c*) average and standard deviation across the whole sample of twelve observers.

as is shown in table 2. The corresponding w/g ratio is shown in the fourth column. Of course, the engineer relies upon the response of photoelectric photometers. On the other hand, the ergonomist is interested in visual responses, that is, in brightnesses, which are supposedly related to behaviour. Contrary to earlier beliefs, it is now known that luminance–brightness discrepancy and its individual variability, are neither due simply to the confusion of brightness with saturation, nor mere artifacts intrinsic to the difficulty involved by the heterochromatic match.

We have tentatively investigated the factors responsible for individual variability, by attending to the changes in eye transmission factor with age. The calculated effects are found to be much smaller than those experimentally observed, in agreement with Smith *et al.*'s (1976) conclusion that "no single variable is sufficient to explain the inter-observer variability".

Table 2.

Observer	Age	Reading on the visual photometer scale (cd/m^2)	Estimated w/g
TG	26	36·8	1·08
FOT	26	3·5	0·11
GF	26	13·6	0·40
MN	28	34·4	1·01
GIU	30	40·0	1·18
SIM	30	52·8	1·55
MAN	35	17·6	0·52
CIN	35	8·8	0·26
RM	37	64·8	1·90
SF	39	40·0	1·18
GC	50	45·0	1·32
LRR	52	48·0	1·41

4. Practical implications

One of the problems the ergonomist is faced with (Grandjean 1979, Östberg 1979) is the optimization of eye–display distance. For this, fine adjustments of accommodation of the lens of the eye are of primary importance. In the case where two or more different hues are simultaneously present on the display, the question arises which is the wavelength focused on the retina. Because of eye chromatic aberration, there are various possibilities. According to the task demand, the selection relies either upon the economy of accommodation effort (Ivanoff 1953) or on the maximum sensitivity (at 555 nm, in photopic vision). By considering the findings of the present experiment, one might wonder whether, in some cases at least, accommodation on a multi-coloured *equiluminous* display is dictated by the brightness sensation, that is, the image focused on the retina is that which appears brightest.

References

FINNEY, D. H., 1962, *Probit Analysis* (Cambridge: Cambridge University Press).

GRANDJEAN, E., 1979, *Arbeitsmedizinische und ergonomische Probleme der Arbeit an Bildschirmgeräten* (Zürich: ETH-Zentrum).

IVANOFF, A., 1953, *Les Aberrations de l'Oeil* (Paris: Ed. de la Rev. d'Opt.).

KAISER, P. K., 1971, Luminance and brightness. *Applied Optics*, **10**, 2768–2770.

KAISER, P. K., BOYNTON, R. M., and HERZBERG, P. A., 1971, Chromatic border distinctness and its relation to saturation. *Vision Research*, **11**, 953–968.

ÖSTBERG, O., 1979, The Health Debate, Second International Word Processing Convention (London, 2–3 May).

PADGHAM, C. A., 1971, The direct estimation of luminosity of coloured light sources. *Vision Research*, **11**, 577–590.

RONCHI, L., MACII, R., STEFANACCI, S., and BASSAN, M., 1980, Brightness and luminance for light emitting diodes. Influence of size and defocus. *Colour Research and Application* (in the press).

SANDERS, C. L., and WYSZECKI, G., 1958, L/Y ratios in terms of CIE chromaticity coordinates. *Journal of the Optical Society of America*, **48**, 389–392.

SMITH, C. V., POKORNY, J., and STARR, S. J., 1976. Variability of color mixture data. I. Inter-observer variability in the unit coordinates. *Vision Research*, **16**, 1087–1094.

WAGNER, G., and BOYNTON, R. M., 1972, Comparison of four methods of heterochromatic photometry. *Journal of the Optical Society of America*, **62**, 1508–1515.

SMITH, C. V., POKORNY, J., and STARR, S. J., 1976, Variability of color mixture data. I. Inter-observer variability in the unit coordinates. *Vision Research*, **16**, 1087–1094.

WAGNER, G., and BOYNTON, R. M., 1972, Comparison of four methods of heterochromatic photometry. *Journal of the Optical Society of America*, **62**, 1508–1515.

Tasks involving contrast resolution, spatial and temporal resolution presented on VDU screen as a measuring technique of visual fatigue

By J. W. H. Kalsbeek and F. W. Umbach

Ergonomics Technology Foundation, c/o Department of Electrical Engineering, Twente Technology University, P.O. Box 217, 7500 AE Enschede, The Netherlands

Whether visual fatigue as an effect of prolonged VDU reading could be measured by ophthalmic tests is not yet solved. In order to do large scale investigations under practical conditions without the intervention of medical specialists an instrument has been developed which allows subjects to be tested at predetermined intervals by presentations on their own VDU screen to which they answer using their own keyboards. Intrinsic properties of CRTs and of the way in which pictures are generated are used to realize tests measuring contrast resolution, spatial resolution and temporal resolution.

1. Introduction

The question of whether there are reversible and irreversible effects of prolonged VDU reading which can be measured by ophthalmic tests is not yet solved. Nevertheless, occupational health specialists are directed by management to screen future VDU users, and unions plead for a regular check up of visual faculties.

So on the one hand there is a pressure to test visual capacities of large numbers of persons. This causes an organizational burden, while often instruments are used of which the applicability to the problem is not clear. On the other hand there is a need to validate vision test instruments in practice on a large population of users. Such large-scale operations call for investigation methods which are easily applied and do not need the intervention of specialists or even test-assistants. In order to create such measuring methods, we have begun to convert classical ophthalmic tests into presentations on VDU screen. Also new ophthalmic tests which hypothetically will fit better the problem of visual fatigue are in preparation. These tests can be applied under normal working conditions on the worker's own VDU at predetermined intervals of hours or days.

The eye-test device that will be described here (patent applied for) differs from classical ophthalmic test instruments in that it is realized by means of a VDU. Some intrinsic properties of CRTs and of the way in which pictures are generated on a VDU are used to realize the tests performed by this device. By its special nature, with this test-device three new opportunities arise. Firstly, because in principle each VDU can be used for this test, the tests can be presented (as an interrupt procedure) on the VDU at which a person is working while he is performing this task. Secondly, because the tests act upon some other properties of the human visual system than do classical ophthalmic tests, new forms of test procedures can be realized. Thirdly, the tests are performed fully automatically. There is no need for a test-assistant and the test data can automatically be handled.

The device can test the following three vision qualities:

(i) The contrast resolution;
(ii) The spatial resolution;
(iii) The temporal resolution.

2. Principle of the tests

The principle of all our tests is that the subject has to recognize characters in a background, like in the Ishahara tests, which distinguish from the background by a different pictorial construction. The intensity of the character increases gradually step by step so that the level of intensity at which the character is recognized can be used as a measure of the quality of the subject's ability on a certain vision property. The characters are randomly chosen by the device from an alphabet; see figure 1.

The screen is divided into an upper part and a lower part. In the upper part the instructions to the test subject are presented, whereas the test picture forms the lower part. The subject responds via his own keyboard by typing in the

Figure 1. Eye test device realized by means of a VDU. The screen is divided into an upper part presenting the instruction to the subject and a lower part showing the test picture.

recognized character. The device compares the answer with the presented character. If the answer is correct, the test stops and the following test starts. If the answer is not correct, the intensity of the character is further increased until a good answer is given.

The results of each test are handled by the device in several possible ways. They can be presented on the VDU after all test items have finished. They can also be stored for later retrieval or sent to a central computer. It is also possible to secure the results against illegal use by constructing the need for a password for output of the data.

All functions of the device are under control of a microprocessor.

3. The contrast resolution test

The contrast resolution test is performed by giving those pixels (elementary picture elements) which belong to the character a brightness different from the brightness of the background, as depicted in figure 2. The total brightness scale has 1024 steps. So if the background is given a brightness corresponding to for instance 512, the character is given in successive stages brightnesses

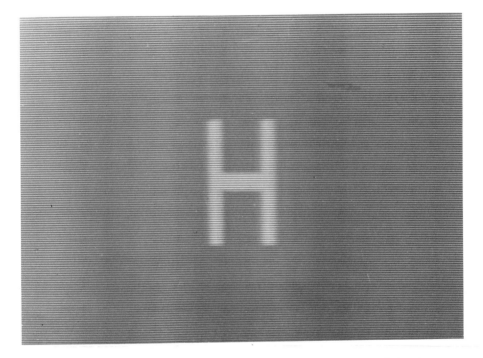

Figure 2. Test picture in the form of a character H. The brightness of the character increases step by step. The level of intensity at which the character is recognized is used as a measure. The size of the character is 4 cm.

corresponding to 512 plus 1, 2, 3 and so on. The time that each step lasts is chosen such that normal response time of the subjects causes only small errors in the measurement. Otherwise the duration of the steps should not be too long. To make the test reproducible, it is (according to Weber's law; see figure 3) necessary that there is a fixed relation between the level of the background brightness and the brightness differences. For Weber's law to hold, the overall luminance should be higher than 100 cd/m². As TV screens have luminances ranging between 100 and 1000 cd/m², this condition can be satisfied.

4. The spatial resolution test

The usual way of measuring the threshold of spatial resolution of the eye is to increase the number of lines per cm in a picture, until they are no longer resolved as separate lines. The lines have a constant brightness difference from the background. However, because there is a relation between brightness modulation depth and spatial resolution at threshold (see figure 4), the measurement can be done in a different way. Instead of changing the number of lines per cm, we can also increase, at a fixed number of lines, the brightness modulation.

With the aid of a VDU, the last method is technically far more easy to realize because we can make use of the property that a VDU picture is composed of horizontal lines. On a 12 inch screen we have, with no interlacing, about 15 lines per cm. With sufficient brightness for Weber's law to hold, the threshold brightness modulation then is about 1%; see figure 3. The threshold level is measured by increasing the modulation depth from zero up until the character is recognized.

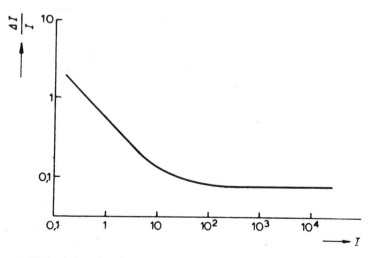

Figure 3. Weber's law showing that a fixed relation is necessary between the level of the background and the brightness differences. Overall luminance should be higher than 100 cd/m².

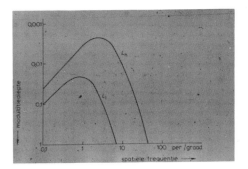

Figure 4. Curves showing the relation between brightness modulation depth and spatial resolution at threshold. Because of this relation, the threshold of spatial resolution of the eye can be measured by increasing the brightness modulation at a fixed number of lines instead of changing the number of lines per cm at a constant brightness difference from the background.

Figure 5. Test picture in the form of a character N. The character is composed of successive more and less bright lines while all the lines of the background have the same brightness.

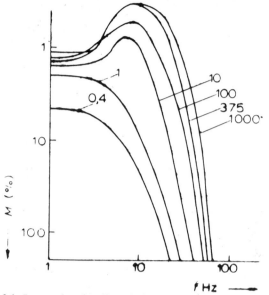

Figure 6. Curve of de Lange showing the relation between the frequency of a flickering light source and the brightness modulation depth needed to resolve the source as a non-steady one.

5. The temporal resolution test

In figure 6 the relation is shown between the frequency of a flickering light source and the brightness modulation depth needed to resolve the source as a non-steady one (Curve of de Lange). The frequency at which, even at 100% modulation, no flicker is recognized is called the critical flicker fusion frequency (CFF). The temporal resolution of the eye normally is measured by determining the CFF of a subject.

Because of the fixed 50 Hz repetition rate of TV frames, it is very difficult to do this kind of measurement by means of a VDU. A simple method, however, is to measure some distinct points of the curve, namely at 25, 12·5, and 6·25 Hz because these are subharmonics of the frame repetition frequency. To make the display test-character flickering at for instance 25 Hz, we simply let the brightness be high in one frame and low in the next frame. For flickering at 12·5 Hz, we use two successive high brightness frames and two low brightness frames. For 6·25 Hz it is four and four. In this way we can measure some samples of the curve of de Lange. The measurement is done by increasing at one of the distinct frequencies, the brightness modulation from zero per cent on.

There is one difference with the precise definition of the measurements for de Lange curve, because here the modulation is not sinusoidal. However, this need not be a cause of errors, because it is possible to design special waveforms of intensity modulation, such that the harmonics of the principle frequency are either weak or higher than 50 Hz.

Section 3.   Visual impairments

Visual impairments and their objective correlates

By P. Rey and J. J. Meyer

Institute of Social and Preventive Medicine, University of Geneva,
Geneva, Switzerland

Results of field studies showed that VDU operators complain more
of visual fatigue and asthenopia than any other group of workers of the
same age. This difference is due to the high level of visual requirement
which characterizes VDU. When operators accumulated visual defects,
they complained more of visual fatigue. To demonstrate this relationship,
however, requires other techniques than routine clinical tests and testing
with sight-screeners. A new apparatus is described which allows the
observer to simulate his working conditions. It can be applied to the
training of the operator in using controls at his workplace or to define,
according to individual visual difficulties, the most appropriate design of
workplace.

1. Introduction

One of the challenges for ergonomists is to understand why VDU operators
complain more than other workers of visual discomfort and fatigue. The aim
of this paper is to show that part of the answer can be found in developing
new tests and new apparatus which would allow the simulation of real working
situations.

2. Method

2.1. *Field studies*

Groups at risk and controls. In all, 312 operators were examined, of whom
211 were between 18 and 35 years of age, and 101 between 36 and 65 years of age.
Three types of workplace were studied:

(*a*) visual display units;
(*b*) other workplaces characterized by high visual strain (engraving, scanning
and watch-making);
(*c*) clerical work.

Appraisal of complaints. Employees were required to express through questionnaires

(*a*) their general feelings of discomfort;

(*b*) their symptoms of visual fatigue at the end of the working day.

(*c*) Their signs of asthenopia (burning, tingling, redness of the eyes, ocular pain, frontal pain, etc.) were checked by direct observation.

Objectivation of visual impairments. Several tests were applied: far and near visual acuity (measured with a sight-screener), near point for accommodation and binocular vision (measured with the near point rule of Clement and Clark), brightness discrimination and resistance to glare (measured with a Mesopto-meter Oculus), flicker-fusion thresholds (measured with a Richez–Meyer Stimulator using modulated light); eye equilibrium was determined with a wing of Maddox.

We called 'disabled' those subjects whose performance was below two standard deviations from the mean performance of young normal subjects (up to 25 years of age), which means: far visual acuity inferior to 9/10; near visual acuity inferior to 10/10; near point for accommodation equal to or over 20 cm; near point for binocular vision equal or superior to 13 cm; hetero-phoria was admitted for a value equal or superior to 6 prismatic dioptres (Rey *et al.* 1974, Meyer *et al.* 1975, 1978, 1979 a).

3. Results of field studies

Complaints appeared to be more frequent among VDU operators than any other group of workers. The lowest proportion of complaints was found in the group of clerical workers. One can ask whether such a difference would be due to age. In fact, a similar prevalence of complaints was discovered in both younger and older workers. Moreover, VDU operators complained more often of visual impairment than other operators of the same age (figure 1).

The effect of work duration on complaints is quite obvious in VDU operators. Let us emphasize that the figure of 75% of complaints in VDU operators working 6 to 9 hours in front of the screen, although very high, is nevertheless quite commonly observed (figure 1).

The second question to be raised is whether the increase of complaints of VDU operators would be due to an excess of eye defects in this particular group. From figure 1, we can conclude that it is not. The proportion of visual defects, as defined under 'Method', is as high in VDU operators as it is in the other group of workers of the same age. It is important to compare operators of the same age, since ageing increases visual defects. In other words, the com-parison we made between groups of workers and within VDU operators on effect of work duration was perfectly valid and we can conclude that the higher frequency of complaints among VDU operators is not due to some selective process but to the higher visual stress.

VDU operators demonstrated an increase in complaints in parallel with increase in severity of eye troubles. This relationship is significant only in the older age group, as shown in tables 1 and 2. However, the borderline between the older and the younger age groups is very low indeed, and most operators of the older group have not yet consulted an ophthalmologist.

Thus we recommend research workers to avoid mixing very young subjects with older ones, since such a mixture could hide part of the visual difficulties encountered by older operators.

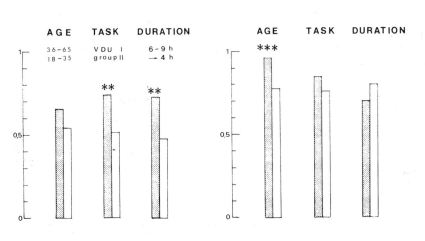

** $p < 0.005$ *** $p = 0.001$

Figure 1. On the left side: proportion of visual complaints for all groups as a function of age, as a function of the task (VDU operators versus other workers), in VDU operators, as a function of the work duration. On the right side: proportion of visual defects as a function of age (all groups), as a function of the task (VDU operators versus other groups), in VDU operators, as a function of the work duration.

Table 1. Number and proportion of complaints in VDU operators according to the level of visual disturbances (brightness discrimination, sensitivity to glare and flicker perception). Age group: 36 to 60 years of age.

	Level of visual disturbances			
Complaints	0	+	+ +	Total
+	18	22	16	56
—	19	13	2	34
Total	37	35	18	90
%	48·6	62·8	88·9	62·2

$\chi^2 = 8.35$, $p \ll 0.05$.

Table 2. Number and proportion of complaints in VDU operators as a function of visual acuity. Age group: 36 to 60 years of age.

Complaints	Visual acuity			
	Good	Poor	Very poor	Total
+	26	18	11	55
—	28	10	2	40
Total	54	28	13	95
%	48·1	64·3	84·6	57·9

$$\chi^2 = 12\cdot0, \ p < 0\cdot01.$$

4. Results of laboratory experiments

Laboratory experiments simulating the visual requirements at VDUs are necessary in order to objectify the visual impairments of VDU operators.

Figure 2 refers to an experimental set-up in which the blinking rate is recorded with strain gauges located at the corner of the eye. Visual fatigue is produced by having the subject watch a TV screen and perform a difficult

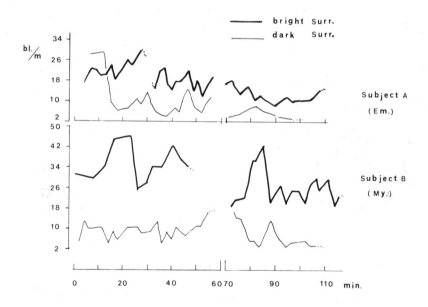

Figure 2. Blinking rate (per minute) as a function of working time for two subjects (one emmetropic and one myopic subject) and two illumination levels: upper curves, bright surfaces surrounding the TV screen, lower curves, dark background surfaces surrounding the TV screen. ——, bright surround; ——, dark surround.

visual task. Two conditions are compared: when the TV screen surrounding is brightly illuminated, and the reverse condition, in which the TV screen is surrounded by darkness. The difference is more pronounced in the myopic eye.

We developed, in our laboratory, a new apparatus (C 45) which gives the subject the opportunity of adjusting a certain number of physical parameters in order to check his own ability in recognizing the gap of a Landolt ring.

First, the observer is able to select the most comfortable distance between his eye and the test object on a continuous scale, the relative size of the object remaining constant. Secondly, the observer is able to reproduce his working conditions; the background luminance as well as the surrounding luminances are adjustable (figure 3). Then, watching the Landolt ring, the observer can adjust the luminance of the test to reach a determined visual acuity, or measure his visual acuity for a given luminance of the test object.

In table 3, four observed conditions are given. Luminances were measured at workplaces with a telephotometer. It is very striking that VDU operators, even though they are working in the same company and in the same room, may be located in very diverse ambient illumination and use their controls in many different ways (Meyer *et al.* 1979 b).

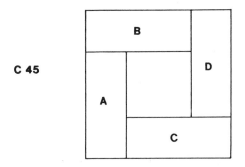

Figure 3. The visual field in the C 45 apparatus.

Table 3. Four workplaces are described in terms of luminance levels before being simulated in a new apparatus called C 45.

Work-place	Screen mean luminance (cd/m²)	A cd/m²	B cd/m²	C cd/m²	D cd/m²
1	1	10	10	10	80
2	1	500	500	500	500
3	9	10	10	10	10
4	9	100	500	500	500

P. Rey and J. J. Meyer

Figure 4 shows that the curves relating the level of recognition of the Landolt ring and the brightness of the test are not superimposed in the four simulated conditions of table 3. The shift between curves is very important indeed. It is also noticeable that the increased brightness of the test object is less and less effective. With this example we should like to demonstrate the possible uses of the apparatus C 45.

The VDU operator can be trained using the controls that he has at his disposal at his own workplace. Easy comparisons can be made between different luminance relationships in order to select the most appropriate. Comparisons can also be made very easily and very quickly between individuals, in order to modify the design of the workplaces taking into account differences between individuals in sensitivity. This instrument can also be applied to the study of visual fatigue taking into account the influence of ageing, correction with glasses, and so on. To summarize, this apparatus is useful in the laboratory but still more so at the workplace.

From our field studies, it is clear that visual impairment in VDU operators is partly related to visual defects. However, one should bear in mind that routine clinical tests are not sufficient since they do not explore brightness discrimination and resistance to glare. Moreover, visual testing should not be used to select good or bad eyes but to adapt the working environment and the visual task to the eye capabilities. In short, our purpose is not selection but ergonomics.

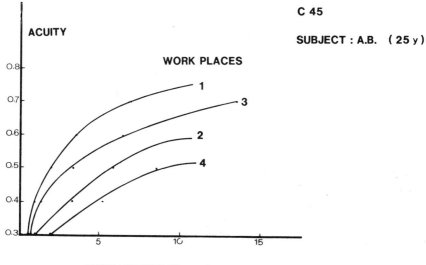

Figure 4. Results obtained with the prototype C 45. Increase of visual acuity as a function of the luminance of a Landolt ring, for the four brightness conditions described in figure 3.

References

MEYER, J. J., KOROL, S., and BABEL, J., 1975, Exploration fonctionnelle des régions rétiniennes maculaires et périmaculaires au moyen de l'ERG de papillotement et détermination des seuils de fusion perceptive d'une lumière intermittente (courbe de de Lange). *Archives d'ophthalmologie*, **35**/3.

MEYER, J. J., KOROL, S., GRAMONI, R., and TUPLING, R., 1978, Psychophysical flicker thresholds and ERG flicker responses in congenital and acquired vision deficiencies. *Modern Problems in Ophthalmology*, **19**, 33–49 (Basel: Karger).

MEYER, J. J., REY, P., KOROL, S., and GRAMONI, R., 1979 a, Plaintes visuelles, déficits fonctionnels et carences vitaminiques. *Médicine Sociale et Préventive*, **24**, 244–246.

MEYER, J. J., KOROL, S., GRAMONI, R., and REY, P., 1979 b, Quelques aspects de la charge visuelle aux postes de travail impliquant un écran de visualisation. *Travail humain*, No. spécial sur les écrans de visualisation, **42**, 275–301.

REY, P., GRAMONI, R., and MEYER, J. J., 1974, La fréquence critique de fusion et la courbe de de Lange, application aux mesures de la fatigue nerveuse et de la performance visuelle. *Travail humain*, **37**, 137–146.

Visual impairments in VDU operators related to environmental conditions

By TH. LÄUBLI, W. HÜNTING and E. GRANDJEAN

Department of Hygiene and Ergonomics, Swiss Federal Institute of Technology, 8092 Zurich, Switzerland

Four groups of office tasks were studied: data entry terminals, conversational terminals, traditional office work and typing.

Eye impairments are observed in every group of office employees but the impairments are more frequent in VDU operators. The impairments persist during leisure time.

High luminance contrasts between screen, source document and surrounding space are associated with an increase of eye troubles. Increased oscillating luminance of characters is associated with lower visual acuity, and with a higher incidence of subjective and objective symptoms of eye irritation including more frequent use of eye drops.

The degree of luminance oscillation of characters must be considered as an important factor for eye strain at VDU workplaces.

1. Introduction

To obtain a survey of the problems caused by the introduction of VDUs, we carried through a field study on different office tasks in Spring 1979.

2. Groups studied

The number of persons examined, their age, sex, working time on keyboards exclusively and the duration of their occupation on keyboards or VDUs are reported in table 1.

The data-entry group, working in banks or book-keeping departments, dealt with one-handed input of numerical data. The work speed was very high (8000–12 000 strokes/hour). The look was directed mainly to the source documents.

The conversational terminal operators dealt with payment orders of home and foreign currencies. They were selected in two different banks, each using a different type of VDU.

The traditional office work group, chosen in one of the banks, dealt with exactly the same task, but in a phase before the introduction of VDUs.

The typists were selected in different companies. During the whole working time they had to type commercial letters or reports, partly from copies, partly from records by earphones.

Table 1. Groups studied.

	n	Age ± s	♀%	>6 h/d	Years ± s	0–1	1–3	>3
				Working on keyboards		Working on VDUs (years)		
Data entry terminals	53	30 ± 8	94	81 %	6 ± 5	17 %	9 %	74 %
Conversational terminals	109	31 ± 12	50	73 %	5 ± 5	46 %	33 %	20 %
– VDU (A): green phosphor	55	34 ± 14	49	62 %	6 ± 5	44 %	18 %	38 %
– VDU (B): white phosphor	54	28 ± 10	52	85 %	4 ± 5	49 %	49 %	2 %
Traditional office work	55	28 ± 11	60	30 %	4 ± 4	—	—	—
Typists	78	34 ± 13	95	65 %	8 ± 8	—	—	—

3. Procedures

3.1. *Methods*

By a *self-rating questionnaire* the operators were asked about physical impairments in different parts of the body including the eyes, about drug consumption and about the evaluation of the working conditions.

Simultaneously we made a *medical examination* of upper extremities and vision. The latter consisted in measurements of heterophorias by the Maddox-Wing Test, of refraction by sciascopy for long distance, of visual acuity and of observations of eye irritations. The visual acuity was measured by 'Scalae Typographicae Birkhäuseri' positioned directly in front of the screen (distance to eye 50 cm, the same lighting conditions as during work, wearer of glasses with correction).

Several lighting conditions such as illumination levels, luminances in the visual field, oscillating luminances of characters and screen were measured.

3.2. *Oscillating luminances of characters*

The light emission of the stimulated phosphor on a cathode ray tube screen is not steady. A periodic impulse response is caused by the repeated refreshment of the decaying light emission of the fluorescent phosphor. The impulse response is determined by the kind of phosphor (decay time), by the refreshment rate and by the luminance levels of characters and of the background. We call this periodic impulse response of the fluorescent phosphor, *oscillating luminance*. We describe the oscillating luminance with the *Uniformity Figure (UF)*. The UF is defined as pulse base divided by pulse height during one cycle.

Figure 1 shows the equipment for measuring UF, the definition of UF, drawn on a harmonic oscillation, and gives two examples of UF. In the upper example (UF = 0·2) the pulse base is very low, in the lower picture the pulse base is increased by the nearly steady high illumination level of the screen.

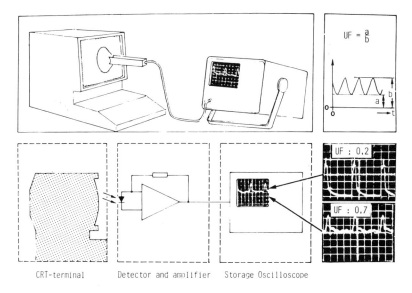

CRT-terminal   Detector and amplifier   Storage Oscilloscope

Figure 1. Procedure for measuring the Uniformity Figure (UF) of the oscillating luminance.

The *oscillating luminance of characters* was measured by focusing the optic system on a completely illuminated field of about 1 mm². The *oscillating luminance of the screen* was measured, when focusing on the whole screen. The UF was measured under the lighting conditions chosen by the operator himself for his work.

In our study the refreshment rate was 50 Hz. Group 'A' had green phosphor, group 'B' white phosphor. In our cases UF is mostly influenced by the brightness of characters.

4. Results

4.1. *Illumination levels*

The illumination levels, measured on the source documents of each workplace, are reported in table 2.

Three results can be deduced:

(1) The mean values correspond to the recommended illumination levels for office jobs.

(2) The range of values at VDU workplaces is large since 90% of the values lie between 100 and 1900 lx.

(3) The illumination levels are somewhat higher at the data-entry terminals than at the conversational terminals; we assume that this tendency reflects the different visual tasks of the two groups.

Table 2. Illumination levels (lux) on source documents.

	n	Median (lx)	90%-range
Data-entry terminals	53	550	140–1900
Conversational terminals	109	430	110–1400
Traditional office work	55	500	100– 800
Typists	78	800	400–3200

$F = 10 \cdot 7, \; p < 0 \cdot 01.$

4.2. *Luminances and contrasts*

Luminances and contrasts in data-entry terminals and conversational terminals are presented in table 3.

Luminance levels were found to be significantly higher in data-entry terminals. This finding supports our assumption that data-entry operators adjust their lighting conditions in such a way as to have good reading conditions of source documents, while operators on conversational terminals choose good reading conditions on the screen.

Luminance levels of reflections are lower than character luminances. We conclude that operators usually do not suffer from partial glare blindness but that reading is rendered more difficult. Luminance contrasts of near and far vision fields are very high. All contrasts are higher than the recommended values reported in ergonomic guidelines.

Table 3. Luminances (cd/m²) and contrasts of luminances.

	Luminances			
	Data-entry terminals (53)		Conversational terminals (109)	
	Median	90%-range	Median	90%-range
Source documents	163**	56–515	108**	34–280
Background of screens	7**	2– 50	4**	1– 11
Characters	37	7– 84†	33	9– 77‡
Reflections (max.)	32	6–100	17	5–120
	Contrasts of luminances			
Source document: screen	21 : 1	7 : 1–50 : 1	26 : 1	10 : 1–87 : 1
Characters: screen	2 : 1**	1 : 1–14 : 1†	9 : 1**	2 : 1–31 : 1‡
Window: screen	312 : 1	28 : 1–1200 : 1	300 : 1	87 : 1–1450 : 1

**t-test, $p < 0 \cdot 001$; †$n = 33$; ‡$n = 61$.

4.3. *Oscillating luminance*

Table 4 shows the measured luminance oscillation of characters and screens. The uniformity figure of total screen surface is high. We assume that these small oscillations do not cause impairment.

Table 4. Oscillating luminance of character and screen (Uniformity Figure: UF).

	Data-entry terminals (33)		Conversational terminals (62)	
	Median	90%-range	Median	90%-range
UF of total screen surface	0·89	0·60–0·99	0·81	0·40–0·96
UF of single characters (≈ 1 mm^2)	0·33**	0·14–0·50	0·11**	0·06–0·45

**t-test, $p<0.001$.

The UF of single characters is very low in conversational terminals. The lower UF-values at conversational terminals are certainly due to the fact that these operators adjust higher luminances of characters in order to get better reading conditions.

We suppose that the measured UF corresponds to the reception of the oscillating luminance of the character on the foveal retina of the focused eye.

4.4. Factor analysis of visual impairments

Table 5 demonstrates a factor analysis of all variables asked for by the questionnaire, related to eye impairments. We could extract only two factors and got a clear distribution of the variables to the two factors. We consider factor one as related to eye fatigue or eye irritation and factor two as related to impaired accommodation.

Table 5. Factor analysis of eye impairments.

		Charge
Factor 1	Pains	0·71
81% of variables	Burning	0·66
	Fatigue	0·64
	Shooting pain	0·53
	Red eyes	0·49
	Headaches	0·42
Factor 2	Blurring of near sight	0·79
19% of variables	Flicker vision	0·62
	Blurring of far sight	0·45
	Double images	0·45

4.5. Incidence and persistence of visual impairments

The incidence of fatigue and shooting pain in eyes and the persistence of impairments in the four different groups are reported in figure 2. Three results can be deduced:

(1) The incidence of visual impairments is high in the two VDU-groups and in typists; it is moderate in traditional office work.

(2) Impairments persist frequently until sleeping time; in fact some operators in the two VDU-groups and some typists said that they cannot watch television or read during leisure time.

(3) In data-entry terminals the incidence of impairments apparent the next morning is still important; however, it is nearly zero in traditional office work.

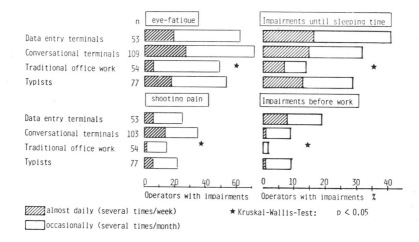

Figure 2. Incidence and persistence of eye impairments.

4.6. *Impairments and contrasts*

By means of the measured surface luminances, we computed various contrast indices. The relation between these contrasts and impairments is shown in figure 3. As shown in table 3, the measured contrasts are above recommended values. The result is not surprising: the higher the contrasts, the more frequent the eye impairments.

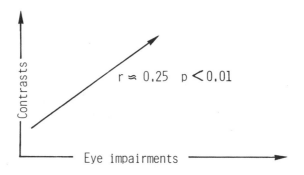

Figure 3. Luminance contrasts and eye impairments.

4.7. Impairments and reflections

Annoying reflections on screens have been reported by 45 % of the operators. We found a correlation between measured intensity of reflections and reported annoyance, but no relation between the measured luminance of reflections and eye impairments.

4.8 Impairments and oscillating luminance of character

In the group of conversational terminals 'B' we measured the uniformity figure of characters on each individual VDU.

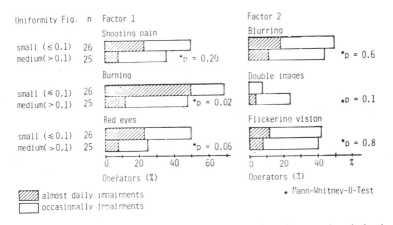

Figure 4. Oscillating luminance of characters and eye impairments (eye irritation and impaired accommodation).

Each operator uses the same type of VDU apparatus. Characters are not sharp; they are produced by white phosphor and have a great oscillation. We divided the group in two parts: one of 26 operators with a low UF ($\leqslant 0.1$), the other with a moderate UF (> 0.1). The measured differences in luminance oscillation are mainly due to the adjustment of character brightness by the operators and partly also to the illumination levels of the room. Figure 4 shows the incidence of some eye impairments for each of these two subgroups. Complaints of eye irritations (factor 1 of factor analysis) are more frequent in the group with strongly oscillating luminances, while complaints of impaired accommodation (factor 2 of factor analysis) seem to be independent of the degree of the luminance oscillation.

Further relations between UF and visual parameters are presented in figure 5. Not only complaints but also physical findings of eye irritation and frequent use of eye drops are associated with a low UF, i.e. with a high luminance oscillation.

The annoying impression of flickering characters is not significantly dependent on the oscillation level.

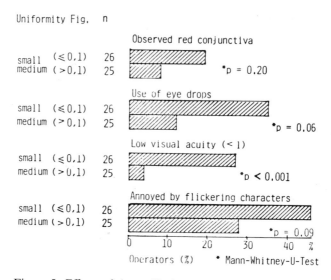

Figure 5. Effects of the oscillating luminance of characters.

The most striking result is shown by the visual acuity: *the group with low UF has a great incidence of operators with decreased visual acuity figures.*

The oscillation as well as the luminance contrast between character and screen are caused to a large extent by the adjusted brightness of the character. We calculated the Pearson correlation for each of these two variables and found between visual acuity and the logarithm of contrast $r = -0.41$ and for the UF $r = 0.46$. Figure 6 shows a three-dimensional presentation of these variables.

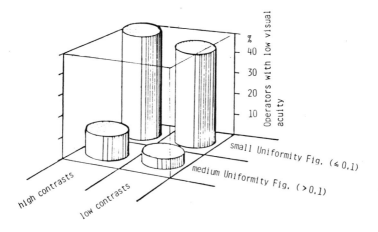

Figure 6. Visual acuity in relation to contrasts between characters and background and to oscillating luminance of characters.

The luminance oscillation level clearly separates the incidence of low visual acuity ($\leqslant 1$), while the contrast shows nearly no influence on the visual acuity.

5. Conclusions

As observed by Hünting *et al.* (1980), operators at VDU workplaces often show constrained postures due to visual distance (legibility), to inadequate workplace dimensions as well as to the uniformity of tasks. The same group of operators also shows an increased incidence of eye impairments.

These two types of work-load may induce in some operators a state of general fatigue accompanied by more or less specific symptoms of postural strain and eye strain. These symptoms may persist during leisure time. In the group of data entry terminals some operators report that even after sleep they do not find complete recovery. We must conclude that continuous work at VDUs is associated with a high work-load, which may produce in some operators excessive fatigue and to some extent even health injuries.

The present study revealed significant relations between lighting conditions on the one side and the incidence of eye impairments on the other. In the frame of our investigation the oscillating luminance of characters seems to be an important cause of visual impairments. The most striking result is revealed by the relationship between the uniformity figure and the visual acuity: the greater the oscillation of luminance, the lower the visual acuity. We assume that a lowered visual acuity might increase the load of a visual task.

Two detailed results must be pointed out: the uniformity figure seems to have no influence on the symptoms related to accommodation but mainly on symptoms revealing eye fatigue or eye irritation. Furthermore, the incidence of persistence of visual impairments is not influenced by the degree of luminance oscillation.

We deduce from our study that a 'flicker-free screen' is not the only valuable criterion to evaluate a terminal display; the uniformity figure or other value describing the degree of oscillation of character luminances might be as important a parameter as the visible flicker of characters.

Acknowledgment

We thank Dr. med. W. Steinebrunner for his medical advice for eye examination of operators.

References

GUNNARSSON, E., and ÖSTBERG, O., 1977, The physical and psychological working environment in a terminal based computer storage and retrieval system. National Board of Occupational Safety and Health, Report 35, Stockholm.

HÜNTING, W., LÄUBLI, TH., and GRANDJEAN, E., 1980, Constrained postures of VDU operators. In: *Ergonomic Aspects of Visual Display Terminals* (this volume), p. 175.

LAVILLE, A., TEIGER, C., LANTIN, G., and DESSORS, D., 1979, Quelques caractéristiques de la fatigue visuelle provoquée par le travail de détection sur microfiches. *Travail humain* (in the press).

MEYER, J. J., REY, P., KOROL, S., and GRAMONI, R., 1978, La fatigue oculaire engendrée par le travail sur écrans de visualisation. *Sozial- und Präventiv-medizin*, **23**, 295–296.

Visual fatigue in VDT operators

By M. J. DAINOFF

Miami University, Oxford, Ohio, U.S.A.

A field investigation was conducted in which a large group of clerical VDT operators were interviewed concerning their attitudes towards their jobs and office computerization. A smaller subset of this group was examined more intensively for one work week, during which time optometric measurements were taken, and a mood/physical symptom check-list administered. Results indicated a relatively high incidence of visual system complaints among workers who frequently used VDTs. However, these appear to be relatively independent of non-visual sources of stress. No consistent pattern of optometric measurements was found to be related to subjective complaints.

1. Introduction

The following is a brief report of a two-part field investigation of VDT operators. The focus was on visual fatigue as well as other ergonomic and job-related problems.

An earlier review of the literature (Dainoff 1979) indicated relatively widespread complaints of visually related problems among users of VDTs in clerical occupations (e.g., Östberg 1975). Involvement of ophthalmic structures in such visual problems has been postulated, particularly in regard to' fatigue of intrinsic and extrinsic eye muscles (Östberg 1977); however, objective evidence has been difficult to obtain. Höller et al. (1975) were able to demonstrate small acuity deficits resulting from 2- to 4-hour working times at VDTs. On the other hand, it is possible that social–psychological factors relating to the use of the computer itself (job pressure, response to office automation, fear of technological unemployment) were making a major contribution to observed operator complaints.

Accordingly, this study is an attempt to obtain objective indications of visual disorder along with corresponding subjective measures, both of specific physical and emotional state as well as broader job-related attitudes. We attempted to accomplish the above by subjecting a small group of VDT operators to a relatively intensive analysis of one week of work. The analysis included daily optometric screening plus questionnaire administration. In addition, a larger group of operators was interviewed about their jobs.

2. Method

2.1 *Subjects*

Two groups of subjects were examined. Group I was a heterogeneous collection of 90 clerical workers from 15 different offices/organizations in the region of south-western Ohio, U.S.A. Most of the workers were female, predominantly young, and were approximately equally drawn from the following job classifications: (*a*) word processing; (*b*) financial; (*c*) record maintenance/retrieval; (*d*) data-entry. With regard to a self-description of the percentage of the total work day each worker spent actually looking at a VDT screen, workers ranged from 0 to 100% with an average of 47%.

Group II participants were 23 persons who worked in a single centralized library cataloguing service. Their average VDT looking time was 75%; otherwise they were demographically similar to Group I.

2.2. *Interview procedure*

A standardized interview format was developed following the 'funnel technique' of Bouchard (1976), in which questions are initially general, but later become specific. An abbreviated version of the question sequence is as follows: (1) What do you most/least like about your job? (2) What do you most/least like about office computerization? (3) How satisfied are you with your physical surroundings—including furniture, office equipment, storage space, lighting? (4) Do you wear glasses? Are they satisfactory? (5) Is the lighting adequate? (6) Has your job had any effect on your health? Each interview took approximately 15 min and was tape-recorded. The words 'stress' and 'eye strain' were never used by the interviewer.

2.3. *Optometric screening procedure*

An industrial visual screening device (Bausch & Lomb Orthorater, Type 71-21-42) was used to obtain measures of acuity, lateral phoria, and vertical phoria, at both the near (0·35 m) and far (6·1 m) distances. Measures were taken binocularly, and corrective lenses were worn if used during work. Subjects were trained to take their own measurements under supervision.

2.4 *Mood and physical symptom questionnaire*

A 37-item check-list was developed using items from two sources. Twenty-four items were taken from the Profile of Mood States (POMS; McNair *et al.* 1971); these items comprised the *vigour*, *fatigue*, and *tension* scales of that profile. The POMS is designed to be sensitive to fluctuations of moods and feelings.

An additional 13 items were included which specifically related to physical symptoms expected to be relevant to VDT operators. Examples of such items were: 'eyes hurt', 'hard to focus', and 'neck/shoulders hurt'. Subjects were instructed to indicate, using a five-point scale, the extent to which the feelings expressed by each item had occurred within the previous hour.

2.5. *Research design*

All subjects in Group I were interviewed using the standardized format described above. Group II subjects were studied more intensively over a 5-day work week. Daily measurements of optometric function and mood/physical state for each subject were made both before and after work. At the conclusion of the work week, they too were interviewed as above.

3. Results

3.1. *Interview coding and weighting*

Individual responses to each of the interview items were content-coded into one of 32 response categories. These categories comprised four major classifications: (I) primary health-related symptoms; (II) ergonomic comments; (III) computer system comments; (IV) job comments. In addition, a subset of the above categories, defined as being of particular interest to this investigation, was subjected to more intensive analysis. This subset, which we call the weighted response categories, included all the response categories subsumed under category I plus category IV-B (complaints about job pressure). The table includes a listing of the classification categories.

In the second stage of analysis, responses judged as falling into one of the weighted response categories were assigned weights reflecting whether the response occurred during the beginning (least specific questions), middle, or end (most specific questions) of the interview sequence. Our assumption was that a given response appearing early on would be more salient/important to the subject, and should, therefore, be more highly weighted. (The weighting was only applied to Group II subjects who were not aware of the initial purpose of the interview.)

3.2. *Interview results* (*Groups I and II*)

The number and percentages of persons responding to a given category were tabulated, and the results appear in the table. It will be seen that complaints about eye strain were the fourth most frequently appearing response, occurring 45% of the time. Moreover, if we combine all categories relating to *visual* effects (I-B, I-C, I-CC, I-E), the percentage of persons who made at least one response in at least one of these categories was 75·21.

Finally, with regard to the weighted response categories, the correlations of proportion of work time spent looking at VDT screens with visual fatigue (I-B) and VDT lighting complaints (I-CC) were moderate and significant ($r = 0·28, 0·39; p < 0·01$). However, the corresponding correlation with physical

Number, percentages, and rank order of number of people responding per category.

Response category		Number of people responding		
		Number	%	Rank
IA	Stress	51	42·15	6
I-B	Visual fatigue	55	45·45	4
I-C	Lighting complaints	45	37·19	8
I-CC	VDT lighting complaints	45	37·19	9
I-D	General fatigue	35	28·93	
I-E	Needs glasses	41	33·88	
II-A	Crowding	52	42·98	5
II-B	Noise	19	15·7	
II-C	Privacy	12	9·92	
II-D	Aesthetic	41	33·88	
II-E	Furniture	15	12·4	
II-F	Keyboard	2	1·65	
II-G	Heat/air	17	14·05	
II-H	Environment +	27	22·31	
III-A	Computer efficiency	98	80·99	1
III-B	Challenge	44	36·36	10
III-C	Down time	59	48·76	3
III-D	Response time	21	17·36	
III-E	Training problems	8	6·61	
III-F	Hostility	8	6·61	
III-G	Local problems	31	25·62	
IV-A	Job enjoyment	68	56·2	2
IV-B	Job pressure	29	23·97	
IV-C	Ignoring employees	9	7·44	
IV-D	Other management problems	15	12·4	
IV-E	Boredom	32	26·45	
IV-F	Distraction	10	8·26	
IV-G	Atmosphere +	46	38·02	7
IV-I	Local problems	32	26·45	
IV-J	Security	6	4·96	
IV-K	Pay/benefits +	5	4·13	
IV-K	Pay/benefits −	7	5·79	
	Total	121		

stress (I-A) was non-significant ($r = 0·19$) and significantly *negative* for job pressure (IV-B; $r = -0·19$, $p < 0·05$). Thus, visually related complaints seem to be relatively independent of other non-visual stressors.

3.3. *Optometric results* (*Group II*)

Unlike Höller *et al.* (1976), we found no significant pre-post work difference on any of the optometric measures. A detailed examination of individual data indicated patterns of optometric changes which were idiosyncratic across subjects, but quite consistent within subjects. We were unable to discern any obvious relationship between these objective measures and subjective responses.

3.4. *Questionnaire results (Group II)*

With regard to the POMS mood scales, subjects showed significantly ($p < 0.05$) more fatigue and tension after work than before. There was also a significant ($p < 0.05$) pre–post work increase in physical complaints, the largest of these being visual symptoms. 'Eye strain' was reported by 30·1% of the subjects at the beginning of work, but this had increased to 62·2% after work. Likewise, there was a 24·9% increase in 'blurry vision'. Finally, there was a tendency for subjects whose VDT screens had a non-reflecting surface to have fewer complaints about eye strain.

4. Discussion

This study provides yet another demonstration of a high incidence of reported visual complaints associated with VDT use. There is some evidence to suggest that these problems are unrelated to non-visual job demands and anti-computer attitudes. Attempts, however, to find objective (optometric) measures corresponding to these complaints remain problematic.

Acknowledgments

This research was carried out in collaboration with my student, Mr. Alan Happ, and Professor Peter Crane, now at the University of Pittsburgh.

References

BOUCHARD, T. J., JR., 1976, Field research methods: Interviewing questionnaires, participant observation, systematic observations, unobtrusive measures. In *Handbook of Industrial and Organizational Psychology*, edited by M. D. Dunnette (Chicago: Rand McNally).

DAINOFF, M. J., 1979, *Occupational Stress Factors in Secretarial/Clerical Workers* (Cincinnati, Ohio: National Institute of Occupational Safety and Health).

HÖLLER, H., KUNDI, M., SCHMID, H., STIDL, H. G., THALER, A., and WINTER, N., 1975, *Arbeitsbeanspruchung und Augenbelastung an Bildschirmgeraten* (Vienna: Ed. Automationsausschuss des Gewerkschaftsbundes der Privatangestellten).

McNAIR, D. M., LORR, M., and DROPPLEMAN, L. F., 1971, *Manual: Profile of Mood States* (San Diego, California: Educational and Industrial Testing Service).

ÖSTBERG, O., 1975, CRTs pose health problems for operators. *International Journal of Occupational Health and Safety*, November–December, 24–52.

ÖSTBERG, O., 1977, Towards standards and TLVs for visual work. Paper read to the 2nd World Congress of Ergophthalmology, Stockholm, 13–16 June.

Section 4.   Performance at VDTs

Visual reading processes and the quality of text displays

By H. Bouma

Institute for Perception Research, IPO, P.O. Box 513, 5600 MB Eindhoven,
The Netherlands

The notion of quality of an alphanumeric display basically refers to
its suitability to the user. Visual processes involved in the use of such
displays are in particular search and reading. Recent advances in the
understanding of the processes involved enable us to envisage how visual
search and reading may proceed from a VDU and to investigate specific
questions as to quality. Factors involved turn out to include optical
quality, lay-out and the proper use of colour.

1. Introduction

Text is displayed for the purpose of reading. Therefore the quality of text
concerns the ease with which users are able to find and read their information.
With many present electronic displays reading is far from easy. There are difficulties in body posture, in reading distances, in eye adaptations, in recognition, in search, and in memorizing. Some solutions for these problems are
well known and just need to be implemented on a massive scale. Other difficulties are less tractable.

The present paper starts from insights into the visual processes of reading.
Notions from recent visual research in reading will be applied to alphanumeric
displays. We concentrate on the required quality of symbols, such as letters and
words, and on the formatting and lay-out of the information. For a classic work
written before the revival of reading research in the seventies, see Tinker (1954).

Two relevant task distinctions should be kept in mind. Firstly, reading
connected text is different from reading separate, non-redundant codes and
numbers. In connected text, the meaning of a sentence or paragraph is dominant and not every word needs to receive equal attention. In separate symbols,
every single letter or digit can be relevant. Secondly, reading proper is different
from visual search. Reading is the intake of information one wants. Search is
the intake of information one does *not* want in order to locate the information
that one does want. Not only the task itself should be considered, but also the
perceptual faculties involved, which may well have wide individual differences.
For more comprehensive papers on reading and visual search, see Bouma
(1978, 1979).

2. Visual processes of reading

Both in reading and in visual search, the eyes move in quick jumps rather than smoothly. The jumps, called saccades, are so fast that no useful information can be picked up during their occurrence. In between the jumps, however, the eyes are steady and the steady retinal images allow for recognition. The visual analysis necessary for this is concentrated around the visual axis, which on the retina corresponds to the central fovea. When we fixate on a certain object, we rotate our eyeballs so that the object is imaged on the fovea and we focus the optics of our eye to get the image sharp. It is only in the fovea and in the immediately adjacent area (the parafovea) that detail vision is sufficiently accurate for the recognition of normal print. We shall further leave the slow focusing processes (accommodation) out of account.

Because of the succession of eye saccades and eye fixations, we can distinguish three different visual processes, which have to function in close time-relationship:

(*a*) The control of eye saccades and of eye pauses (section 3).
(*b*) Recognition processes during a single eye pause. We shall deal separately with the recognition of characters (section 4) and with the horizontal extent of the recognition area, to be called visual reading field (section 5).
(*c*) Integration of information picked up during successive eye pauses (section 6).

For the variables 'luminous contrast' and 'colour', we shall briefly work out some of the insights (section 7) and finally some general conclusions will be formulated.

3. The control of eye saccades

When a person is reading connected text, three types of eye saccade occur (figure 1): (*a*) rightward saccades of 8 ± 4 letter positions: *reading saccades*; (*b*) leftward saccades, usually small: *correction saccades*; (*c*) large leftward saccades from the end of one line towards the beginning of the next line: *line saccades*. All types of saccade may be very different for different texts and different subjects. Figure 2 gives distributions of saccade size and pause duration for subjects reading the same text. Both the combined data of seven subjects and the individual data of two subjects are shown. For general papers on eye control see Levy-Schoen and O'Regan (1979) and Rayner (1978).

(*a*) Reading saccades are based on a routine motor programme, the parameters of which are influenced by global text properties. The extent of the horizontal visual reading field is of direct influence. Saccade extent and pause duration have independent controls, with the constraint that correction saccades become necessary if eye fixation leads text processing by more than working memory capacity.

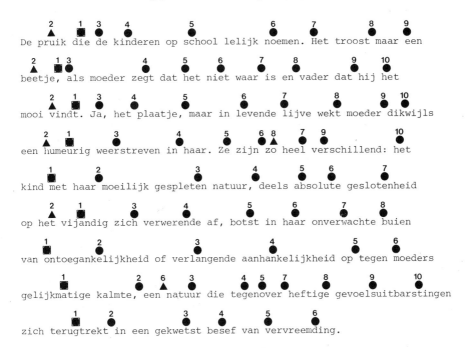

Figure 1. Eye fixations in the silent reading of a paragraph of Dutch text. Three different types of eye saccade are indicated: reading saccades (circles), correction saccades (triangles) and line saccades (squares). Numbers indicate the order of fixations within each line.

(*b*) Correction saccades often occur directly after line saccades. They occur at other moments as well, more so in difficult than in easy texts and more often in unskilled than in skilled readers.

(*c*) Line saccades start before the end of a line is reached and do not quite reach the beginning of the next line. Their moment of occurrence is determined by visual information from the right visual field. Since by then eye fixation is close to the right-hand line ending, the ending can clearly be seen and successive lines can be allowed different line endings, without the reading process being disturbed. So the endings of lines need not be vertically aligned. The horizontal extent of line saccades is controlled by visual information in the left visual field, concerning the far left-hand text margin, which therefore should be in a straight vertical line (in typographers' terms: justified) with a sufficiently wide margin (Gregory and Poulton 1970). The vertical extent of line saccades is controlled by perceived inter-line distance. If this vertical component is inaccurate, the eye may mistakenly jump over two or perhaps even three lines. This is clearly inefficient and in the case of unconnected code numbers the reader may not even notice that he has missed out one or two lines. A rough estimate of the minimum admissible

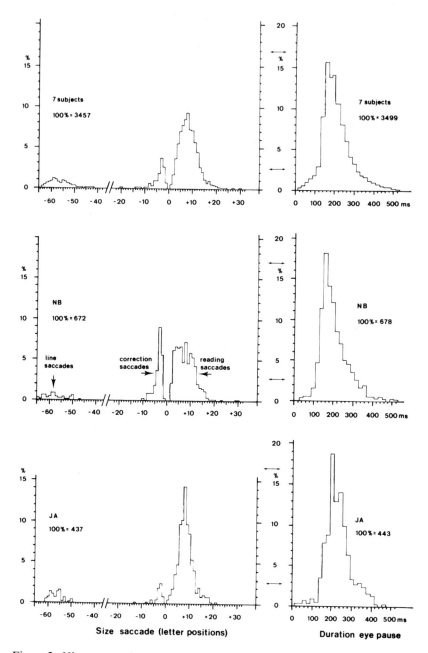

Figure 2   Histograms of saccade extent (in letter units) and of eye pause durations. The
upper graph gives combined results of seven subjects reading the same paragraph, whereas the middle and lower graphs show the results of two separate
subjects.

value of line distance over line length (line angle) appears to be about 1/30, corresponding to about 2°.

As a consequence, line distance should increase with line length. It follows that for large line lengths, line distance should be large and print density (number of letters per unit area) will be low. Therefore, if a high density is required, line length should be restricted (figure 3). An example can be found in newspapers, where a high print density is achieved by using relatively narrow columns. If only a single column of text is used, it is of advantage to have the page vertically oriented. Most electronic text display units are horizontally oriented (aspect ratio 3 : 4), probably because they are directly derived from normal television screens. It seems advantageous to use screens vertically oriented (aspect ratio 4 : 3), thus resembling the standard format of A4 sheets ($\sqrt{2}$: 1) or, if oriented horizontally, in a two-column mode, particularly if a high density of letters is required.

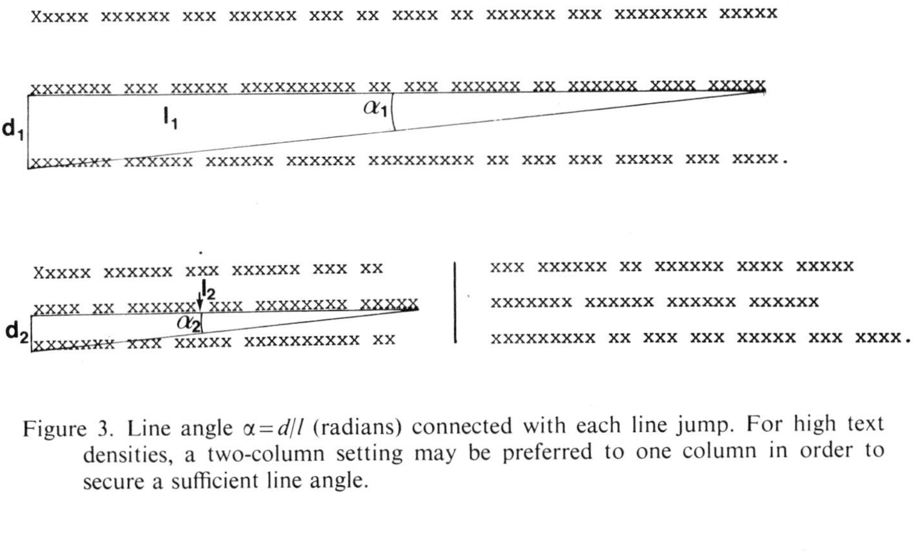

Figure 3. Line angle $\alpha = d/l$ (radians) connected with each line jump. For high text densities, a two-column setting may be preferred to one column in order to secure a sufficient line angle.

4. Character recognition

During each eye pause, characters are recognized in foveal and parafoveal vision. Quick and correct recognition requires that the characters are acceptable, identifiable and distinctive.

Acceptability is the degree to which the character configurations suit the internal notions that readers have built of such characters. There may well be certain cultural differences in these mental notions, such as in the handwritten versions of 1 and 7. New forms can be taught, but on a massive scale this is not at all easy.

Identifiability concerns clear and sharp letter details, which should stand out clearly. This is particularly important for the inner details which are surrounded by other elements, for example in e, a and s. The line elements should contrast sharply with the background and be homogeneous. Stroke width should be between 10 and 15% of x-height. Letter size is probably not very critical, but letter details should stand out to ensure sufficiently quick recognition.

Distinctiveness means that each character should be very different from other characters, in particular from those that are visually somewhat similar such as I–1; S–5. For example, extensions of descending letters (p, q . . .) and ascending letters (b, d . . .) should be at least 40% of x-height.

All three notions can be tested in experiments. Figure 4 gives part of a confusion matrix, which indicates for a certain typeface how e, o, and c are confused in a letter reading test. Confusion matrices indicate the letters of relatively poor legibility, and also the configuration factors which cause this.

		Response			
		e	o	c	other
Stimulus	e	24	23	05	48
	o	03	58	04	35
	c	19	11	43	27

Figure 4. Part of a confusion matrix for lower-case letters. It indicates percentages of correct (main diagonal) and incorrect answers. The confusion matrix is helpful for finding letters that tend to be confused because of visual similarity (Bouma 1971).

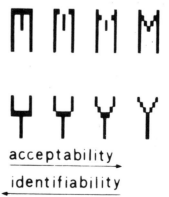

acceptability

identifiability

Figure 5. Two examples of a conflict between acceptability and identifiability (Bouma and Leopold 1969).

Particularly in the case of code numbers, which have little redundancy and in which each symbol has to be recognized on its own strength, it is important to have each symbol optimally designed. The three requirements may be conflicting, in which case a suitable compromise has to be found. Figure 5 gives an example for two matrix characters. In figure 6 a character set is given

Figure 6. A set of alphanumeric symbols as designed in a 7 × 11 matrix. Optimum acceptability, identifiability and distinctiveness have been aimed at, and these have been checked by preference ratings and by analysing confusions from legibility experiments (Bouma and Leopold 1969, Bouma and van Rens 1971).

for a 7 × 11 matrix, which has been designed on the basis of the above requirements (Bouma and Leopold 1969, Bouma and van Rens 1971). In passing, it may be remarked that the design of the widely applied seven-segment digits is far from optimal (van Nes and Bouma 1980).

5. The visual reading field

At the point of fixation (central fovea) and in an adjacent parafoveal area, visual information can be picked up during an eye pause. Somewhat farther from fixation, vision is insufficient for this. We speak of the useful visual area as the *visual reading field*. How far the visual reading field extends and how its boundaries are determined are both practically and theoretically important.

Let us first consider visual acuity as a possible limiting factor. Visual acuity reflects the smallest detail of a certain standard object (called optotype) that can be seen. The best optotype is the Landolt C, in which the detail is the gap in one out of four possible orientations. The reciprocal of the smallest gap size seen (in units of minutes of arc visual angle) is defined as visual acuity. For assessing visual acuity outside fixation, the optotypes are flashed for say 100 ms, which prevents eye fixations on them. It turns out that visual acuity is a relevant indicator of the recognizability of a single letter as a function of eccentricity.

This is no longer the case if more letters are present than just one. The recognition of an embedded letter is much worse than that of a single letter (figure 7). In fact, the horizontal field in which an embedded letter can be recognized is only about 30% of the field in which a single letter can be recognized. Consequently, the visual reading field for embedded letters is much narrower than visual acuity would indicate. This is due to adverse interactions between adjacent letters. These interactions have unexpected properties (Bouma 1978). Here we just list them: the effects of interference are strong, they operate over a wide retinal distance, they are mainly directed towards the fovea, they are specific for certain letter features and they are less expressed in the right than in the left visual field (at least for readers of languages that are read from left to right).

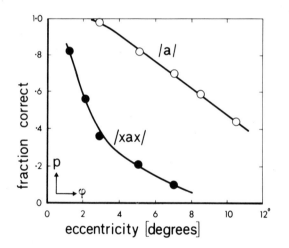

Figure 7. Embedding randomly chosen target letters between two letters x (indicated as /xax/) makes recognition scores in eccentric vision drop sharply as compared with the non-embedded situation (indicated as /a/). The diameter of the corresponding useful visual field shrinks to about 30% of its non-embedded value. One degree visual angle corresponds to four letter positions (Bouma 1970).

For code numbers without much redundancy, only a few symbols can be picked up in a single glance. For words the situation is somewhat different because, with sufficient word knowledge, only part of the information needs to be seen in order to arrive at a correct recognition. If insufficient details are seen, subjects have a strong tendency to guess and they usually respond with words that resemble the stimulus word. Due to the interference properties, word recognition is better in the right than in the left visual field (figure 8). The precise relations between letter recognition and word recognition (see Bouwhuis and Bouma 1979) are outside the scope of this paper.

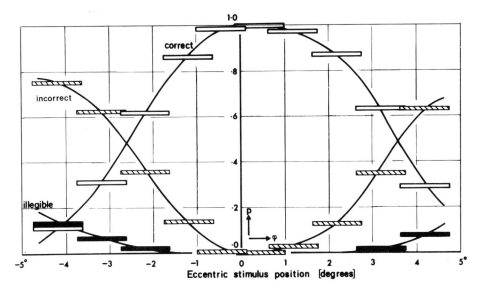

Figure 8. Recognition of isolated Dutch words as a function of retinal eccentricity on both sides of fixation. One degree visual angle corresponds to four letter positions. Bar width indicates average word length. Note the higher correct scores for words right of fixation and the high fraction of incorrect word responses (from Bouma 1973).

Because of the large retinal distances of adverse interactions, lines above and below the one read will interfere with parafoveal word recognition unless line distances are sufficiently large. If lines are too closely spaced, the extent of the visual reading field is decreased so that less information can be picked up in a single eye pause. So far there are insufficient experimental data for precisely assessing where the limits are, but our present estimates for running text of good quality may be seen in figure 9.

Thus a wide visual reading field is a second perceptual factor which calls for a sufficient inter-line distance. Since non-redundant code numbers already have a narrow reading field, inter-line distances for code numbers can be less than for running text.

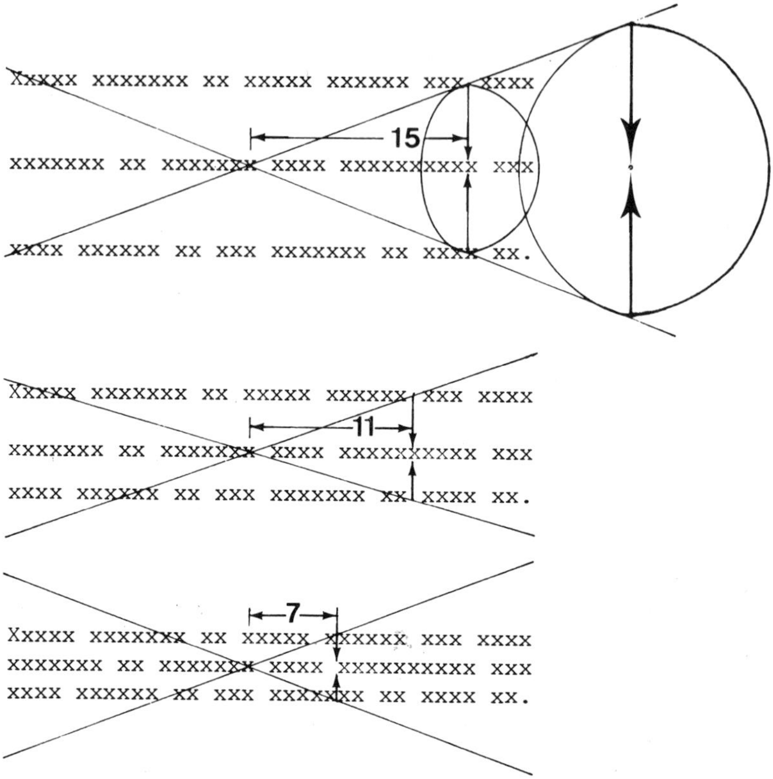

H. Bouma

Figure 9. Schematic diagram, indicating the interference zones, when fixation is at the crossing point of the oblique lines. The oblique lines delineate the interference areas, and any contours present within an interference area make recognition at the centre of this area more difficult. It follows that the visual areas around fixation, which are free from such interference by the two adjacent lines of print, decrease with decreasing line distance, from 15 letters from fixation (upper) to 7 letters (lower). It is assumed that the interference is active over retinal distances of about 40% of eccentricity.

6. Timings

In the reading of connected text, the eye makes some four fixations each second, successive fixations being some eight characters apart. If text quality is good and lines are sufficiently far apart, the visual reading field during each fixation can easily be as wide as 20 letter positions, 8 left of fixation and 12 right of fixation (figure 10). Thus most words can be read in more than one fixation. Nevertheless, the subjective impression is that each word is recognized only once.

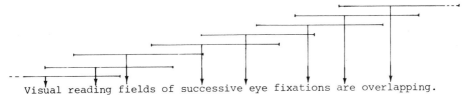

Visual reading fields of successive eye fixations are overlapping.

Figure 10. Estimate of the horizontal extent of the visual reading field during successive eye pauses if text quality is good and inter-line distance large. The estimate is based upon the recognition of isolated words at both sides of fixation and, right of fixation, is probably on the conservative side.

This effect indicates a certain flexibility of the recognition system and it makes reading less dependent on the precise fixation position and saccade timing. However, in order to know the extent of this flexibility, a direct insight into timings is necessary. Now it turns out that in parafoveal vision, recognition takes more time than in foveal vision (figure 11). This indicates that the moment of correct recognition is not only determined by the moment a word appears within the visual reading field, but also by the position relative to fixation where it appears.

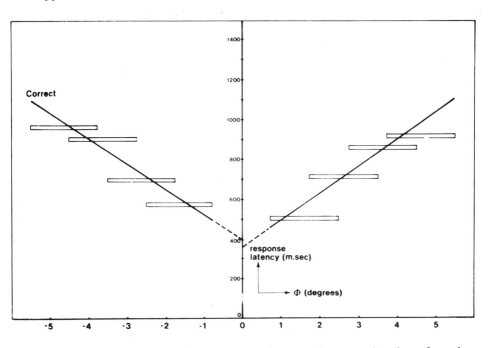

Figure 11. Response latency for correct word recognition as a function of word eccentricity. One degree corresponds to four letter positions. The farther from fixation, the slower the recognition process proceeds (Schiepers 1974, 1980).

Consider the usual reading situation. A word first appears in right para-foveal vision, where recognition takes a relatively long time. During the next eye fixation, 200 ms or so later, the same word appears in foveal vision, where recognition is faster. Thus it may well occur that the quicker foveal processing just makes up for the earlier parafoveal presentation in such a way that a single recognition results from the two successive presentations. This hypothesis is somewhat speculative as yet, but it would help us to understand why recognition for the reader occurs only once, whereas the word appears within the visual reading field at least twice. There remain problems, of course, for example whether a possible third presentation left of fixation has some function (for example in controlling correction saccades), or whether the third presentation is suppressed. However this may be, any influence on eye saccades by the recognition process should be timed relative to moment of recognition (entry in working memory) rather than to moment of appearance in the visual reading field. This is a recent area of research and quantitative conclusions for text displays cannot be drawn as yet. However, it is clear by now that extra delays occur in the recognition process if text quality is insufficient.

7. Contrast and colour

Finally, we shall briefly consider luminous contrast and colour to show the relevance of some of the theoretical notions. We shall focus particularly on the visual reading field.

If luminous contrast is varied experimentally, it turns out that parafoveal word recognition is critically dependent on contrast value (figure 12). The lower the contrast, the narrower is the visual reading field. Parafoveal recognition provides more insight into this matter than foveal recognition. Such experiments therefore indicate what contrast values can be tolerated without undue disturbance of the reading process. Obviously, contrast at a visual display unit in a working station is also dependent on any reflections in the screen.

These contrast experiments are also relevant to the reading of coloured text. The available evidence indicates that the legibility of coloured text depends on luminous contrast and not on the colour itself. Thus dark colours (brown, blue) on a dark background as well as light colours (yellow, green) on a light background have low contrast values and consequently legibility of such text is poor, because the visual reading field is very much restricted and visual recognition is delayed.

The colour itself may well be visible far from fixation, thus giving rise to a wide 'conspicuity area' (Engel 1971, 1977, 1980), but the coloured letters and digits can only be *read* very close to fixation. This indicates that colour is a useful aid for visual search, i.e. if a reader knows what colour he should look for, it helps him in quickly locating the required information, but the actual reading of the information depends on luminous contrast and not on colour.

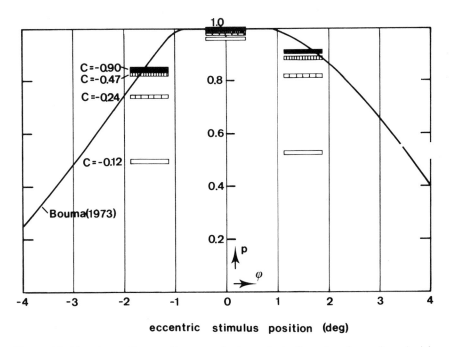

eccentric stimulus position (deg)

Figure 12. Fractions of correctly recognized words in foveal and parafoveal vision for four values of luminous contrast $C = (L_d - L_b)/L_b$ where L_d is the luminance of the dark letters and L_b the luminance of the bright background (from Timmers 1978, Timmers, van Nes and Blommaert 1980).

A second function of colour is that it causes perceptual grouping of objects within the same range of colour and contrast, though quantitative effects cannot be specified as yet.

8. Conclusion

Problems connected with visual display units can be approached by determining in practice what the complaints are and engaging in a trial-and-error procedure for minimizing inconveniences for the actual users. This approach is at present indispensable. However, good engineering should rest on solid insight into the functions that the displays have to fulfil so as to avoid unacceptable situations occurring. In the case of visual display units, the insight concerns processes of reading and visual search, for which tasks VDUs should be optimally geared.

Present research on reading processes is sufficiently far advanced to enable us (a) to formulate rules of thumb that can easily be applied in practice, and (b) to design perceptual tests which are indispensable for knowing intrinsic qualities of visual display units already in a prototype stage. Consequently the costly and cumbersome trial-and-error procedures, which have left us with so many poor visual working stations, have to be considered obsolete.

References

BOUMA, H., 1970, Interaction effects in parafoveal letter recognition. *Nature, London,* **226**, 177–178.

BOUMA, H., 1971, Visual recognition of isolated lower-case letters. *Vision Research,* **11**, 459–474.

BOUMA, H., 1973, Visual interference in the parafoveal recognition of initial and final letters of words. *Vision Research,* **13**, 767–782.

BOUMA, H., 1978, Visual search and reading: eye movements and functional visual field: a tutorial review. In *Attention and Performance VII,* edited by J. Requin (Hillsdale, N.J.: Erlbaum), pp. 115–147.

BOUMA, H., 1979, Perceptual functions. In *Handbook of Psychonomics,* Vol. 1, edited by J. A. Michon, E. G. J. Eykman and L. F. W. de Klerk (Amsterdam: North-Holland), Chap. 8, pp. 427–531.

BOUMA, H., and LEOPOLD, F. F., 1969, A set of matrix characters in a special 7×8 array. *IPO Annual Progress Report,* **4**, 115–119.

BOUMA, H., and VAN RENS, A. L. M., 1971, Completion of an alpha-numeric matrix display with lower-case letters. *IPO Annual Progress Report,* **6**, 91–94.

BOUWHUIS, D. G., and BOUMA, H., 1979, Visual word recognition of three-letter words as derived from the recognition of the constituent letters. *Perception and Psychophysics,* **25**, 12–22.

ENGEL, F. L., 1971, Visual conspicuity, directed attention and retinal locus. *Vision Research,* **11**, 563–576.

ENGEL, F. L., 1977, Visual conspicuity, visual search and fixation tendencies of the eye. *Vision Research,* **17**, 95–108.

ENGEL, F. L., 1980, Information selection from visual display units. *Ergonomic Aspects of Visual Display Terminals* (this volume), p. 121.

GREGORY, M., and POULTON, E. C., 1970, Even versus uneven right-hand margins and the rate of comprehension in reading. *Ergonomics,* **13**, 427–434.

LEVY-SCHOEN, A., and O'REGAN, K., 1979, The control of eye movements in reading. In *Processing of Visible Language,* Vol. 1, edited by P. A. Kolers, M. Wrolstad and H. Bouma (New York: Plenum Publishing Co.).

VAN NES, F. L., and BOUMA, H., 1980, On the legibility of segmented numerals. *Human Factors* (in the press).

RAYNER, K., 1978, Eye movements in reading and information processing. *Psychological Bulletin,* **85**, 618–660.

SCHIEPERS, C. W. J., 1974, Response latencies in parafoveal word recognition. *IPO Annual Progress Report,* **9**, 99–103.

SCHIEPERS, C. W. J., 1980, Response latency and accuracy in visual word recognition. *Perception and Psychophysics,* **27**, 71–81.

TIMMERS, H., 1978, An effect of contrast on legibility of printed text. *IPO Annual Progress Report,* **13**, 64–67.

TIMMERS, H., VAN NES, F. L., and BLOMMAERT, F. J. J., 1980, Visual work recognition as a function of contrast. *Ergonomic Aspects of Visual Display Terminals* (this volume), p. 115.

TINKER, M. A., 1954, *Legibility of Print* (Minnesota: Minnesota University Press).

Visual word recognition as a function of contrast

By H. Timmers, F. L. van Nes and F. J. J. Blommaert

Institute for Perception Research, IPO, Den Dolech 2, Eindhoven, The Netherlands

In an experiment concerning the effect of decreasing contrast on the legibility of Dutch three-letter words, percentages of correct responses and corresponding voice-response latencies were measured. The correct score for foveal stimulus presentation remained almost constant when contrast was decreased, whereas at $1 \cdot 5°$ parafoveal presentation correct scores decreased from 90 % to 50 % when contrast was diminished from 0·90 to 0·12. For such a contrast decrement, foveal latencies increased by about 50 ms and parafoveal latencies by about 150 ms. A decrease of text–background contrast will therefore impair normal reading processes; this has consequences for text presentation on visual display units.

1. Introduction

Legibility is a property of texts which has to do with the *visual* processes involved in reading. Readability, on the other hand, is a property related to the *cognitive* processes functioning while the text is read. It is possible to speak about the legibility of isolated words, or even letters, whereas the term readability only makes sense for combinations of words or sentences that are, for instance, easy or difficult to understand. The legibility of text is determined by a large number of factors that pertain either to

dimensions and distances, of and between the characters, words and lines constituting the text, or

luminance and colour, of these characters and their background.

One example of the first group of factors is character or letter size: its effect on legibility can easily be observed in daily life, where one is confronted with all sorts of printed material. A second, often neglected, example of this group is the distance between successive lines of text, on paper or visual display units: if the inter-line distance is too small, reading is made more difficult.

An example of the other group of factors is the luminance of the text character-background: it determines the adaptation of the retinal area concerned and therefore defines the spatial (and temporal) resolving power of the eye for such text parts. The luminous contrast between characters and background is another example of this same group of factors. In normal print this contrast is generally well above a level at which legibility is negatively influenced (Tinker 1963), so its importance may be less apparent than that of letter size. But, for text presentation on visual display units, contrast may be at a lower, perhaps critical level, for instance when bright surfaces are reflected in the display screen. Data on the relationship between legibility and text–background contrast are therefore of obvious practical importance; yet such data are scarce. They are also of interest from a more theoretical viewpoint, since they will clearly increase our knowledge about the essentials of the reading process.

The present experiment explored some aspects of legibility as a function of contrast, viz. the probability of correct recognition and the response latencies for isolated three-letter words from the Dutch language. The main reason for choosing this stimulus material was the availability of a considerable amount of experimental data, as well as a theoretical model on the recognition of such words with high text contrast (Bouma 1973, Bouwhuis and Bouma 1979).

2. Method

2.1. *Stimuli*

160 different Dutch three-letter words which are fairly common (frequency of occurrence $> 10^{-5}$) were used as stimuli. They were typed on white paper through new carbon-tape; this results in homogeneously black letters with sharp boundaries. A 'Courier 10' typeface, lower case, was used. The contrast C between letters and paper was high, viz. 0·90, according to the following definition of contrast:

$$C = \frac{L_p - L_c}{L_p},$$

where L_c is the luminance of the black characters and L_p that of the white paper. Texts which are produced in the way described may be considered to have excellent quality and thus represent a good reference when certain factors, e.g. text contrast, are selectively degraded. In the actual experiment, four levels of contrast were used: 0·90, 0·47, 0·24 and 0·12, at a constant background luminance of 150 cd/m². The stimuli were presented in a two-channel tachistoscope at three retinal positions, viz. with the middle letter at 0°, i.e. foveally, and at $-1\cdot5°$ and $+1\cdot5°$ parafoveally. The distance between the centres of two adjacent letters was 2·5 mm, i.e. it subtended an angle of 0·25° at the chosen viewing distance of 57 cm. The stimulus presentation time was 100 ms. This is shorter than the visual reaction time, so that eye movements by the subjects could not systematically influence the results of the experiment. A blank field, provided only with a suitable fixation mark, preceded and succeeded each stimulus. This field also had a luminance of 150 cd/m².

2.2. *Procedure*

For every subject, the experiment was divided into two sessions, with one day between sessions. The first session started with 40 practice trials at a contrast of 0·36. In all further trials, the other four contrast levels were combined with four blocks of the 160 different stimuli in a Graeco-Latin square to determine the order of stimulus presentation for each subject. Thus each stimulus word was presented four times. The retinal position at which a stimulus was presented was randomly varied within stimulus blocks.

Stimulus presentation was self-paced. The subjects were instructed to respond accurately, but as fast as they could, by saying the word they perceived aloud. Response latencies were measured by means of a voice switch (see Schröder 1977).

2.3. Subjects

Twelve members of the IPO staff acted as subjects; they all had a visual acuity, either natural or corrected, of at least 1·0 for both eyes (determined with a Landolt C chart). Binocular vision was used.

3. Results

The first measure of word recognition employed, namely the percentage of correct responses, is depicted as a function of contrast in figure 1. These data, averaged across the twelve subjects, show that with diminishing contrast the *foveal* correct score hardly changes, whereas *parafoveal* correct scores decrease from about 90% to 50%. Most of this decrement occurs when contrast is reduced below 50%. Figure 1 also shows that there is a difference in correct score of about 6% in favour of the presentation in the right visual field; qualitatively this fits in with the results of Bouma (1973).

The inset of figure 1 shows the word 'recognition' as an example of text which is read at a viewing distance equal to that of our experiment, namely 57 cm. The added scale denotes the subtended visual angles of letter strings in text read at such a distance. Imagine an eye fixation at the 'r' or 'recognition': then figure 1 gives an indication of how reading performance declines with decreasing text contrast at an eccentricity equal to that of the first 'i' in 'recognition'.

The second measure of word recognition used—i.e. latency of the correct verbal responses—averaged across subjects, is shown as a function of contrast in figure 2. At all three stimulus locations decreasing contrast has a clear effect on latency: for foveal presentation, latencies increase by about 50 ms when contrast decreases from 0·90 to 0·12, whereas for parafoveal presentation the same decrease of contrast results in latency increases of about 150 ms. Most of this increment occurs when contrast is diminished below 50%. A small but consistent difference, independent of contrast, is found between the two parafoveal conditions: presentation in the right visual field yields slightly shorter latencies.

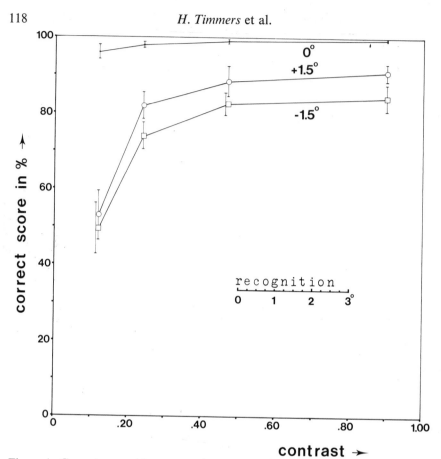

Figure 1. Correct recognition scores, in per cent, for Dutch three-letter words as a function of text–background contrast C at three retinal locations (see text for the definition of C). The thin vertical lines at each data point indicate standard deviations of the mean. See text for explanation of the inset.

4. Discussion

In normal fluent reading, three basic visual processes are operative. (1) Saccadic eye movements, i.e. eye jumps between successive fixation points. During such movements there is no useful perception and therefore no contribution to the recognition of words. (2) Recognition therefore has to take place in the pauses between saccades and is limited to an area surrounding each fixation point, called the visual reading field. (3) Integration of the fragments of text recognized during successive eye pauses (see e.g. Bouwhuis and Bouma 1979, Legein and Bouma 1980).

To what extent do the results of the present experiment relate to those normal reading processes? Our data demonstrate that parafoveal word recognition, in particular, deteriorates when the luminous contrast between text and

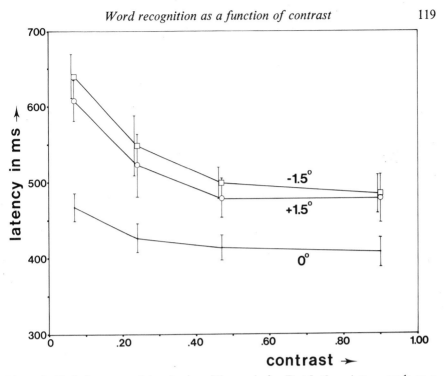

Figure 2. Verbal response latencies in milliseconds for Dutch three-letter words as a function of text–background contrast at three retinal locations. The thin vertical lines indicate the standard deviations of the mean of each data point.

background is reduced. Deterioration shows up both in the probability that the word presented is recognized correctly and in the time needed for correct recognition (see also Bouwhuis *et al.* 1978). It should be noted that these effects are already apparent at modest retinal eccentricities, in terms of the visual angles that letter strings subtend at normal viewing distances, as is illustrated by the inset in figure 1. The results described may therefore be interpreted as showing that a reduction of text contrast will result in an impairment of normal reading processes, because of (*a*) a shrinkage of the visual reading field, and (*b*) an increase of recognition latencies: such increases will interfere with the normal time relationships within the integration process mentioned above.

Obviously, a number of differences exist between our stimuli—three-letter words, typewritten in black 'Courier 10' letters on white paper—and a typical VDU presentation, featuring luminous matrix letters on a darker background. As was mentioned in the introduction, the latter difference implies another adaptational state of the eye, with lower resolving power. In any case, it appears justifiable to conclude that if visual display units are operated in such a way that text contrast is low, reading such text is impeded *in a quantifiable way*. Low text contrasts may exist in quite a few display situations; for example, an ignorant application of colour in systems like Viewdata or Teletext may lead to colour combinations of text and background that have too low a luminous contrast, and are therefore hard to read.

References

BOUMA, H., 1973, Visual interference in the parafoveal recognition of initial and final letters of words. *Vision Research*, **13**, 767–782.

BOUWHUIS, D. G., and BOUMA, H., 1979, Visual word recognition of three-letter words as derived from the recognition of the constituent letters. *Perception and Psychophysics*, **25**, 12–22.

BOUWHUIS, D. G., SCHIEPERS, C., SCHRÖDER, U. O., and TIMMERS, H., 1978, Temporal structure of visual word recognition responses. *IPO Annual Progress Report*, **13**, 83–93.

LEGEIN, C. P., and BOUMA, H., 1980, Visual recognition experiments in dyslexia (in the press).

SCHRÖDER, U. O., 1977, A controlled voice switch. *IPO Annual Progress Report*, **12**, 137–139.

TINKER, M. A., 1963, *Legibility of Print* (Iowa State University Press).

Information selection from visual display units

By F. L. ENGEL

Philips Research Laboratories, Eindhoven, The Netherlands

Colour can be a very useful expedient for improving the surveyability of electronically displayed text. With the introduction of Viewdata and Teletext, the use of colour in text displays has increased considerably. Its appropriate application, however, requires a subtler approach than is standard today.

To that end the 'conspicuity area' is proposed as a means for assessing more quantitatively the influence of colour on the visual prominence of embedded entities of text. Experimental evidence for the relevance of this concept is given.

1. Use of colour in Teletext and Viewdata

Teletext and Viewdata are new electronic developments, that enable the user to obtain on the screen of his adapted home TV-receiver, in alphanumeric and/or simple graphic form, a wide variety of information services, relating for instance to consumer interests, entertainment, news and encyclopaedic data. The user selects specific 'pages' of information by means of a small numeric key pad. Figure 1 (a) shows a sample of a typical page that can be called up from Prestel, the Viewdata system of the British Post Office, at present in experimental operation.

In normal typography, variables like different type size, bold face, italics or interline spacing are frequently used to improve the layout (see e.g. Hartley 1978), thus supplying the reader with global information about the structure of the text. Precisely these global cues markedly increase the legibility of the text, since they enable the reader to skip those parts that are irrelevant for him and to read with greater care the regions of interest. Due to the limited spatial resolution of the electronic page, most of these typographic facilities are not available in Viewdata and Teletext. In fact, colour is frequently used there as a substitute. In view of the substantial amount of search, selection and global reading required for finding the desired information in such systems (see van Nes and Tromp 1979), the extensive use of colour for structuring and emphasizing parts of text seems justified.

However, a closer look at figure 1 (a) which is in fact one of the principal menu-pages of Prestel, reveals that, although the colours certainly enliven the image, they clearly violate the grouping that exists in the text itself (see e.g. the broken Gestalt of the word 'PRESTEL' and that of the price '0p–3p' of item 1). Furthermore, reading is hampered by the distracting influence of certain conspicuous colour contrasts, leading to an unintended emphasis on less relevant parts (see e.g. the red '3p's in figure 1 (*a*). Both influences of colour (grouping and emphasis) can be perceived more clearly by eliminating the meaning of the text as in figure 1 (*b*).

From this it may be concluded that, although colour is indeed a powerful means of improving the legibility of electronic text displays, its property of grouping and emphasizing parts of a text is not always optimally applied. The latter problem has also been remarked upon by Reynolds (1979). In the following we present a method of quantifying the 'visual conspicuity' or prominence of (coloured) entities in their background, making it possible to access the use of colour in text displays in a more systematic way.

2. Conspicuity area

When we are looking at a still picture, the movements of our eyes are characterized by brief periods (100–400 ms) during which the eyes remain fixated at a certain position and during which visual information is taken in. These fixation pauses are alternated by rapid movements towards other positions, during which perception is negligible. Since, in general, only a fraction of the image

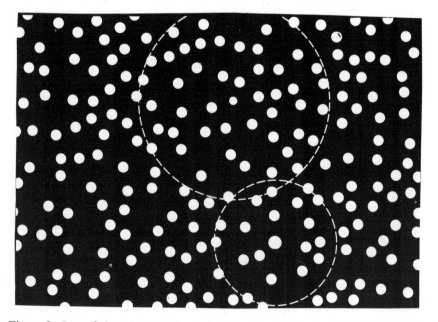

Figure 2. One of the test patterns used in the investigations described. The dashed circles approximate the conspicuity areas of the two deviating spots.

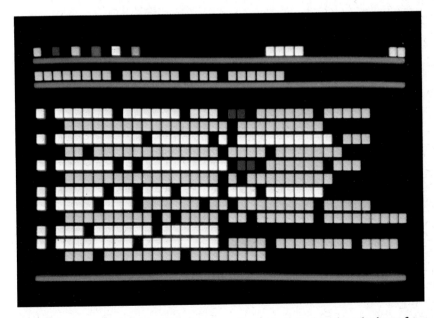

Figure 1. (*a*) A sample of a Viewdata-image, as it can be called up by telephone from Prestel, and can be displayed in colour on an adapted home TV-receiver. (*b*) By converting the alphanumeric characters of (*a*) into rectangles of the same colour, the influence of the colours on the layout becomes more apparent.

can be perceived in a single eye-fixation pause, it is relevant to ask what factors determine the successive choices of fixation position. In the context of this question, we advocate the application of the notion of "visual conspicuity" (Engel 1976). We assume visual conspicuity to be the external or involuntary determinant of information selection by eye movements, as opposed to other determinants under voluntary control, having a more cognitive or internal origin (see, for example, Bouma (1978) for more details on the latter influences in reading).

Figure 2 depicts the 'conspicuity area' of two test spots whose diameters differ from the fixed diameter of the background spots. The conspicuity area represents the field in which one has to fixate, in order to discover the relevant object by virtue of its sensory differences (in size, colour, etc.) with regard to the surroundings. A larger area then corresponds to a more conspicuous object. In practice, the areas are not quite circular; the radius R averaged over the border eccentricities in eight directions is used as a measure of their size. Since the conspicuity area is also conceivable as centred around the line of sight, its border can be determined straightforwardly by requiring the observer to fixate a central mark at the monitor, and, while doing so, to let him try to discover the location of a given test object in successive tachistoscopic presentations of, relative to the fixation mark, shifted versions of the same test object background pattern.

In the following, some experimental evidence is given to show the relevance of the conspicuity area; for a full account see Engel (1971, 1974, 1977).

3. Experimental evidence

We experimented with patterns like that in figure 2, with two special spots, one larger and the other smaller than the surrounding background spots. Before each session one of the two (e.g. the larger) was labelled 'target' and the other 'non-target'. It was the observer's task to find the target as fast as possible, but at the same time to avoid fixation on the non-target.

As an example of the results obtained, figure 3 gives for a series of 48 presentations the cumulative number of times the given target was found as a function of search time.

It was found that our data could be described rather well by assuming that the successive eye fixations during search are arbitrarily positioned over the display, while during each fixation a field of the size of the relevant conspicuity area is checked for the target. This assumption enabled us to derive in a second way, viz. from the slope of the exponential approximation of the cumulative search-time data (Engel 1977), the effective radius (r) of the corresponding conspicuity area (see figure 4, upper line).

The linear relation found ($r = 0.8\ R$) corroborates the assertion that the conspicuity area constitutes a useful concept for assessing visual search.

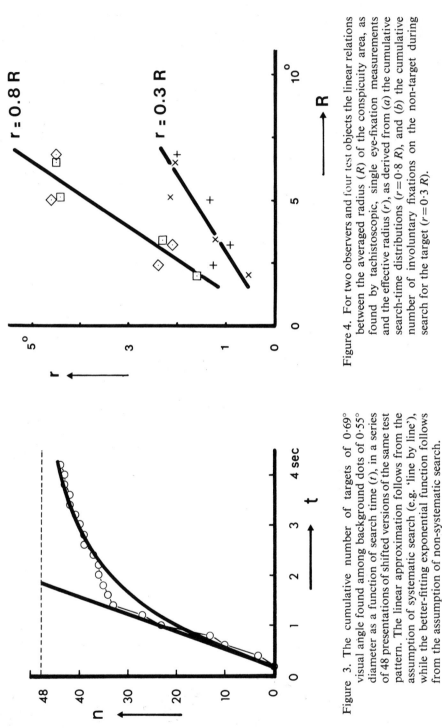

Figure 4. For two observers and four test objects the linear relations between the averaged radius (R) of the conspicuity area, as found by tachistoscopic, single eye-fixation measurements and the effective radius (r), as derived from (a) the cumulative search-time distributions ($r = 0.8\,R$), and (b) the cumulative number of involuntary fixations on the non-target during search for the target ($r = 0.3\,R$).

Figure 3. The cumulative number of targets of $0.69°$ visual angle found among background dots of $0.55°$ diameter as a function of search time (t), in a series of 48 presentations of shifted versions of the same test pattern. The linear approximation follows from the assumption of systematic search (e.g. 'line by line'), while the better-fitting exponential function follows from the assumption of non-systematic search.

With regard to the non-targets, it followed from the eye-movement recordings we made during the search experiments that they were nevertheless involuntarily fixated. The extent to which this happened was found to be directly related ($r = 0.3 \, R$) to the size of the corresponding non-target conspicuity area (see figure 4). Thus, the occurrence of involuntary, reflex movements of the eyes could also be related to the relevant conspicuity area.

Although the described results are related to randomly positioned objects that differ in size, instead of to regularly positioned characters that differ in colour, it is claimed that the conspicuity area constitutes a significant tool for assessing the influence of colour in electronic text displays as well as for research on information selection from visual display units in general.

Acknowledgment

I am very grateful to N. V. Philips' Gloeilampenfabrieken for covering the cost of using coloured illustrations in this paper.

References

BOUMA, H., 1978, Visual search and reading: Eye movements and functional visual field: A tutorial review. *Proceedings of the 7th International Symposium on Attention and Performance* (Hillsdale, N.J.: Erlbaum), pp. 115–147.

ENGEL, F. L., 1971, Visual conspicuity, directed attention and retinal locus. *Vision Research*, **11**, 563–576.

ENGEL, F. L., 1974, Visual conspicuity and selective background interference in eccentric vision. *Vision Research*, **14**, 459–471.

ENGEL, F. L., 1976, Visual conspicuity as an external determinant of eye movements and selective attention. *Philips Research Reports Supplements*, **6**, 1–92.

ENGEL, F. L., 1977, Visual conspicuity, visual search and fixation tendencies of the eye. *Vision Research*, **17**, 95–108.

HARTLEY, J., 1978, *Designing Instructional Text* (London: Kogan Page).

VAN NES, F. L., and TROMP, J. H., 1979, Is viewdata easy to use? *IPO Annual Progress Report*, p. 14.

REYNOLDS, L., 1979, Teletext and viewdata a new challenge for the designer. *Information Design Journal*, **1**, 2–14.

Experimental investigations for optimal presentation-mode and colours of symbols on the CRT-screen

By G. W. RADL

Technischer Überwachungsverein Rheinland, Cologne, F.R. Germay
and University of Trier, F.R. Germany

Methods and main results of four different experiments for the adaptation of information presentation on VDUs to the human perception are described. The first experiment shows that frames can bring an improvement in readability and visual comfort, when the VDU is positioned unfavourably under optical conditions which can cause glare effects. The second experiment demonstrates that coloured symbols bring an advantage in readability of the information on the screen, when the use of colour is not connected with a decrease of the luminescence level on the display and colours are situated within the yellow–green part of the spectrum. The performance of man in identifying colours of simple symbols on different coloured backgrounds on a colour TV screen was investigated in the third experiment. The results are an impressive demonstration of the problems in the application of multicolour CRT displays. In the last experiment it was found that the presentation-mode of dark characters on a light background on the VDU screen provides better readability and higher visual comfort than the presentation of light characters on a dark background.

1. Use of frames when a VDU is positioned unfavourably

1.1. *The question*

Is it possible to improve readability with light symbols on a dark background on the screen, when the VDU is positioned unfavourably in an optical environment which causes glare effects (e.g. windows or bright walls)? What effects do different frames have?

1.2. *Method*

Subjects had to complete letter series on a paper sheet by transcribing letters which were presented on the screen, and had to identify numbers which were short-term presentations on the display, both tasks to be done in a standardized form. All subjects carried out the tests with an unframed unit as well as with frames varying in width and form. The performances of the subjects with the different frames were compared, and also their subjective ratings of visual comfort.

1.3. *Illumination conditions*

The green–yellow symbols on the screen had a brightness of $120 \, cd/m^2$, the brightness of the screen background was $18 \, cd/m^2$. Glare was produced by luminous discharge lamps (4000 K) which were situated behind semi-transparent Plexiglass. The part of the optical background behind the screen which was used to produce glare consisted approximately of $75°$ in the centre of the visual field. Its brightness was $4200 \, cd/m^2$. Subjects were situated at a viewing distance from the VDU screen of 60 cm. The illumination level on the workplace was 500 lx.

1.4. *Subjects*

The subjects were 22 male and female persons between 22 and 42 years, all experienced with work on VDUs.

1.5 *Results*

Figure 1 shows the results of completing the letter series tests and demonstrates the influence of the frame-width on the perceptual performance in transcribing letters from the VDU screen as well as on the ratings of visual comfort on a scale between 0 and 7.

It can be shown that the width of the frame had a systematic significant effect on the reading performance and also on the rated visual comfort. However, the widest frame was not the best. It is probable that the widest black frame caused a too low adaptation level of the eye. In further experiments, it

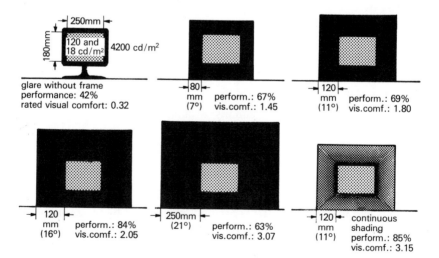

Figure 1. The frames used and their effects on performance in a letter-transcribing test and on the rated visual comfort. The performance is related to the individual's performance in a tested presentation situation without glare (100%). The rating scale for visual comfort ranged from 0·00 (worst) to 7·00 (best).

was shown that a frame with continuous shade from black at the VDU screen to white at the outside produced a further improvement.

1.6. *Conclusions*

Under unfavourable positioning of the VDU, caused by a too bright optical environment, frames can bring an improvement in VDU-readability and visual comfort. However, it is to be pointed out that frames do not present an ergonomically ideal solution. Their application should be limited to cases where units of past technical generations have to be used under unavoidable glare conditions.

2. Effects of coloured symbols on a VDU screen

2.1. *The question*

What symbol colour is best, when light symbols are presented on the dark background of the VDU screen?

2.2. *Psychophysical factors*

The effect of the spectral sensitivity of the eye is well known (Hartmann 1977). As figure 2 shows, the brightness sensitivity of the human eye is greatest at a wavelength of 555 nm. Also known is the effect of the chromatic aberration of the optical system which can make the eye short-sighted for blue–violet up to 1·5 dioptres (Le Grand 1957).

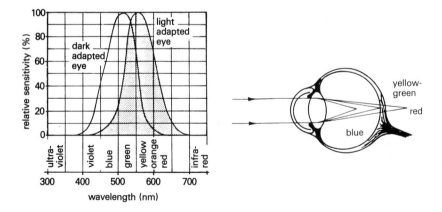

Figure 2. Spectral sensitivity and chromatic aberration of the eye.

2.2. *Methods in the experiment*

White and six different symbol colours were produced using CRTs with different phosphors and coloured Plexiglass filters. Figure 3 shows the colours used within the German Standard colour diagram (DIN Farbenkarte) (which is similar to the Munsell-diagram). The different luminescences of the coloured signs were also measured. Under laboratory conditions and at a well designed workplace, illuminated with 500 lx without glare and without reflections on the screen, the individuals had to do a task similar to those described under the first experiment. They were forced by the letter-transcribing test to make eye movements between the screen and the well illuminated paper sheet. The duration of the test run under each condition was 10 minutes. After the tests with all seven symbol colours the individuals had to compare each colour condition for the symbols with every other (21 comparisons) under the aspect: Which of both would you prefer on the VDU at your workplace?

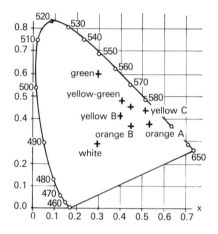

Figure 3. The used symbol colours within the standard colour diagram.

2.4. *Subjects*

The subjects were 30 males and females between 19 and 42 years, all with experience in VDU work and all without eye and colour defects.

2.4. *Results*

Figures 4 and 5 demonstrate some of the results. The investigated symbol colours produced only relatively small differences with respect to the readability, and not all differences are significant; but high and significant differences are found with respect to the ratings in the paired comparison test. The brightness and the contrast of the symbols on the VDU screen seem to be more important than the symbol colours in any case when they are within the recommended area of the spectrum.

2.6. *Conclusions*

Coloured filters which are placed in front of a tube with white or coloured light-emitting phosphors to reduce the bandwidth of the spectrum, but also the

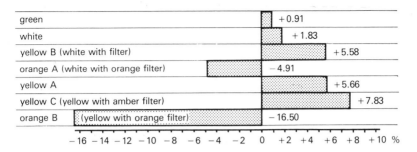

Figure 4. Relative performance in the letter-transcribing test related to the individual's average performance under all colours.

luminescence, normally bring no advantage. Only tubes with phosphors which transform the full energy of the electronic beam into a reduced band within the yellow–green region can be recommended. When such coloured symbols are preferred by man, it seems to be caused mainly by psychological factors rather than by physiological mechanisms. This finding could also be verified by practical experiences since the investigation.

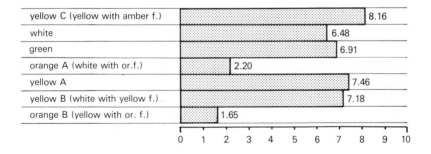

Figure 5. Preference scores of the different symbol colours. The scale ranged from 0 (no preference in all comparisons) to 10 (preferences in all comparisons of each colour with every other).

3. Discrimination of coloured symbols on different coloured backgrounds on a TV screen

3.1. *The question*

What effects do different combinations of symbol and background colours have on the detection rates of small symbols, on the rate of correct colour discrimination, and on the reaction time?

3.2. Method

In the experimental study subjects were required to detect as quickly as possible and to name the colour of small moving squares on a TV monitor with different coloured backgrounds. Five symbol colours and seven background colours (six colours as shown in figure 6 and 'grey with 40% visual noise') were used. All trials involving a single background colour were presented in one block. Symbol size (three levels), symbol velocity (fast and slow), directions of the symbol movements and illumination level (10 lx and 480 lx) were also systematically varied. Observer performance was quantified by registering the proportion of correctly and incorrectly named symbol colours, the percentage of symbols not detected and the reaction time.

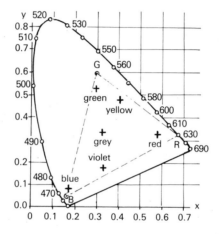

Figure 6. The used colours and the limitations of the colour TV screen within the standard colour diagram.

3.3. Subjects

The subjects were 30 well sighted young men.

3.4. Results

Figure 7 shows that the various combinations of symbol/background colour produced error rates between 4% and 95%. The accuracy and speed of perception were also influenced by the symbol size and to a lesser extent by the symbol velocity and the direction of motion. The level of illumination had a comparatively small influence.

3.5. Conclusions

In view of the high error rates observed in this study, careful preliminary consideration is required for the colour-coding of symbols of TV-displays.

I would like to point out that it is necessary to differentiate between three kinds of colour use on VDUs:

Colour is used in a *one-colour display* as demonstrated in investigation two, and this can be done without problems.

Colour is used for *better structuration* and to make orientation easier. This is connected with some problems but is not impossible.

Colour is used as a *code-element*. This causes difficulties because man's colour discrimination abilities seem to be very limited.

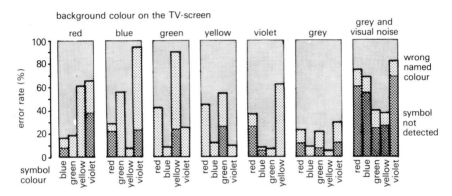

Figure 7. Error rate for the different symbol/background colour combinations.

4. Positive and negative presentation mode

4.1. *Question*

Can differences be found between positive and negative presentations even during a short working period with the VDU? (The term 'positive presentation' is usually used in Germany for 'negative contrast' and means dark symbols on a light background.)

4.2. *Method*

The performances, the error rates and the ratings of visual comfort were compared, when the individuals had to solve standard tasks which simulated the visual performance during data and text input with a VDU from a paper sheet. The same VDU was used for both presentation modes with a refreshing rate of 66 c/s to avoid flicker when using positive presentation. The tasks were carried out under good illumination conditions (500 lx) at an ergonomically well designed workplace.

4.3. *Subjects*

The subjects were 24 males and females, all participants of an introductory course in text communication.

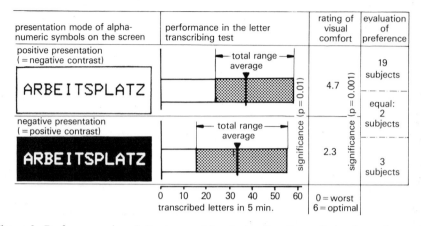

Figure 8. Performance in a letter-transcribing test and ratings of visual comfort and of preference under positive and negative presentation modes of the alphanumeric symbols on a VDU screen.

4.4. *Results*

The results are shown in figure 8. The differences are significant and can be interpreted on the basis of physiological optics. Positive presentation causes a higher average luminescence level on the screen. Visual acuity and the depth of focus of the eye increase (Hartmann 1977, Häusing 1976). Too large brightness-differences between the screen and the paper sheet are avoided.

4.5. *Conclusions*

Positive presentation (= dark symbols on a light background) was found to be significantly better than negative presentation. Positive presentation can be recommended not only on the basis of the results of this experiment but also for the following reasons:

The adaptation conditions for the eye are better, especially when eye movements between the VDU screen and a paper sheet often occur.

The sensibility for discomfort glare, which is often reduced by practically unavoidably bright optical environment, is reduced.

Positive presentation is also an effective and ergonomically ideal method for avoiding reflections on the screen.

Today VDUs with positive presentation are technically possible and can be produced at acceptable cost.

References

BRIGHAM, F. R., HAINES, A., RADL, G. W., and SCHNADT, H., 1979, *Bewegte Farb-symbole auf Fernsehbildschirmen*. Report No. T/RF 36/RF 360/61603 (Köln: Technischer Üeberwachungsverein Rheinland).

HARTMANN, E., 1977, *Optimale Beleuchtung am Arbeitsplatz* (Ludwigshafen: Kiehl Verlag).
HÄUSING, M., 1976, Colour coding of information on electronic displays. In *Proceedings of the 6th Congress of the International Ergonomic Association* (Santa Monica, California: The Human Factors Society), pp. 210–217.
LE GRAND, Y., 1957, *Light, Colour and Vision* (New York: Wiley).
RADL, G. W., 1980, *Ergonomie. Arbeitsplaetze mit Bildschirmgeraeten.* Report No. 128011 (Paderborn: Nixdorf Computer AG).
RADL, G. W., 1980, *Vergleich von Positiv- und Negativdarstellung auf Bildschirmen im Hinblick auf die Erkennungsleistung und auf die erlebte visuelle Beanspruchung* (Düsseldorf: Akzente, Studiengemeinschaft 'Akzeptanz neuer Bürotechnologien').
WAGNER, D. W., 1973, Farbmessungen an Fernseh-Farbbildroehren nach dem Dreibereichsverfahren. *Die Farbe*, **22**, 31–43.

Improving the legibility of visual display units through contrast reversal

By D. Bauer and C. R. Cavonius

Institut für Arbeitsphysiologie, Universität Dortmund, Postfach 1508,
D-4600 Dortmund 1, F.R. Germany

Observers attempted to identify letters on a television terminal, which were presented either as conventional light letters on a dark background (positive contrast) or as dark letters on a bright background (negative contrast). Both the error rate and the time required to perform the task were significantly reduced when negative contrast was used.

1. Introduction

From the viewpoint of sensory physiology, it is clear that conventional visual display units (VDUs) leave a great deal to be desired. Many of the problems arise from the fact that VDU technology was taken over directly from the television industry, with the result that the luminance, resolution, and frame rate are far from optimum for the efficient transfer of information.

Of these, luminance (or its physiological counterpart, adaptation level) has the most pervasive influence, since it directly affects visual acuity, contrast sensitivity, pupil diameter, and speed of accommodation. In general, visual acuity and contrast sensitivity both improve as adaptation level is raised (for a review, see Westheimer 1972). Good visual acuity is necessary if errors are to be avoided: for example, at a normal viewing distance the difference between the letters O and D in one common type font consists of moving four dots through 1·2 minutes of arc. Since normal acuity is generally defined as the ability to discriminate objects that subtend 1·0 minutes, discriminating between these letters forces the user to operate at close to his limit of resolution. Contrast sensitivity, which is of importance in any task that requires the user to discriminate between brightness levels in spatial patterns, also improves at higher adaptation levels.

Secondary but none the less significant advantages in a higher adaptation level include a smaller pupil and more rapid accommodation. Increasing the luminance from 10 cd/m² (which is approximately the mean luminance of many VDUs) to 100 cd/m², for example, reduces the diameter of the pupil from about 4 mm to 3 mm. This reduces optical distortions and significantly improves the depth of field. The latter effect is of considerable importance to older users, who have lost much of their ability to accommodate. However, younger observers also benefit from higher luminance: the data of Cakir *et al.* (1978) suggest that raising the luminance from 10 to 30 cd/m² doubles the speed with which accommodation can be changed from 0·3 to 1·0 m.

However, raising the adaptation level carries a severe penalty: the visual system becomes more sensitive to flicker. Within the range of luminances covered here, the so-called Ferry–Porter law holds: the highest frequency at which flicker is seen increases linearly with luminance, by about 10 Hz for each tenfold increase in luminance. Thus, a VDU with a 50 Hz refresh rate that is just at the threshold for flicker perception at 10 cd/m² will flicker violently at 100 cd/m². Since flicker is one of the most disturbing features of VDUs (e.g. Cakir *et al.* 1978, pp. 157–160), it is easy to understand why conventional VDU practice has been to keep screen luminance low by keeping the screen as dark as possible, using light letters on a dark background. To determine the frequency at which flicker disappears, eight observers with normal vision were allowed to adjust the repetition frequency of a P4 (white) phosphor display screen that was operated at 200 cd/m², without any pattern; the frequency had to be raised to 90 Hz before all flicker disappeared when peripheral vision was used. To be well beyond flicker threshold, a repetition rate of 100 Hz was used in the experiments to be described except when a conventional display was simulated, in which case the European convention of 50 Hz was used.

In selecting an appropriate luminance for the VDU screen, the following criteria were used: large contrast steps between the screen and its surroundings should be avoided, as these tend to degrade acuity; and the luminance of the screen should resemble that of other material, such as typed documents, that the user may have to consult while using the VDU, so as to avoid unnecessary changes in adaptation level, which reduce visual sensitivity. Measurements of typical documents on a desk that received an illumination of 550 lx, which is just above the 500 lx that is prescribed as a minimum for office work in Germany (Opfermann and Streit 1979), showed that they had a mean luminance of 80 cd/m². This value was used as representative of the worst case that would be encountered in practice.

2. Experiment 1: character recognition test

2.1. *Method*

In this test, we wanted to simulate a common situation in which the user must look back and forth between the VDU and some other display (such as a typed document). The observers began each trial by looking at a small (6 × 10 mm) numeric display located at eye level behind the VDU, and about 0·9 m from the observer. As soon as the observer identified a number flashed on the display, he shifted his gaze as rapidly as possible to the VDU, which was a Hazeltine 1500 with P4 phosphor, modified to work at a frame rate of either

50 or 100 Hz. A four-letter nonsense word was briefly displayed on the VDU; the observer attempted to read the word and type it on the VDU keyboard. By asking the observer to report only four letters, we hoped to minimize problems of retention and errors of typing; but by using nonsense words, we prevented him from filling in his response by guessing the identity of a real word.

Suitable parameters of the task were chosen in pilot work. The numeric display presented either the number '4' or the number '6', at random, every 660 ms for 490 ms. The observer demonstrated that he had identified the '4' or '6' by pressing the corresponding key on the numeric part of the VDU keyboard. The program logic required the observer to press the key while the number was present or within 170 ms after it had disappeared. This task was hard enough to ensure that the observer paid full attention to the numeric display at the beginning of the trial, but easy enough to allow him success in identifying the number in the great majority of trials. A successful key-press caused the display controller to present the four-letter nonsense word on the VDU for 340 ms, beginning 70 ms after the key-press had occurred. Each letter was formed of a conventional 6×8 dot matrix, 4·3 mm high and 3·0 mm wide; the closest distance between adjacent letters was approximately 0·4 mm. The letters were presented in blocks of 100 words, and the total number of errors and the specific errors were recorded, as well as the time that was required to complete each block. After two practice blocks, two blocks of conventional positive-contrast letters (i.e. light letters on a low, 4 cd/m² background), and two blocks each of positive-contrast letters on a bright background (80 cd/m²) and negative-contrast (dark letters) on an 80 cd/m² background were presented in counterbalanced order.

2.2. Observers

The observers were 13 men and 10 women with normal vision, between the ages of 23 and 47. All had experience with standard typewriters; about half had some, but none extensive, experience with VDU terminals. They wore their usual spectacle correction, if any.

2.3. Results

The results are given in figure 1, in which the abscissa gives the number of errors made (out of a possible 800), and the ordinate is the proportion of the 23 observers who made the specified number of errors *or less*. These cumulated proportions have been transformed by plotting on a Gaussian probability ordinate, so that the fact that the cumulated data can be described by a straight line means that the distribution of errors across observers was approximately normal. The arrows in figure 1 show the mean errors for the group: 102 for high luminance, negative contrast (H−); 137 for low luminance, positive contrast (L+); and 144 for high luminance, positive contrast (H+). Thus, changing from the conventional L+ condition to the negative contrast H− condition reduced the mean error rate by 26%. The H+ condition was especially

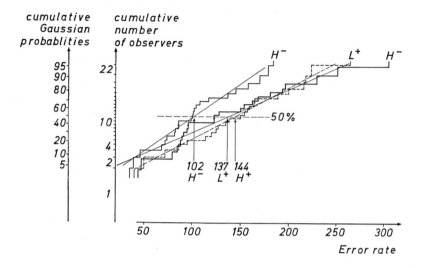

Figure 1. The ordinate gives the cumulative number of observers who made as many errors as, or less than, a given value on the abscissa, under the following conditions: H−(solid line): high luminance (80 cd/m²), negative contrast; L+ (dashed line): low luminance (10 cd/m²), positive contrast; H+(solid line): high luminance (80 cd/m²), positive contrast.

unsatisfactory, and was dropped from the later experiments. Also, observers complained that the bright letters were too dazzling.

3. Experiment 2: detection of discrepancies

3.1. *Method*

This experiment measured the speed and accuracy with which observers detect discrepancies between characters on a VDU, and similar material typed on paper. Two conditions were compared: conventional positive contrast, with 50 Hz repetition frequency (L+); and negative contrast, high background (H−), with 100 Hz frequency. To simulate a work situation, the observers set their own brightness and contrast: in L+ they set the brightness of the background so that flicker was just invisible (< 10 cd/m²); and the letters to between 40 and 65 cd/m². In the L+ condition, the room illumination was reduced to 270 lx, to improve the contrast of the letters. In the H− condition, all observers set the letters to be as dark as possible, and the background within the range 50 to 70 cd/m². In this condition the room illumination was set at 550 lx.

The four-letter nonsense words were presented in blocks of 100 words. The observer set his own pace: pressing the space bar on the terminal caused one word to appear for 340 ms at a random location within a 6 × 8 cm rectangle on the screen. The observer then looked to a sheet on which 100 nonsense words were typed in IBM Orator (a sanserif, 3·1 mm high font that resembles the electronically generated characters). The observer's task was to draw a pencil line through any letter that differed from the ones just presented. A total of six blocks of 100 characters were given, with a short pause between blocks. The first two blocks were for practice; only the last two positive contrast and last two negative contrast blocks were used in the data analysis. A counterbalanced ABBA order was again used.

3.2. Observers

Observers were 12 men and 7 women from the original group of observers.

3.3. Results

Figure 2 (*a*) compares the error rates and figure 2 (*b*) the times to complete the task for H− and L+ presentation. The results are plotted in the same manner as in figure 1. The ordinates are the proportions of the 19 observers to make a given number of errors or less, or to need the specified time or less. The Gaussian means are 27 errors in the H− and 35 errors in the L+ presentation. Thus, changing from the conventional L+ presentation to the negative contrast, high level condition reduces the mean number of errors by 23%. A similar improvement can be seen in the figure of performance time: the mean drops from 12·2 min in the L+ condition to 11·25 min in the 'negative contrast' H− condition, which is an improvement of about 8%.

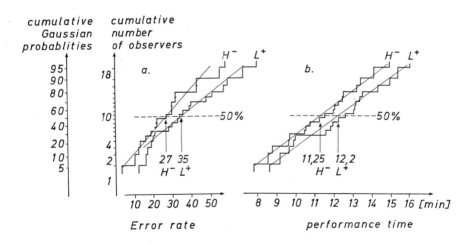

Figure 2. (*a*) The ordinate gives the cumulative number of observers who made as many errors as, or less than, a given number on the abscissa, under the following conditions: H−: high luminance, negative contrast; L+: low luminance, positive contrast. (*b*) Cumulative number of observers who took as much time as, or less time than, a given value on the abscissa. Conditions as in (*a*).

3.4. *Observers' evaluation*

Since no display is of much value if potential users dislike it, the observers' evaluations of the positive and negative contrast displays were solicited by means of a questionnaire. All but one observer favoured the negative contrast display, commenting that it was easier to read and more comfortable to use. Positive contrast was described as requiring more effort and as being more tiring. Even observers who had experience with conventional displays preferred the negative contrast display. The one observer who indicated a slight preference for positive contrast actually performed better, by every measure, when using the negative contrast display.

Acknowledgments

We thank Matthias Bonacker for conducting the experiments, and Peter Wilms for developing the computer programs.

References

CAKIR, A., REUTER, H. J., V. SCHMUDE, L., and ARMBRUSTER, A., 1978, Untersuchungen zur Anpassung von Bildschirmarbeitsplätzen an die physische und psychische Funktionsweise des Menschen. *Forschungsbericht der Humanisierung des Arbeitslebens* (Bonn: Der Bundesminister für Arbeit und Sozialordnung).

OPFERMANN, R., and STREIT, W. (editors), 1979, *Arbeitsstätten* (Wiesbaden: Deutscher Fachschriften-Verlag).

WESTHEIMER, G., 1972, Visual acuity and spatial modulation thresholds. In *Handbook of Sensory Physiology*, VII/4, *Visual Psychophysics*, edited by D. Jameson and L. M. Hurvich (Berlin, Heidelberg, New York: Springer-Verlag), pp. 170–187.

Error detection at visual display units

By S. BAGNARA

Istituto di Psicologia del C.N.R., Rome, Italy

In one experiment, VDU operators were asked to detect two different types of error: letter substitution, and word or part of a sentence repetition. Subjects showed significant differences in detection performances as a function of the types of error. The results are discussed in terms of differences in mental processes involved and in task demands.

1. Introduction

VDU operators may be requested to detect errors in complex texts. The errors to be detected can be different in type and require various levels of knowledge and processing. For instance, when one of the internal letters in a word is upper case while all the others are lower case, the detection of the error does not necessarily call for knowing the meaning of the word itself; detection may occur on the basis of a visual analysis of the word and requires only the limited knowledge of the upper case and lower case forms of the letters in the alphabet used. On the other hand, when part of a sentence is repeated, an operator has to know the meaning of the sentence to detect the error; greater knowledge is needed and the processing should be deeper and more demanding (Craik and Lockhart 1972).

Some authors maintained that visual reading can be performed through relatively independent stages, mechanisms, or codes (Posner 1978). Kolers (1973) pointed out that recognition of words does not occur by the piecemeal recognition of their letters, and that reading connected discourse does not proceed by the serial recognition of the single words. Furthermore, Lott Holmes (1973) proposed that letter identification, word identification, and comprehension of meaning are distinct tasks that can be performed independently on the same visual information. Each task would call for specific mechanisms which can work relatively independently and in parallel (Henderson 1974).

It is well known that prolonged working at VDU leads to symptoms of eyestrain (Cakir 1978) and visual fatigue (Bedwell 1978). These symptoms seem to be related to the task demands; in fact, Cakir (1978) found that programmers declared much less eye strain than data-entry operators, when using the same equipment. On the basis of the independent stages of processing model, these differences may be conceived as determined by the different task demands for accurate visual analysis. It can be hypothesized, in fact, that prolonged work at VDUs should impair performance when accurate visual analysis for detecting errors is needed, and that it should have little or no influence when error detection taps higher-level mechanisms, relatively independent of visual analysis. An experiment was undertaken to test these hypotheses.

2. Methods

2.1. *Subjects*

Six VDU operators, male, normally sighted, mean age 35 years, all working at VDUs for one year or more, took part in the experiment.

2.2. *Procedure*

Nine news articles were presented to the subjects through a commercial VDT (Linotype VDP 300). The first two articles were considered as a practice session, and the others as the experimental session. The contents of the articles were as follows: (*a*) practice session: (1) health care, (2) cycling; (*b*) experimental session: (1) editorial on the political strategy of an Italian party, (2) football, (3) letter to the editor on heroin addicts, (4) short story, (5) trade union strategy, (6) football, and (7) crime. The articles were always presented in this order. There were 144 errors randomly distributed through the seven experimental articles (one error per 50 words, on average). There were two different types of error: (*a*) 72 errors consisted of substitutions of one of the internal letters in a word; (*b*) 72 errors consisted of repetitions of a word or part of a sentence. The subjects were asked to read the articles looking for errors. They were also requested to signal detections by putting the errors between brackets. Speed was not even named and no information about the types of error was given. The experimental task lasted 105 min on average; the differences in the time taken to perform the task between the fastest and the slowest subject was 12 min. The VDU and the VDU workplace characteristics followed the recommendations listed in Cakir *et al.* (1979). At the end of the experimental session, omissions were computed as a function of time course, divided in quarters of an hour.

3. Results

The results showed a clear relationship between subjects' performances in error detection and time course (see table). Subjects detected more errors at the beginning than at the end of the experimental task (92·1 % vs 81·9 % in the first quarter and in the last one, respectively). This decrement did not depend on the different contents of the articles, in fact there is a clear difference also

Error detections and omissions (in percentages) as a function of time course.

	Time course (in quarters of an hour)							
	1	2	3	4	5	6	7	Mean
Detections	92·1	91·6	93·1	91·3	88·8	87·5	81·9	89·5
Missed:								
Substitutions	5·1	3·3	4·8	4·7	9·5	10·0	9·7	6·8
Repetitions	2·8	5·0	2·0	4·0	1·6	2·2	8·3	3·7
Total omissions	7·9	8·3	6·8	8·1	11·1	12·2	18·0	10·5

between the second and sixth quarters, when subjects were reading articles with similar content.

Omissions of letter substitution errors were about twice as frequent as omissions of repetition of a word or part of a sentence, and the distributions as a function of time course were quite different. The omissions of the first type of error increased linearly from about 5% up to 10%; while the second type of error omissions showed a marked increase only at the end of the experimental session, in the last quarter of an hour.

Two *t*-tests for correlated samples on arcsine transformations of omission percentages showed that the differences between the two distributions of omissions were statistically significant ($t(5) = 2·73$; $p < 0·05$) in the first period of time considered, and were not significant in last quarter. Two further *t*-tests showed there were no significant differences between the first and the last periods considered for both types of omission; however, in the case of word or sentence repetition errors a *t* value (2·43) very close to the significance level was obtained (*t* value for $p < 0·05 = 2·57$).

4. Discussion

The results can be summarized as follows: (*a*) error detection decreases as a function of time course; (*b*) the deterioration in performance is due mainly to an increase in omissions of errors of word or sentence repetition; and (*c*) omissions of letter substitution errors also increase, without approaching, however, a statistically significant level.

These data seem to indicate that working at a VDU produces a significant decrement in performance when tasks require detailed analysis of the visual material presented after a period longer than the one we used. The decrement in letter substitution error detection is apparent, but it does not reach significance in a task lasting 105 min.

Furthermore, the data showed that different task demands bring about different patterns in performance deterioration: the two types òf error yield different distributions in detection along the time considered. The increase in omissions of word or sentence repetition errors cannot easily be attributed to VDU characteristics, as in the case of the other type of errors. It seems more appropriate to explain it by assuming that the detection of word or sentence repetition errors calls for a mechanism devoted to meaning or conceptual analysis, independent from that involved in the accurate visual analysis required by the other type of error. The two mechanisms may differ in fatigue appearance and in their relations to VDU characteristics.

If this notion is tenable, it can be hypothesized that VDU characteristics determine visual fatigue as a function of the demands of the tasks the operators are requested to carry out. The VDU operators would be likely to note visual fatigue symptoms when the task to be performed requires detailed visual analysis of the material presented at the VDU; on the other hand, when their tasks demand higher level (i.e. semantic, or conceptual) analysis of the same material, the VDU operators would not note the same symptoms, at least not at the same frequency. The differences in eye-strain symptoms between various groups of VDU operators that Cakir (1978) found might easily be explained on the basis of this suggestion, the groups having to carry out tasks demanding different levels of analysis.

References

BEDWELL, C. H., 1978, Assessment of eyestrain and difficulty of viewing visual display units. Paper presented to the Conference on Eyestrain and Visual Display Units, Loughborough, 15 December 1978.

CAKIR, A., 1978, Incidence and importance of eyestrain among VDU operators. Paper presented to the Conference on Eyestrain and Visual Display Units, Loughborough, 15 December 1978.

CAKIR, A., HART, D. J., and STEWART, T. F. M., 1979, *The VDT Manual* (Darmstadt: Inca-Fiej Research Association).

CRAIK, F. I. M., and LOCKHART, R. S., 1972, Levels of processing: A framework for memory search. *Journal of Verbal Learning and Verbal Behavior*, **11**, 671–684.

HENDERSON, L., 1974, A word superiority effect without orthographic assistance. *Quarterly Journal of Experimental Psychology*, **26**, 301–311.

KOLERS, P. A., 1973, Three stages of reading. In *Psycholinguistics and Reading*, edited by F. Smith (New York: Holt Rinehart & Winston), pp. 28–49.

LOTT HOLMES, D., 1973, The independence of letter, word, and meaning identification in reading. In *Psycholinguistics and Reading*, edited by F. Smith (New York: Holt Rinehart & Winston), pp. 50–69.

POSNER, M. I., 1978, *Chronometric Explorations of Mind* (Hillsdale: L. Erlbaum).

Method of calculating inspection time of samples on visual display by measurement of eye movement

By K. Noro and K. Tsuchiya

University of Occupational and Environmental Health, Japan School of Medicine, Kitakyushu, Japan

Results of the experiments for visual counting inspection are described. A model which satisfies the results is constructed. The counting times are estimated by the model. Estimated and observed counting times are compared. A procedure for calculating counting time is proposed.

1. Introduction

According to the research of Noro and Kurabayashi (1968), the time required for counting varies with the complexity of objects being inspected and the strictness of inspection standards. What is most important in the process of visual inspection is the inspector's eye movements. Recently, Kowler and Steinman (1977) experimentally investigated the function of eye movement to count objects in a small visual field (2·3°). The result obtained from the experiment with repetitive patterns suggests that counting did not require saccades. Noro (1980) conducted a series of experiments with the objects in a larger visual field. He reported that even dots scattered within such a wide visual angle of the sample can be counted with not so many saccades. This result gave a quantitative explanation of subitizing (or immediate apprehension) and counting (the objects are counted one by one) processes defined by Kaufman *et al.* (1949) for perception of the number of objects through measurements of eye movements. Other findings of the above study are as follows:

(1) The counting time varies with the symmetry of specific samples.

(2) The human visual process also varies with the number of dots present on the samples. The number of dots that divides the two processes (subitizing and counting) is put at four, according to the results.

(3) The visual characteristic of the sample which exerts an overall influence on the counting task is the number of dots present on each of five circular sections of the sample.

(4) The entire process of eye movement is divided into the period during which the eyes do not move after sample presentation and the period during which the eyes move and respond to the presented sample. The former period is required to establish fixed elements, such as physiological response and light adaptation, to discriminate symmetry. The

latter period is required to count and report the number of dots present on the sample.

Noro (1980) constructed a visual information model for counting from the above findings.

The present paper introduces the model and proposes the procedure for calculating counting time.

2. Experiment

2.1. *Subject*

A student was employed as subject.

2.2. *Method of measuring eye movements*

This study adopted electro-oculography to measure eye movements.

2.3. *Stimulus*

The stimulus samples had black dots scattered on a white background. The number of black dots ranged from two to ten per pattern. Three different types of patterns were prepared for each set of black dots. One type of pattern has dots symmetrically arranged, while the other two had dots placed at random. The total number of the patterns belonging to one type was nine.

2.4. *Procedure*

The subject counts and reports the number of black dots on each pattern (sample) projected onto a screen by a slide projector located behind him. The samples presented subtended 25·8° horizontally and 17·6° vertically, and the black dots subtended 0·37°. This work is performed when time is not limited.

3. Visual features of samples

After comparison of various indexes, the numbers of dots or the configurations of dots in different parts of each sample were adopted as the visual features. (Each sample was divided into five circular parts. The numbers of dots in the respective divisions were used as data.)

4. Relationship between visual features of samples and counting time

Multiple regression equations were obtained to predict the time until the start of eye movement and the number of saccades after the start of eye movement. They are summarized in the table.

Multiple regression equations for prediction of the time (Y) to the start of eye movement and the number of saccades (S) from the start of eye movement to the start of response†.

Random or symmetrical	Number of dots	Equation	Multiple correlation
R	2–4	$Y_1 = 0 \cdot 088 + 0 \cdot 238\,(X_4 + X_5)$	$0 \cdot 991$
R	2–4	$S = 0 \cdot 833 + 0 \cdot 500\,(X_1 + X_2 + X_3) + 0 \cdot 833\,(X_4 + X_5)$	$0 \cdot 882$
R	5–10	$Y_1 = 0 \cdot 201 + 0 \cdot 073 X_1 + 0 \cdot 015 X_2 + 0 \cdot 033 X_3$	$0 \cdot 516$
R	5–10	$S = 2 \cdot 190 + 0 \cdot 960 X_1 + 0 \cdot 855 X_2 + 0 \cdot 469 X_3$ $+ 0 \cdot 300 X_4 + 0 \cdot 575 X_5$	$0 \cdot 728$
S	2–10	$Y_1 = 0 \cdot 358 - 0 \cdot 082\,(X_1 + X_2 + X_3) + 0 \cdot 033\,(X_4 + X_5)$	$0 \cdot 670$
S	2–10	$S = 1 \cdot 978 - 1 \cdot 402 X_1 + 4 \cdot 25 X_2 + 1 \cdot 271 X_3 + 0 \cdot 13 X_5$	$0 \cdot 900$

† Y: counting time, S: number of saccades, X_i: number of dots in the dividend part i.

5. Proposed counting time model

The model which satisfies the findings of Noro (1980) consists of a six-stage, three-branch tree structure as shown in figure 1. The process of estimation is performed in three subprocesses in accordance with the model. Using the equation in the table, the calculating procedure for each subprocess is as follows:

The time (Y_1) to the start of eye movement is estimated.

The number of saccades between the start of eye movement and the start of response is estimated. The time between the start of eye movement and the start of response is estimated by equation (1):

$$Y_2 = S \times D \qquad (1)$$

where

S = number of saccades as estimated by equation S of the table,

D = fixation duration.

D is defined as the time when the sum of square errors between estimated and observed counting times is minimized.

Thus, the time required (Y) to count is calculated by equation (2):

$$Y = Y_1 + Y_2. \qquad (2)$$

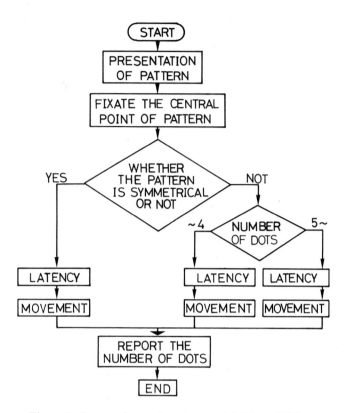

Figure 1. Proposed counting time model (Noro 1980).

6. Estimation of counting time

The counting times estimated by the model are plotted in figures 2 and 3. These figures show that fit between estimated and observed counting times is good for both random and symmetrical patterns.

7. Procedure for calculating counting time

In general, there exist samples and objects of various characteristics and sizes. The procedures applicable commonly to such samples and objects are described below.

(i) Determine the desired counting accuracy or, in other words, the percentage of correct counts.

(ii) Describe the visual characteristics of objects to be inspected. The items to be described are as follows:

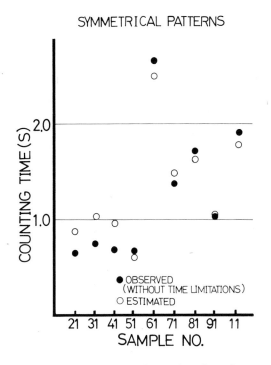

Figure 2. Observed and estimated counting times for symmetrical patterns.

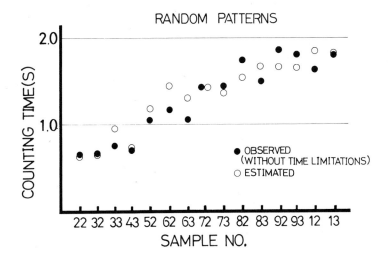

Figure 3. Observed and estimated counting times for random patterns.

(*a*) Angles at which the sample subtends the visual field horizontally and vertically.

(*b*) Visual characteristics of objects to be counted. Describe the shape and size of objects. Visual angle per fixation.

(*c*) Regularity of arrangement of objects to be counted: random or symmetrical.

(iii) Determine the visual field which conforms to the desired accuracy. This item differs from (*b*) in (ii). It points to the visual field per inspection.

(iv) Determine the number of saccades. From (*b*) in (ii), (iii) and the number of objects, estimate the required number of saccades.

 (v) Determine the scanning method: decide whether to count all objects in a sample at a time or to count objects in a few subgroups. This is closely related to the method of object presentation.

(vi) Estimate the counting time by the proposed model.

References

KAUFMAN, E. L., LORD, M. W., REESE, T. W., and VOLKMANN, J., 1949, The discrimination of visual number. *American Journal of Psychology*, **62**, 498–525.

KOWLER, E., and STEINMAN, R. M., 1977, The role of small saccades in counting. *Vision Research*, **17**, 141–146.

NORO, K., 1980, Determination of counting time in visual inspection. *Human Factors* (in the press).

NORO, K., and KURABAYASHI, T., 1968, Judgment time and its application on visual inspection task. *Japanese Journal of Ergonomics*, **4**, 221–226.

Application of SAINT for the analysis of visual performance and workplace layout

By K.-F. Kraiss

Forschungsinstitut für Anthropotechnik, D–5307 Wachtberg-Werthhoven, F.R. Germany

It has been shown that operator behaviour and visual performance in rather complex control/monitoring tasks may be predicted fairly accurately by network models. The effort for this simulation is significantly simplified by the application of the SAINT simulation language.

1. Introduction

In many practical instrumentation applications, it is mandatory to know in advance whether and to what degree an operator can fulfil the tasks he is expected to do, given the amount and type of information presented to him.

As an example, take the following arbitrary situation (see figure 1) that may have been identified as being critical in the course of a system development process (Kimmel 1980):

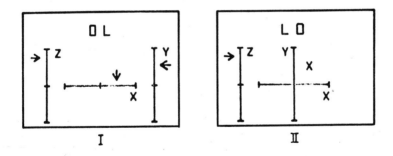

Figure 1. Two display configurations for the described control/monitoring task.

Three independent stochastic processes with a bandwidth of $\omega = 2\cdot07$ must be stabilized simultaneously by manual control using three scales presented on a CRT screen. Scales X, Y are served by the operator's right hand using a two-dimensional joystick while the Z-axis is controlled by the left hand with a one-dimensional stick. In addition two binary digits showing 'L' or 'O' are shown side by side in the upper part of the screen. Any time a digit shows 'L', a push-button has to be kept pressed with the left or right foot respectively. Both digits are driven randomly at a 1 second interval. Both states are equally probable ($p(L) = p(O) = 0·5$).

It is obviously difficult to say beforehand and without experimentation whether this complex task can be handled by one operator and which display configuration is better adapted to the task. To answer these questions, the task and the operator performance must therefore be simulated.

Numerous efforts have been made to model human control and monitoring behaviour. The most prominent examples are the cross-over and the optimal control models (Sheridan and Ferrell 1974). Both are rather restricted when it comes to application. Alternatively human behaviour may be modelled as a sequential decision process. This involves a transition from a simultaneous multi-loop to a sequential single-loop control. In this case, any loop is served only in specific time intervals, the sequence of which is determined by experience, objective criteria, priorities or by accident. Thus modelling starts with a detailed analysis of the assumed or requested (normative) sequence of actions down to elementary operator functions. Subsequently a task network is synthesized from these elements. Linkages and transition probabilities between tasks are selected in such a way that the model behaves realistically under dynamic conditions.

2. The SAINT simulation language

Model generation is significantly simplified by the application of a simulation language called SAINT (System Analysis of Integrated Networks of Tasks) (Wortman and Duket 1978, Wortman *et al.* 1978).

SAINT is a network modelling and simulation technique for the design and analysis of complex man–machine systems. It provides the conceptual framework for representing systems that consist of discrete task elements, continuous state variables, and interactions between them. It facilitates an assessment of the contribution system components make to overall system performance.

It is the ability to combine models of dynamics (e.g., aircraft equations of motion) with models of discrete activity sequences (e.g., operator actions) that permits the systems analyst to describe both hardware and human performance in the context of a single model.

Since it is not possible to describe SAINT here in detail, only the most essential features needed to understand the model described later are mentioned. For discrete event simulation, a graphical-network approach to modelling is taken, whereby a user of SAINT describes the system to be analysed via a network model and auxiliary descriptions. For continuous process representation, the user is expected to provide Fortran statements of the relevant state equations to be solved. Mechanisms are provided for creating an interaction between the discrete and continuous components of the model.

The discrete task-oriented component of the SAINT model consists of nodes and branches, each node representing a task. Tasks are described by a set of characteristics (e.g., performance time duration, priority, resource requirements). Branches connecting the nodes indicate precedence relations and are used to model the sequencing and looping requirements among the tasks. Complex precedence relations have been designed into SAINT to allow predecessor–successor relationships which are deterministic, probabilistic, and conditional. Resources, either human actions or hardware equipment, perform the tasks in accordance with the prescribed precedence relations, subject to resource availability. The precedence relations also indicate the flow of information through the network. The symbol used to model a task in SAINT is illustrated in figure 2.

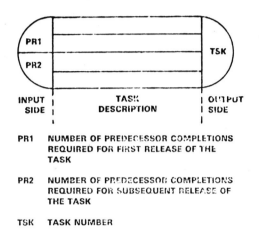

PR1   NUMBER OF PREDECESSOR COMPLETIONS
       REQUIRED FOR FIRST RELEASE OF THE
       TASK

PR2   NUMBER OF PREDECESSOR COMPLETIONS
       REQUIRED FOR SUBSEQUENT RELEASE OF
       THE TASK

TSK   TASK NUMBER

Figure 2. Task symbol.

The centre portion of the task symbol contains all task description information, such as performance time characteristics, statistics to be collected, and attributes to be assigned. It is subdivided into rows, with each row containing a specific type of descriptive information about the task. Further, each row is divided into two parts. The left-hand part contains the task description code. It is used to identify the type of information that appears in the right-hand part of the row. The output side of the node contains the task number (TSK). In addition, the shape of the output side indicates the branching operation to be performed upon task completion. The four branching types included in SAINT are deterministic, probabilistic, conditional take-first, and conditional take-all. Their shapes are depicted in figure 3.

The second component of a SAINT model is the state variable description. The SAINT user defines these state variables by writing the algebraic, difference, or differential equations that govern their time-dependent behaviour. The use of state variables in SAINT is optional. The SAINT user writes the state variable equations in a Fortran subroutine.

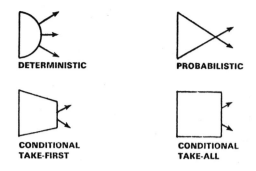

Figure 3. Task branching symbolism.

In SAINT, simulated time is advanced in accordance with the type of system being modelled. If no state variables are included, simulated time is advanced from one task completion to the next. When state variables are included in the model, time is also incremented in steps between scheduled task completions for the purpose of updating the values of the state variables. The step size is a function of user-specified accuracy requirements. The interactions between tasks and state variables are initiated either by tasks being completed or by state variables crossing specified threshold values.

SAINT was developed in ANSI standard Fortran and consequently, is machine-independent. The task network data is punched on cards in free-form. The SAINT includes an extensive input error-check feature to assist users debugging their models. For production runs, users can select a more efficient non-error-checking version of SAINT. SAINT also includes provisions that allow formatting model outputs so they can be processed by available statistical analysis packages.

3. Modelling the control/monitoring task using SAINT

A reasonable strategy for the simultaneous control of three processes (see figure 1) seems to be to check first all instrument pointers and select the one with the largest deviation. Subsequently the operator starts to control the relevant process and closes this loop according to the cross-over model. While still controlling, the operator checks the other two processes using peripheral vision. As soon as one of the other two pointers shows a larger deviation, attention and control activity is shifted over to this process. Feedback of the old loop is interrupted. The model thus resolves a simultaneous three-axis control into a threefold one-axis control that is sequentially worked upon.

The upper part of figure 4 shows how this verbally described strategy translates into a SAINT-model. Task 1 (RANDUP 1) is used to generate and filter three statistically independent Gaussian noises needed to disturb the three processes. By tasks 3 to 5, labelled DEVINST, the actual deviation of each instrument is determined. For each check a fixation time (TIME) of 0·3 s is inserted, which seems to be a representative value. In addition each of these tasks is attached to a resource (RESR). Three different resources simulate the situation where all instrument pointers can be inspected simultaneously, as may be the case for a high display integration. If only one resource for all three tasks is available, a sequential instrument scan is modelled, as may happen with widely separated instruments.

CONTROL (task 6) manages the switch-over of control activity from one process to the next. This action is assigned a duration of 200 ms corresponding to a simple reaction task.

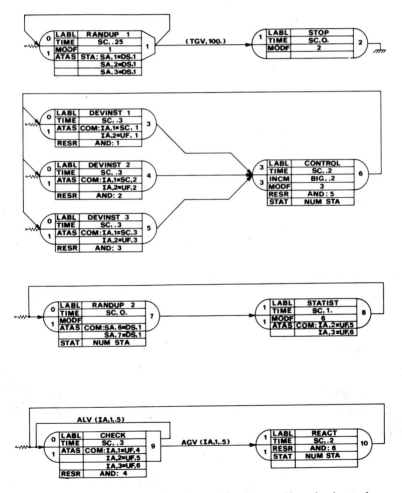

Figure 4. SAINT-model for the combined control/monitoring task.

The lower part of figure 4 represents the monitoring of the two additional digits in figure 1. Both indicators are controlled by task RANDUP 2 which yields two independent random digits (O, L) every second.

Monitoring is modelled by tasks 9, 10 (CHECK and REACT). The operator monitors continuously both binary indicators and determines whether a change in status has taken place. This observation may take about 0·3 s. If the status has changed, the relevant reaction is stimulated (REACT). Since this is a simple expected reaction, 200 ms seems to be a reasonable guess for this task. Subsequently observation is continued, given the resource assigned to task 9 is not otherwise busy; otherwise, task 9 has to wait until the resource becomes available again.

In figure 4 task 9 is depicted as having its own resource (RESR 4), a separate 'eye' so to speak for the observation of both binary indicators. If the same is true for tasks 1 to 3, all information on the screen (see figure 1) can be seen at one glance, as may be the case for small screens.

On the other hand the effect of an entirely sequential scan may be portrayed, if only one resource is attributed to tasks 3, 4, 5 and 9. A suitable assignment of resources is therefore a means to study the effect of various instrumentation

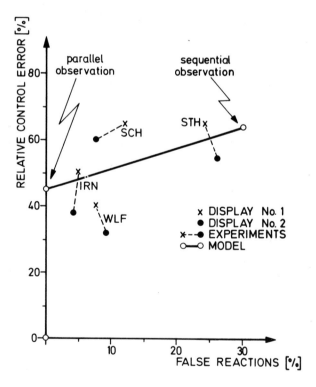

Figure 5. Comparison of experimental and analytical results.

alternatives. The described network represents a well structured, relatively simple model for a rather complex control/monitoring situation. It may be emphasized that modelling is primarily based on the assumption that the operator applies the outlined normative strategy. In addition, assumptions have been made concerning fixation and reaction times based on data available from the literature. For the manual control part McRuer's cross-over model was applied.

In figure 5 a comparison between experimental (--) and analytical (—) results is depicted. It may be seen that the model predicts an optimal performance for parallel instrument scanning showing a relative control error of about 45% and no wrong reactions at all. For a sequential scan of the display items, this deteriorates to 64% relative control error and 30% wrong reactions. Experimental data are available for four subjects and both display alternatives. For all subjects display 2 yields better results than display 1, probably because in the second configuration two scales (X, Y) can be checked simultaneously. The performance of the four subjects varies widely but is grouped around the line predicted by the model. This reflects differences in scanning and controlling strategy applied by the subjects. Subject IRN is, for example, able to absorb information from the screen almost simultaneously, while subject STH prefers a sequential scanning mode. It may, however, be stated that the model predicts this variance in behaviour correctly and is thus a reliable means of estimating system performance at an early design stage.

References

KIMMEL, K. R., 1980, Die Bewertung von Anzeigen durch den vom Menschen übertragenen Informationsfluβ bei Regelaufgaben. Kybernetik Kongreβ, Mainz, March 1980, to be published by Oldenbourg-Verlag.

SHERIDAN, T. B., and FERRELL, W. R., 1974, *Man Machine Systems* (Cambridge, Mass.: MIT Press).

WORTMAN, D. B., and DUKET, S. D., 1978, *Simulation Using SAINT: A User-Oriented Instruction Manual*, AMRL-TR-77-61 (Ohio: Wright-Patterson AFB).

WORTMAN, D. B. *et al.*, 1978, *The SAINT User's Manual*, Aerospace Medical Research Laboratory, AMRL-TR-77-62 (Ohio: Wright-Patterson AFB).

Design of VDU operator tasks

By E. Tintori Pisano

Institute of Occupational Health, Ergonomics Section, Milan, Italy

The special aspects of field work are outlined to show the scope of ergonomic problems in practical situations. Those which can be solved by means of information available in the literature are listed. For those where knowledge is defective, attempts to define the main variables called into play and to analyse their relations on the basis of existing tasks compared with the demand of specific human processes, and extrapolation to future tasks, are briefly summarized.

1. Introduction

The content of this paper is derived from a field study, where an ergonomic evaluation was carried out into the design of a computerized telecontrol system, concerning an electricity network in a highly urbanized area. The evaluation also included some design criteria, which were meant to be an improvement where the ones previously adopted were not judged to be conducive to operators' health and comfort and, consequently, to system efficiency.

The case seems to be a somewhat representative example of the constraints that fieldwork is subject to, which often act as an impairment to the scientific value of studies; particularly that caused by pressure of time, in this case six months, and by no experimental work being allowed. Other pertinent constraints included those posed by hardware, by only very limited modifications still possible in the software, and by an already existing building. Furthermore, the problem was compounded by the fact that operators had not been informed about the design in progress and were unaware of the possible implications of computerization. The organization structure of the company and its system component orientation rather than system interface made the collection of data rather circumscribed.

2. Task variables

The project to be examined covered the area of system performance, the output of which is to receive electricity supply from power stations, to make some voltage transformation and to distribute it, in spite of whatever alteration or emergency occurs.

Most work concentrated on visual displays (a huge control panel, four CRTs, some small specialized devices), keyboards, teleprinters, work-station, control-room layout and lighting, while the computer was to be accepted as it was. For the rest, some human operations were mentioned and defined, but there was no actual design of the operators' task as such and no relevant information was provided to assess workload.

The ergonomic study has tended to define the tasks of human operators in the new system on the basis of actual operations to be done, in order to see which abilities are implied and what compatibility exists between them and the equipment provided; on the other hand it has also investigated what changes the human operator must undergo in respect of his past experience and existing or attainable skills. Information has been derived from documents, from what was reported by the present operators during interviews, from the ergonomists' surveys of their current activity, and from meetings with the company managers and technical staff. Operations to be done can be summarized as follows:

poor motor activity substantially limited to digitation of keyboards and ordinary movements for telephone calls, writing and reading;

routine activity such as repetitive operations and quantitative adjustments in the process, adopting the company procedures;

information and instruction exchange with other departments or units, internal and external to the company;

monitoring the control operated by the computer on the process, by observing all visual and graphic displays, where ordinary and anomalous events are represented and described;

selection of additional information needed both about correction and compensation made by the computer, in case of ordinary alteration or emergency left to be solved by the human operator;

diagnosis of emergency events, as deriving from punctual monitoring, detection and correlation of significant variables;

actions undertaken, resulting in commands, sometimes iterative commands, to the computer to operate machines and/or regulate process variables.

Variation compared with operations performed until now can be summarized as:

considerable reduction in operator movement;

introduction of digitation of keyboards;

removal of a good deal of hand-written recording;

monitoring of the process interposed by the computer, which means loss of direct contact, felt as deprivation of information, and also more concise presentation of information and different physical modality of presentation;

allocation to the computer of the operations dealing with the most simple alterations in the process;

computer feedback at some level of errors and computer control of the number of operations possible for a given system component.

The scant attention paid to the design of operator task has given no evidence about the present operators' old habit of devising simulated emergency situations and of designing operational strategies: such activity has played the role of balancing undemanding waiting time with overloaded attention and concentration required during emergencies. Even more important, it reduces uncertainty about emergency features and improves strategic behaviour.

3. Human abilities

First of all, the human need to walk around has been preserved by transmitting everywhere in the building, and not only in the control room, auditory signals acting as reinforcement of visual signals. A new skill is then to be acquired, that is, eye–hand coordination, which is supported by:

location of keyboards and most-used visual displays in the same horizontal visual angle;
forward and backward adjustability of keyboard case, lateral to desk centre;
key setting as a function of sequence, priority, and frequency of use as well as of operators' stereotypes. This is also for the purpose of memorizing keys so that they can be digitized on the basis of tactile perception.

Human memory storage and recall of routine operations, as well as simple decision processes, are lightened in the computerized system, but some additional operations are still to be allocated to the computer in order to avoid loading the operator with the necessity of shifting from simple to complex levels of activity.

A further load to short-term memory derives from the representation on the CRT screen of portions of the process one by one; unfortunately, existing constraints prevent information from being organized and presented in alternative ways.

The demand on perceptual abilities is mainly concerned with visual perception, as most information is conveyed through it by means of panels, digital, analogue and graphic displays, in addition to printed documents. Environmental variables and signal chracteristics have been reviewed for the purpose of making human perception not only possible, but also comfortable in front of the new physical modality of information presentation. As for the environment the following can be mentioned:

general layout allowing the operator not to have to adjust his eyes and/or head too often, on the basis of calculations on visual angles;
distance of displays from the operator's eye calculated according to angular size and density of symbols and characters;
quantity, direction and colour of light considered;
integration of natural and artificial sources as well as of general and local lighting;
reflectance of surfaces and luminance contrast taken into account;
specular reflection and glare control on the screen.

With regard to signals, produced on an 8×6 dot matrix, examination has been mainly devoted to legibility of alphanumeric characters and symbols, which has lead to the revision of luminance contrast, of density ratio, and of symbol features appearing ambiguous. With respect to this the basic criterion has been to maintain the customary ones and then to look for uniformity or compatibility all through the displays present in the control-room. If that is so, no additional decoding ability is required provided that the existing noise produced by some redundant symbols is eliminated.

Other linguistic requirements are the same as before with the advantage of some quantitative reduction of performance in this field, due to decreased communication with other technicians.

The dialogue with the computer is strictly programmed and there is no freedom left to the operator, who is asked to operate the system with very little knowledge about computer performance: this is a situation that, on a different scale, reproduces traditional work divisions.

The analysis of the present task has shown that the decision level is where the highest number of human operations cluster, while the computer gives no substantial support to the very complex decisions to be taken to solve emergency situations. The best way to analyse it has appeared to be the definition of the number of possible choices and the identification of hierarchy recognized by human operations, in order to draw out the main factors underlying decision strategies and to have them aided by the computer information-processing.

In the absence of help like this, which could not be provided because of the constraints mentioned before, the diagnosis stage is still very critical even if it is the most creative and interesting in the operators' opinion: uncertainty will always be the same and will lead to a task perception at least similar to the past one. In fact, in the operators' internal model the major emphasis is put upon their permanent state of alertness, from which derives perceptual load, much more than from sensory stimulation; another reason is that visual perception implied in process control is rather different from what is demanded in information retrieval systems or in conversational dialogues, as representations are stored in the operator's memory and therefore his observation of the screen is nothing but search for relevant details.

4. Quantitative assessment

As emergency events may be predicted only in relation to the time of the year and to technical programmes, which is less relevant, a survey has been made of emergencies which have occurred in the last year in six out of the 19 distribution stations, compared with the frequency and time needed to overcome it, and then contrasted with the time taken by routine operations. A coefficient has been determined to transfer these historical data to the whole network; the daily occurrence of events has been assumed to be normally distributed. Results have been examined for each of the three usual work shifts and include routine activity and emergency situations classified within five groups of increasing gravity. The sixth group, which is the most critical, has been left out as each event of this kind always takes many hours to be solved and requires the joint actions of at least two operators; at present one event of this group takes place on an average once in nine days but increases to a three-day frequency in the new situation because of the centralization of the control. Considering that such an event may occur at any time and that the duration of the others overlaps routine operations, it is apparent that shift structure has to be modified and the full job cannot be committed to two operators only, as it was in the company design, under pain of intolerable stress and lack of efficiency. It must be added that stress may derive also from shortage of time for customary simulation of a possible emergency, as mentioned before.

5. Results

Results will be available within a few years, as the full implementation of the system will take such a long period; this means that feedback reliability may be impaired and therefore discussion could be particularly useful among those who have met similar situations. For the time being the main issue is a message to researchers to work in the direction of the synthesis of tasks, in order to have in view whatever is the specialized area of interest or the finding aimed at: there is need of methods, techniques, approaches, maybe even attitudes, that are closer to the dimensions and complex relations experienced by people in real-life circumstances. In such a way single variables examined by research work can enter the whole scope of problems and can be connected with each other, up to the identification of factors not yet investigated.

Section 5. Postural problems

Postural reactions related to activities on VDU

By A. LAVILLE

Laboratoire de Physiologie du Travail et Ergonomie, CNAM, Paris, France

A work analysis has been effected as well as systematic postural observations with two groups of female operators doing two different kinds
of tasks on a visual display terminal. The postural observations are discussed with the help of the results obtained from work analysis. They
show that the required speed of execution, usually imposed by an apparent
simplification of work, is an important factor for postural immobilization.
   One may interpret this postural immobilization as a factor to maintain
a stable system of reference allowing a precise dimensioning of visual
and motor space coordinates.
   Thus, the arrangement for dimensioning the workplace and its physical
ambience are not sufficient to allow the adaptation of tolerable postures
over many hours and days of work. One must take into account the
actual content of the task as well as speed obligations. This is important,
since computerized systems, in their very short response delays, favour
a high degree of speed in work rhythms.

1. Introduction

Posture can be defined in a general way as the organization of bodily segments in space according to gravity forces. From this representation of
posture, studies have been made that concern anthropometric characteristics
in an active population, biomechanical laws that determine the limits of the
respective mobility of corporal segments and the role of psychophysiological
functions that regulate postural position (cf. *Sitting posture*, edited by Grandjean 1969, Berthoz 1978). These findings, often established in youthful, healthy
and handicap-free populations, have, however, been complemented by the
study of diversified populations; in particular, modifications induced by age in
postural organization have been more or less taken into account within limits
that remain very narrow (Marcelin 1975). Thus has been developed the notion
of internal conditions, i.e. functional state and variability thereof that determine postural regulation. At the same time, specific studies made upon postures
adopted according to the characteristics of executed tasks have integrated yet
another aspect of finality in postural regulation; posture also functions as a support in the activity of information-finding as well as motricity in a constructed
spatial environment (Laville 1968, Grandjean 1969, Teiger *et al.* 1974). Posture
then depends upon characteristics of the task to be performed as well as the

conditions in which that task is being performed. However, among these external parameters, one considered primarily the dimensional characteristics of the elements of work position: the necessity for precision and force to be exerted, i.e. the factors that determine in the first place motricity and only in the second place, the activity of information-finding.

The characteristics of the compromise achieved between the internal conditions (anthropometric and functional state of the operators) and external parameters (task exigencies and dimensional environment of this task), have been refined by subjective data produced by systematic enquiries (Grandjean 1969). A variety of norms have thus been submitted to allow a theoretical establishment of an ergonomic conception of job function from a postural point of view. If these norms are applied to the actual work situation on a visualizing screen, they orientate projects towards the dimensional conception of a job function that would be both unique and generally applicable to any task that necessitates the use of such a technical apparatus (Cakir *et al.* 1978).

The studies from which we report a few results have operated a work analysis as well as systematic postural observations upon two groups of women operators doing two different kinds of tasks on a visualizing screen. The results of these postural observations are discussed with the help of the results obtained from work analysis. These data are contrasted to results obtained from previous studies, either of an experimental nature, or in an actual industrial work situation.

2. Results

We shall compare two types of registering activity upon a terminal screen:

one being simple registering, i.e. direct transcription of figures (simple data collecting);

the other one being figured registering, i.e. interpretation and encoding of information as well as registering thereof (data ciphering and collecting).

In the first case, this simple registering activity is carried on at very high speed and there is a strict control of performance. In the second case, pressure upon performance is somewhat lower but is not altogether absent.

2.1. *Postural observations*

Systematic observations of the positioning of corporal segments have been effected with the help of a pre-established grille: they apply principally to position of the head and upper trunk in the different spatial dimensions (simple registering: 68 observations upon 7 operators, figured registering: 275 observations upon 11 female operators).

These observations attempt to answer two questions.

(1) For each of these tasks, does there exist a unique type of posture?

If one takes as a reference the posture most frequently adopted within each of the two groups (interindividual postural mode), one is led to the conclusion that this represents only a very low percentage in the observations that have been conducted: 15% in the simple registering work, 12% within the figured registering work. Each element being taken singly (see figure 1), percentages of postural mode are higher, differences between the two situations bearing essentially upon the fact that three elements in simple registering present no interindividual variability whatsoever. On the other hand, the number of combinations of positions is clearly higher within the group doing the figured registering (103) than within the one doing the simple registering (16). There seems thus to exist a larger homogeneity in postures within the simple registering group than in the other.

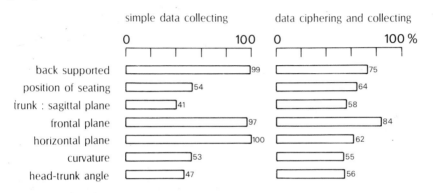

Figure 1. Group modal position for each part of body: occurrence frequency (per cent).

(2) Is there a difference between the two groups according to the postural immobilization criterion?

If one adopts as reference the postural mode of each of the female operators and if one calculates the frequency with which it is adopted, one may appreciate the degree of postural immobilization of the female operators (intra-individual variations); one notes that individual postural mode is found, in the average, in 73% of systematic observations in simple registering and 34% in figured registering.

For each female operator, the average number of observed combinations of positions is 2·6 in simple registering, and 13·6 in figured registering.

Finally, for each female operator, the reproduction of the position of each postural element is observed with a clearly higher frequency in the case of simple registering than in the case of figured registering (figure 2).

From these few elements of information, it appears that the immobilization is without question higher in the simple registering group than in the figured registering one.

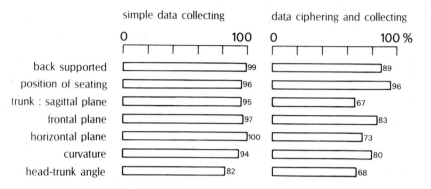

Figure 2. Individual modal position for each part of body: occurrence frequency (per cent).

2.2 *Distance between eye and task*

In these types of task, the three places where visual information input is principally effected are the screen, the keyboard and documents. However, looking towards the keyboard has probably only a re-calibrating function of the motor space of the hands without any use of clear and precise data-retrieving; these glances are very short, of the order of a few hundred milliseconds. Thus, we shall not take into account the distances between the eye and the keyboard that would then have a different status from distances between eye and screen or eye and document.

The results of measuring the distances between eye and task cannot be interpreted in absolute terms because these depend in part on the functional state of each female operator's eyesight, the disposition of workplace and the positioning of each of the elements. If one compares the collected values, one becomes aware of two facts:

in both work situations, the variability of the eye to document distances is higher than that of the eye to screen distances;

the variability of eye to screen distances and eye to document distances is lower in the case of simple registering than in the case of figured registering.

Table 1. Comparision of eye to task distances.

		Operator 1 Simple registering	Operator 2 Figured registering
Eye to screen	Mean	45·4 cm	88·5 cm
	σ	1·8	4·7
Eye to document	Mean	45·2 cm	50·4 cm
	σ	2·1	10·5

3. Discussion

If one assigns to posture the role of supporting the data retrieving activity as well as motricity, one may isolate the postural determining factors linked to the task by an analysis of visual activity, the primordial modality of data-retrieving as well as by the analysis of keyboard fingering activity.

Visual activity, in our perspective, can be apprehended with the help of two clues: one is the percentage of time spent in orientating the eyes towards the screen, the document and the keyboard, the other is the duration of looks in each of those directions.

The results (table 2) show that in the case of simple registering, the reading of the document is privileged and it may be supposed that the looks towards the screen have a mere controlling function of the registered data; looks towards the keyboard play a part of initial dimensioning in the space where the hand functions. In the case of figured registering, looks towards the screen and document have both rather similar characteristics and it may be inferred that they have an analogous status: looks towards the keyboard conserve their role of motor space dimensioning.

One may thus suppose that clearly privileging the direction of glances towards a single element of the task produces a first cause of postural immobilization. A second cause is probably the speed in executing the task. In previous experiments (Laville 1968), we had shown that for sensori-motor precision

Table 2. Visual examination. N = number of operators, m = average, σ = standard deviation, n = number of measurements.

	Average time spent in looking at different parts of work (as percentage of work time)			
	Simple data collecting ($N=6$)		Data ciphering and collecting ($N=5$)	
	Mean	σ	Mean	σ
Screen	18	0·09	30	12·8
Document	70	0·10	28	7·9
Keyboard	10	0·03	15	10·7
Other place	2		27	

	Average duration of glances used to look at different parts of work (seconds)					
	Simple data collecting			Data ciphering and collecting		
	N	Mean	σ	N	Mean	σ
Screen	187	0·91	0·81	588	1·54	1·94
Document	387	2·81	15·28	533	1·49	1·48
Keyboard	201	0·41	0·37	324	1·27	1·15

A. Laville

tasks, the distance eye to task was shorter as speed of execution was higher, and that this speed was also associated with a greater stability of that distance (see figure 3).

In some industrial tasks (e.g. garment) (Teiger *et al.* 1974), parcellized and with high productivity obligations, it has been shown that the seamstresses' posture was stable in time for the whole duration of their eight-hour work day and that this stability was achieved through a high degree of tension in postural muscles, increasing with the duration of work.

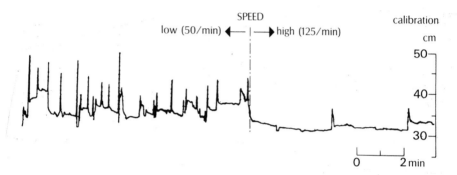

Figure 3. Record of eye–task distance during experimental work: modification of distance and variability with speed of sensori-motor activity.

One may establish a comparison between the parcellization of the seam-stresses' work and that of the simple registering task: that parcellization allows the imposition of productivity obligations and thence the rapidity of execution. In the case of figured registering, the complexity of the task diminishes the productivity obligations that may be imposed and thence the rapidity of execution.

One may interpret this postural immobilization as playing the part of maintaining a stable system of reference that allows a precise dimensioning of visual and motor space coordinates; postural activity can therefore be considered as a positioning activity of corporal segments in relation to gravitational forces as well as significant information concerning the environment and the various places of activity. In this interpretative system, the head/upper-trunk ensemble appears as a privileged element from which calibration of space is effected on the one hand, and on the other hand, the organization of other corporal segments. The head is the location of visual, auditive and labyrinthic sensors, and is linked to the upper trunk by cervical vertebrae and the muscles of the neck (Wyke 1972), the latter being particularly rich in proprioceptive receptors; thus the role of head-positioning in space appears through recent studies as the central element out of which are organized the main systems of reference of the body in relation to the environment as well as organization of corporal segments between themselves (Cohen 1961, Paillard and Beaubaton 1978, Paillard 1971, Bizzi *et al.* 1972). From this fact, one may consider posture not solely as support to visual-motor activity but as taking part in this particular activity (Teiger 1978).

Posture is determined by the intrinsic conditions of man at work: anthropometric dimensions, biomechanical characteristics, and conditions of visual function, among others. It is also determined by external constraints linked to the execution of the task: among these, the required speed of execution, habitually imposed through an apparent simplification of work, is an important factor.

The postural immobilization that it provokes requires a high degree of contraction of postural muscles and is an obstacle to blood circulation, both factors increasing in the course of time (Pottier *et al.* 1967, Teiger 1978).

Thus, the arrangement of the dimensional space of the workplace and its physical ambience are not sufficient to allow the adaptation of tolerable postures throughout many hours and days of work. One must take into account the actual content of the task as well as speed obligations, the more so because computerized systems, in their very short response delays, favour a high degree of speed in work rhythms.

Acknowledgments

I thank D. Dessors, R. Kandaroun, A. Kerguelen and L. Pinsky for their assistance.

References

BERTHOZ, A., 1978, Rôle de la proprioception dans le contrôle de la posture et du geste. In *Du Contrôle Moteur à l'Organisation du Geste*, edited by H. Hecaen and M. Jeannerod (Paris: Masson), pp. 187–224.

BIZZI, E., KALIL, R. E., MORASSO, P., and TAGLIASCO, V., 1972, Control programming and peripheral feedback during eye-head coordination in monkeys. In *Cerebral Control of Eye Movements and Motion Perception*, edited by Dichgans and E. Bizzi. Karger Basel Bibliotheca opht. n° 82, pp. 220–232.

CAKIR, A., REUTER, H. J. V., SCHMUDE, L., and ARMBRUSTER, A., 1978, Untersuchungen zur Anpassung von Bildschirmarbeitsplätzen an die physische und psychische Funktionsweise des Menschen, *Forschungsbericht der Humanisierung des Arbeitslebens* (Bonn: Der Bundesminister für Arbeit und Sozialordnung).

COHEN, L. A., 1961, Role of eye and neck proprioceptive mechanisms in body orientation and motor coordination. *Journal of Neurophysiology*, **24**, 1–11.

FOURCADE, J., MARTIN, J. P., JACO, J., and DEFAYOLLE, M., 1975, Attention visuelle—posture. Contribution à l'étude du système. *Le Travail Humain*, **38**, 119–132.

GRANDJEAN, E. (editor), 1969, *Sitting Posture* (London: Taylor & Francis Ltd).

LAVILLE, A., 1968, Cadence de travail et posture. *Le Travail Humain*, **31**, 73–94.

MARCELIN, J., 1975, L'état ostéo-articulaire des travailleurs de 40 à 50 ans. Recommandations ergonomiques. In *Age et Contraintes de Travail*, edited by A. Laville, C. Teiger and A. Wisner (Paris: NEB), pp. 87–113.

PAILLARD, J., 1971, Les déterminants moteurs de l'organisation de l'espace. *Cahiers de Psychologie*, 14, 261–316.

PAILLARD, J., and BEAUBATON, N., 1978, De la coordination visuo-motrice à l'organisation de la saisie manuelle. In *Du Contrôle Moteur à l'Organisation du Geste*, edited by H. Hecaen and M. Jeannerod (Paris: Masson), pp. 225–260.

POTTIER, M., DUBREUIL, A., and MONOD, H., 1967, Les variations de volume du pied au cours de la station assise prolongée. *Le Travail Humain*, 30, 111–122.

TEIGER, C., 1978, Regulation of activity: an analytical tool for studying work-load in perceptual motor tasks. *Ergonomics*, 21, 203–213.

TEIGER, C., LAVILLE, A., and DURAFFOURG, J., 1974, *Tâches répétitives sous contrainte de temps et charge de travail.* Lab. de Physiologie du Travail et d'Ergonomie du CNAM, Rapport n° 39.

WYKE, B., 1972, Articular neurology review. *Physiotherapy*, 58, 94–99.

Constrained postures of VDU operators

By W. Hünting, Th. Läubli and E. Grandjean

Department of Hygiene and Ergonomics, Swiss Federal Institute of Technology, Zurich, Switzerland

In a survey at various VDU workplaces, the following results were obtained:

Constrained postures at VDU workplaces and in typists are in some operators associated with physical impairments in hands, arms, shoulders and neck.

Medical findings on muscles, tendons and joints confirm the reported complaints.

The greater the keyboard height above desk, the higher the incidence of impairments at VDU workplaces.

The more hands and forearms are rested the lower the incidence of complaints.

Low working levels can only be recommended if adequate supports for the source documents with independently adjustable height are provided.

Several other recommendations for a proper design of VDU workplaces are deduced from the present study.

1. Introduction

An important consequence of the introduction of VDUs at workplaces is the integration of operators in a man–machine system. The space of action of the employee is restricted; the movements are limited and stereotyped in fingers, hands and arms. The position of the head is imposed by visual angle and visual distance; the position of the hands is given mainly by the keyboard and to some extent by the source documents. Many jobs have a repetitive character with special demands on vigilance.

All these elements further *constrained postures*, which are characterized by

a restriction of free movements, and

long-lasting static postural efforts.

At first, static efforts may produce painful fatigue in the muscles concerned (localized fatigue). These troubles are short-lived and reversible. If the static load associated with high work-speed in fingers and hands is repeated daily over a long period of time, more or less permanent aches will appear; this second stage may also involve tendons and joints.

Symptoms of this kind were reported for keyboard operators by Ferguson (1971), Hünting *et al.* (1980), Nakaseko *et al.* (1975) and also for VDU operators by Östberg (1980), Elias *et al.* (1980), Smith *et al.* (1980), Laville (1980) and others.

It is reasonable to assume that inadequate workplace designs might generate or aggravate such physical impairments. This state of affairs was the background of the field-study presented here.

2. Investigated groups and their jobs

The following groups of operators were studied:

    53   operators on data-entry terminals,
    55   operators on conversational terminals with a movable keyboard,
    54   operators on conversational terminals with a sunk keyboard,
    78   typists, and
    55   employees occupied with traditional office work.

The first three groups were working on VDUs; the last two groups served as control groups. The groups show the following job characteristics.

Data-entry terminal operators

Only the right hand is operating the keyboard.
The working speed is mostly high (8000–12 000 strokes/hour).
The look is mainly directed to source documents.

Conversational terminal operators

Both hands operate the keyboard.
The speed is moderate.
The look is directed 50 % to screen and 50 % to source documents.
The terminals with movable keyboards offer a much larger space to rest hands and arms than those with sunk keyboard.

Typists

Both hands operate the keyboard.
The speed is high.
The look is directed sometimes to source documents and sometimes earphones are used.
The employees at the typewriters were full-time typists.

Traditional office workers (without VDU)

operate the keyboard occasionally,
move around,
look in many directions.

These employees had the same job as those on conversational terminals (payment transactions in banking).

3. Methods

The following investigations were carried out:

The physical impairments were recorded with a self-rating questionnaire.
Workplace dimensions and some postures were determined.
Medical examinations of muscles and joints concerned were made.
Skin temperatures of forehead and hands were taken.

The survey of physical impairments was made with a questionnaire illustrated with anatomical drawings of the body, the arms and the hands. Each subject had to rate symptoms such as stiffness, tiredness, pains and cramps for each part of the body. The answers were presented on the following ordinal scale: 'almost every day', 'ocassionally', and 'never or seldom'.

The measurement of workplaces covered such dimensions as seat height, distance seat level to desk and keyboard, keyboard- and table-height above floor, and keyboard-height above table. The frequencies of resting hands and arms were recorded.

The medical examinations covered the palpation of painful pressure points in the area of shoulders, arms and hands. Furthermore, painful reactions to isometric contractions of the forearms (bending, torsion and extension of hands) were checked. Skin temperatures were measured on the forehead and right middle finger.

4. Results of the survey

4.1. *Workplace dimensions*

The 90% range of measured workplace dimensions of all 162 VDU-operators is shown in figure 1. Among the various dimensions we must emphasize the excessive heights of desk and keyboard level above the floor; nearly all exceed the recommended height of 75 cm. The operators compensate the high working level by adjusting a relatively high seat level in order to get an optimal distance seat level to keyboard level of 25–35 cm.

4.2. *Physical impairments*

In table 1 the incidence of pains—involving the answers 'almost daily'—is given. It is interesting to note the high incidence of pains in the groups of data-entry terminal operators on the one side and the low figures in the control group of 'traditional office workers' on the other.

4.3. *Medical findings*

One result of the medical findings is reported in figure 2, which shows the incidence of painful pressure points on tendons, joints and muscles in the area

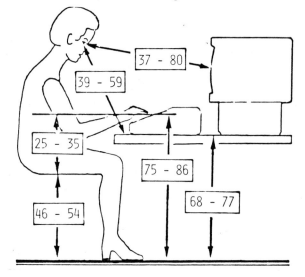

Figure 1. The 90% range of dimensions of the 162 VDU workplaces.

Table 1. The incidence of pains reported from the operators of the groups.

	n	Neck	Shoulders	Right arm	Right hand
Data-entry terminals	53	11	15	15	6
Conversational terminals	109	4	5	7	11
Typists	78	5	5	4	5
Traditional office workers	55	1	1	1	0

of the shoulders. The clinical symptoms in the shoulder area are frequent at data-entry terminals and rare in the control group of traditional office workers. The results of painful reactions appearing during an isometric contraction of the forearms show that muscle pains are observed in 10 to 25% of the operators in the groups data-entry terminals, conversational terminals and typists. The control group of 'traditional office workers' is free of these symptoms.

The palpation of the neck muscles (trapezius) reveals painful indurations in all office work groups. The range of operators having such indurations lies between 14 and 23%. The incidence is particularly elevated in the two groups characterized by high-speed work: the operators of data-entry terminals and the typists.

Table 2 shows the percentages of operators who visited doctors for hand and arm impairments during the last year. A rather large proportion of the operators had seen a doctor for these pains.

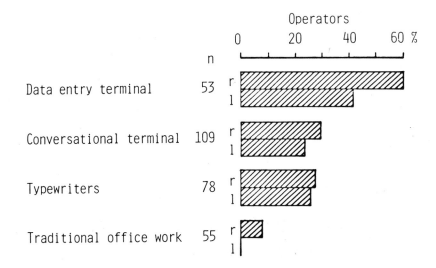

Figure 2. Medical findings: painful pressure points at tendons, joints and muscles in the area of shoulders.

Table 2. Operators who visited doctors for arm or hand impairments.

Groups	n ($=100\%$)	Operators %
Data-entry terminals	53	19
Conversational terminals	109	21
Typists	78	27
Traditional office workers	54	13

4.4. *Skin temperatures*

The skin temperatures, measured in all operators during their working time on the level of the forehead and on the hands, showed for the majority of cases lower values for hands than for the head. For the operators at the data-entry terminals and to some extent also for the typists the gradient of temperatures is related to the incidence of impairments in hands, arms, neck and shoulders: low skin temperature of the hands is associated with a higher incidence of impairments. Similar modifications of the skin temperature in operators with clinical disorders in the area of arms, shoulders and neck were observed by Nakaseko (1975) and by Maeda (1979). These authors assume that compressions of the artery at the neck as well as vegetative reflexes might be the reason of this phenomenon.

All these medical findings support the assumption that constrained postures at office workplaces may produce persistent injuries involving conditions of inflammation and degeneration in the overloaded tissues. Jobs associated with high-speed keyboard operations seem to enhance these effects.

4.5. *Relations between workplace design and impairments*

Our field-study reveals inadequate design of the workplaces on the one side and a certain incidence of physical complaints on the other. These results induced us to analyse the relations between workplace design and physical complaints.

We first studied the relationship between working levels and the incidence of impairments. These results can be summarized as follows. High keyboard levels above floor as well as high desk levels at VDU workplaces are associated with a lower incidence of physical impairments. An example of such a relationship is shown in figure 3 for the group of operators at conversational terminals. The item 'keyboard level above floor' is divided, according to median values, into a lower (< 84 cm) and a higher (> 84 cm) working level group. For each group the percentage of operators with pains or stiffness is reported. It is seen that the lower keyboard level group is associated with a higher incidence of physical impairments in shoulders, neck and back. This result is a great surprise, since it does not correspond with our general ergonomic knowledge.

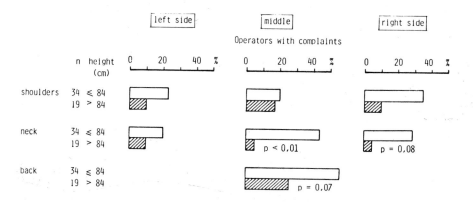

Figure 3. Relationship between keyboard levels above floor and incidence of pains or stiffness at conversational terminals with movable keyboards.

Observations at the workplace gave us an indication which may explain the surprising relations in the VDU groups: nearly all operators had their source documents lying on the desk. Special supports were very rare. Therefore, the higher the desk, the closer the source documents are to the eyes. These considerations lead us to the following conclusion: the higher the desk level, the higher are the source documents; so the better is the posture of head and trunk, resulting in a lower incidence of impairments!

Furthermore, we observed at least in one group that—at the higher keyboard levels—the operators rested forearms and hands more often. This could be another reason for the surprising result.

We do not conclude from these results that high desk or keyboard levels ought to be recommended. *We still believe that lower working levels are better, but only if an adequate support for the source documents with independently adjustable height is provided.*

In a second step we studied the relationship between keyboard height *above desk* and incidence of impairments. In this case an index of impairments was calculated according to the procedure of a Guttman scale. Tingling, cramps, pains, tiredness as well as the frequency of symptoms were taken into consideration for the scale. The operators were divided into a group with an increased incidence of impairments, i.e. with an index higher than the median value of the Guttman scale, and one group with lower incidence of impairments. As in figure 3, we also divided the heights of keyboards above desk into a lower and a higher group. The results for the VDU groups are shown in figure 4. It can be seen that in general the higher keyboard levels above desk are associated with a higher incidence of impairments. The only exception is shown in the group of data-entry terminal operators in the left hand and arm which, in fact, are not used to operate the keyboards. However, our results give no precise indication of the keyboard height needed. Nevertheless, it is obvious

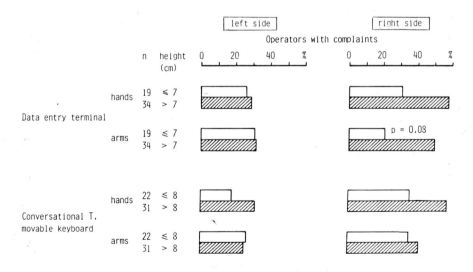

Figure 4. Relationship between keyboard levels above desk and incidence of impairments in hands and arms. (Operators with complaints are those with an index of the Guttman scale higher than the median value.)

that an adequate keyboard height could be obtained by the use of an adjustable support for forearms and/or hands.

These considerations led us to a detailed analysis of the effects of forearm/ hand supports. Special hand supports were never observed in our field-study. But we noted whether hands or forearms rested on the desks or on the keyboards using these elements as supports. The results are shown in figure 5.

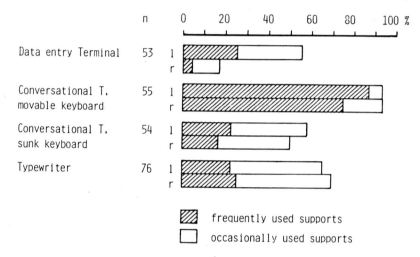

Figure 5. Frequency of hands or forearms rested on desks or on keyboard frames. l = left side, r = right side.

One result is obvious: hands and forearms are rested in nearly 90% of the cases in the group 'conversational terminal with movable keyboard'. In all other groups hand or forearm supports are used rather seldom.

With the movable keyboard, the operators have a large space to rest forearms and hands. With the sunk keyboard they have only a small and obviously insufficient space to rest hands.

We can conclude: hands and forearms are rested if there is a good opportunity!

This conclusion raised the question whether hand supports have an effect on the incidence of impairments. In figure 6 the use of supports is compared with the incidence of impairments. The same procedure was applied to assess the operators with impairments as explained for figure 4. The results show that in all groups the behaviour characteristic 'seldom used supports' is associated with a higher incidence of impairments in hands and arms.

Our results support the general requirement of providing keyboards with an adequate device giving the operator the opportunity to rest hands and forearms. This recommendation is particularly indicated for conversational terminals where operators always have short waiting periods according to the response time of the terminal.

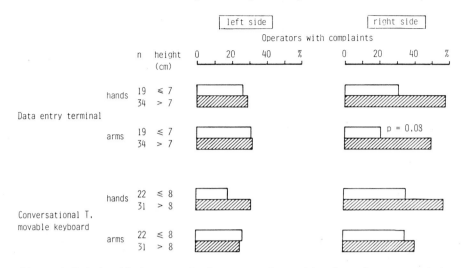

Figure 6. Relationship between the frequency of rested hands or forearms and the incidence of impairments in hands and arms. (A Guttman scale was used to assess operators with impairments as indicated in figure 4.)

5. Conclusions

The survey revealed that physical impairments in hands, arms, shoulders and neck are reported by some employees operating keyboards. In general, the complaints as well as the medical findings are more often observed in the working group at data-entry terminals. Some of the symptoms can be considered as localized fatigue and are reversible. Some other findings show more serious impairments, involving tendons and joints, which might have a more chronic character.

A further analysis of the results revealed relations between the design of the workplaces and the incidence of complaints. These results justify the following recommendations:

Separate devices to adjust the heights of desk- or keyboard-level, the position of the source documents and the height of the terminal display are necessary. Movable keyboards give a greater flexibility and more space to rest hands and forearms; they must be preferred to sunk keyboards.

All workplaces with keyboards should give an adequate possibility of resting hands or forearms. This is especially recommended for jobs on conversational terminals characterized by frequent waiting times.

Acknowledgments

We thank Professor Dr. med. F. J. Wagenhäuser for his medical advice in the physical examination of operators, and Dir. H. P. Unger (Swiss Bank Corporation) for supporting and helping us with our field study.

References

ELIAS, R., CAIL, F., TISSERAND, M., and CHRISTMANN, M., 1980, Investigations in operators working with CRT display terminals; relationships between task content and psychophysiological alterations. *Ergonomic Aspects of Visual Display Terminals* (this volume), p. 211.

FERGUSON, D., 1971, An Australian study of telegraphist's cramp. *British Journal of Industrial Medicine*, **28**, 280–285.

HÜNTING, W., GRANDJEAN, E., and MAEDA, K., 1980, Constrained postures in accounting machine operators. *Applied Ergonomics* (in the press).

LAVILLE, A., 1980, Postural reactions related to activities on VDU. *Ergonomic Aspects of Visual Display Terminals* (this volume), p. 167.

MAEDA, K., 1979, Occupational cervicobrachial disorder in Japan. (Personal communication.)

NAKASEKO, M., 1975, Thermographical study of skin temperature of fingers and hands on the young female workers. Osaka City University, Japan (unpublished).

NAKASEKO, M., NISHIYAMA, K., and HOSOKAWA, M., 1975, Problems of reducing work loads in cash register operation: 1. Comparisons of work loads in usual cash register and electronic cash register operations. *Japanese Journal of Industrial Health*, **17**, 168–170.

ÖSTBERG, O., 1980, Accommodation and visual fatigue in display work. *Ergonomic Aspects of Visual Display Terminals* (this volume), p. 41.

SMITH, M. J., STAMMERJOHN, L. W., COHEN, B. G. F., and LALICH, N. R., 1980, Job stress in video display operations. *Ergonomic Aspects of Visual Display Terminals* (this volume), p. 201.

Field study in newspaper printing: a systematic approach to VDU operator strain

By A. Grieco, G. Molteni and B. Piccoli
and R. Perris

Institute of Occupational Health, University of Milan, Via S. Barnaba 8, Italy

In the largest Italian newspaper industry, the *Corriere della Sera*, the replacement of the old typographic department with a new photocomposition department gave rise to a series of complaints from the 280 workers. The complaints are mainly in relation to environmental factors, such as light and climate, workplace design, screen optical characteristics and job organization.

Taking into account the workers' complaints, the *Corriere della Sera* designers have projected and completed a new VDT workplace in order to improve the ergonomic aspects and, consequently, the quality of work. At the same time, the Ergonomic Section of the Clinica del Lavoro of Milan has been required to programme a field study to evaluate and compare the ergonomic aspects of the old and new workplaces.

The preliminary results of the study of climatic, anthropometric and visual aspects are presented and discussed.

1. Introduction

In the last decade, computer applications have spread widely, involving almost all branches of industry. The reasons are numerous and in particular are due to technological progress in the computer field, both in constructions and in terms of programming level, and to the increased possibilities of application and lower costs.

As a consequence, a larger number of workers come into direct contact with computers, while in some cases, the extended application of computers in a broader range of industrial environments is creating more pressing social problems as far as employment is concerned.

Much has been written about the effects on people of working with computers and much has also been put into practice by computer designers; in fact today's computers are more sophisticated and conform better with the ergonomic requirements than their predecessors. However, at present, many problems remain unsolved, as the frequent national and international debates on man–computer interaction are proving. In particular, the problems still open

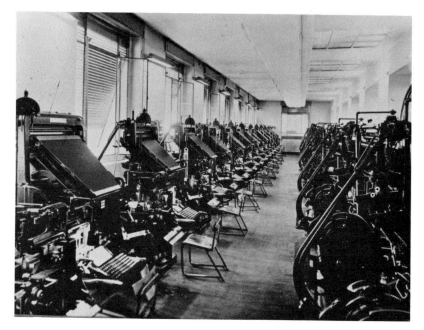

Figure 1. The old typographic department.

Figure 2. The new photocomposition department.

are those concerning the visual and anthropometric aspects of video-terminal workplaces, both deeply discussed in the past years; but besides these two aspects, many other problems are objects of attention, that is, the psycho-sociological aspects such as job organization, job quality and satisfaction, mental work load, fatigue and monotony. Occupational physicians, ergonomists, industrial designers and workers involved in the computerization process especially are paying particular attention to these aspects.

The printing industry is in the front line of computerization, since it currently faces the process of technological evolution that requires the replacement of linotypes with visual display units. In the largest Italian newspaper industry, the *Corriere della Sera*, the replacement of the old typographic department (figure 1) with the new photocomposition department has been gradually carried out in the last three years and is now complete (figure 2).

2. Methods

In the photocomposition department, 280 workers are divided into four shifts of six hours each; the main tasks to be performed by the workers are those of keyboard operator, proof-reader and make-up, and all the workers shift every other week to different tasks. The mean age of the workers is 38 years and almost all of them come from the typographic department, so that their experience of the new job is, at maximum, 3 years.

A series of unstructured interviews on selected samples of photocomposition workers brought to light the types of complaints shown in table 1. Taking into account the workers' complaints, the *Corriere della Sera* designers, with the advice of the Ergonomic Section of Clinica del Lavoro of Milan, have projected and completed a prototype of new VDT workplace in order to improve the ergonomic aspects and, consequently, the quality of work. At the

Table 1. Main types of complaints reported from photocomposition department workers.

Environment	
Light	Direct reflections from lights, glare from windows
Climate	Local hot-spots due to air conditioning system
Work place	
Design	Very poor because requires uncomfortable operating posture
Screen	Poor optical characteristics, mainly for screen reflections
Job organization	
Work load	Not predictable, with periods of very heavy work load
Job satisfaction	Dissatisfaction because of monotony and decrease of mental abilities demanded in comparison to previous typographic job

same time the Ergonomic Section of Clinica del Lavoro has been required to programme a field study to evaluate and compare the ergonomic aspects of the old and new workplaces. The programme has taken into account the study and the evaluation of the variables showed in table 2.

Table 2. Variables under study in the photocomposition department of *Corriere della Sera.*

Work and job organization
Subjective complaints
Type and frequency
Comparison between complaints of discomfort and sources of discomfort
Analysis of possible discrepancy between complaints of discomfort and discomfort sources
Mental work load
Environment
Climate
Lighting
Workplace layout and postures
Radiation
Optical characteristics of visual display and result of eye tests

The study is at present in progress and not all the variables have been studied; this is because the prototype of the new workplace was completed only a few weeks ago and is not yet operating in the photocomposition department.

The variables studied are the climate and the anthropometric aspects of workplace, both objects of this paper; the radiation and mental work load study are the objects of the papers of Drs. Terrana and Bagnara. As far as the visual aspect is concerned, the present paper will only discuss the eye tests that have been chosen to study the physiopathological variation of visual performance in VDT users.

3. Results

One of the sources of complaints was the climate and air-conditioning system. The temperature was described as too high, especially at ground level, and the subjective feeling of 'stagnating air' and presence of odours was reported.

The air-conditioning system, as shown in figure 3, has particular characteristics: the air is introduced into the room from grids placed on the floor, and the grids can be easily moved from one place to another, so that it is possible to place them so as to avoid direct draughts on the workpeople. The air is removed through grids located near the walls at a height of 150 cm. Air temperature, velocity, humidity, and radiant heat were measured at three different heights

Figure 3. The air-conditioning system.

from the floor, that is 50, 120 and 200 mm, in six different positions in the room. The results showed an air temperature ranging, in all positions, from 20°C to 23°C, a relative humidity ranging from 45% to 55% and an air velocity of 0·05 m/s. In addition, in every position an increasing air temperature from the lower point of measure to the higher with a gradient of 2·5°C was registered.

As far as anthropometric aspects of the old workplace are concerned, the frequency and types of complaints of discomfort reported by the workers were related to the fact of being forced to maintain incorrect posture. More than 50% of VDT users complain of aching necks and backache during and at the end of their workshift; with minor frequency of headaches, tenderness and parenthesias of legs.

The quality and frequency of complaints do not differ from those described in the literature in similar situations; their source is mainly to be identified in the bad workplace design, though it must be pointed out that every type of posture, including the so-called 'ergonomically correct posture' causes discomfort if it has to be fixed or maintained for too long a time. To reduce the postural discomfort the *Corriere della Sera* designers have built a new prototype of a VDT workplace.

The anthropometric characteristics of the old and new VDT workplaces are shown in table 3.

Table 3. Main anthropometric aspects of the old and new VDT workplaces.

	Old workplace	New workplace
Desk		
Height	680 mm	720 mm
Surface	Matt	Matt
Leg area height	660 mm	700 mm
Leg area depth	650 mm	750 mm
Leg area width	570 mm	850 mm
Chair		
Base	Five point	Five point
Seating height	Adjustable from 390 to 490 mm	Adjustable from 400 to 550 mm
Seat angle	Not adjustable	Adjustable
Front edge of seat	Rounded	Rounded
Seat surface	Not padded	Padded
Back-rest height	370 mm	370 mm
Back-rest adjustability	no	yes
Keyboard		
Height of home row	30 mm	25 mm
Screen		
Height of screen centre from ground	880 mm	950 mm

The VDT users often complain of visual discomfort after different times of exposure, the most frequent complaints of discomfort being burning eyes, lachrymation, frontal and occipital headache, redness, difficulties in fixation, blurred vision or diplopia. All these signs and symptoms, in subjects either with normal vision or with refractive defects, are commonly related to visual stress.

The international literature indicated several factors as sources of these discomforts, that is, postural, environmental work design, personal and in particular, visual, factors (Stewart 1978).

VDT use requires the observation of mainly three visual displays: the screen, the keyboard and the manuscript. Usually, the distance of the visual displays from the subject's eyes ranges from 50 to 90 cm, while the size of the characters and symbols varies between $4 \times 2 \cdot 5$ mm for capital letters, 3×2 mm for small letters and 1×2 mm for some symbols (Cakir *et al.* 1979).

The unaided visual operator, at the viewing distance of 50 cm, needs to read characters properly of that size 1 to 3 diopters of accommodation with a convergence of 6 to 15 prismal diopters and a resolution power of 0·5 to 1 minute of arc, which means from 5 to 10/10 of visual acuity. This high degree of visual performance is demanded of VDT users for many hours a day and

Table 4. Eye tests and physiological correlates with their possible interpretation for the evaluation of visual fatigue in VDT users.

Possible interpretation	Eye test	Physiological correlates
Eye stress	(a) Lateral phoria at near	Not evident visual axes deviations
	(b) Dynamic retinoscopy	Refractive ocular conditions
Amplitude of recovery	(c) Positive relative convergence	Amplitude of convergence and divergence capacity
	(d) Negative relative convergence	
	(e) Amplitude of accommodation	Refractive power of the crystalline
Visual functions impairment	(f) Stereopsis	Tri-dimensional vision
	(g) Visual acuity	Eye resolution power

throughout their working life; the visual functions more involved and, consequently, subjected to an 'easy fatigue' are convergence, accommodation and binocular fusion. Therefore, in our study of visual fatigue in VDT operators, we decided to measure and analyse the above-mentioned visual functions by means of the eye tests shown in table 4, in subjects with normal vision, before and after work at VDTs.

4. Discussion

In the light of the results of temperature values, it is possible to conclude that the discomfort experienced by the workers is mainly due to the very low air velocity, to the higher air temperature at head level and to the fact that the particular characteristics of the air-conditioning system do not ensure a complete removal of air from the room, but instead tend to remove only the lower strata of air, creating, particularly in the upper part of the room, areas of unremoved air; this is responsible for the subjective feeling of still air and presence of odours (Bedford 1948, Fanger 1970).

The working posture has been improved by the new VDT workplace; it is possible to observe in figures 4 and 5 that the main differences between the two workplaces are:

the desk height is lower in the old place, causing an unfavourable position of the hands and arms when using the keyboard;

the height of the screen centre is at 85 cm in the old place and 95 cm in the new one. This aspect is very important in order to ensure a more correct viewing distance and to avoid an excessive bending of the head and of the upper part of the body, responsible for the neckache and backache;

the leg area has been increased, allowing a more comfortable position of the operator;

the anthropometric characteristics of the chair, completely redesigned, in particular the aspects of the seat angle and backrest, both now adjustable.

The optimal configuration of a workplace is necessary, but not sufficient, to eliminate postural discomfort at work. Nevertheless, in our opinion the complaints of postural discomfort among the photocomposition workers will be reduce by the new workplace.

In order to better compare the ergonomic aspects of the two workplaces, we are going to apply the method for evaluation of risks of injury induced by working postures developed at the Clinica del Lavoro of Milan and published by the Comminity Ergonomics Action as a working document (Grieco *et al.* 1979).

The main aims of the method are:

(*a*) it should give a quantitative description of the relative location in space of the different parts of the body in any work posture whatsoever, and of the size of the angles formed between them in cases where these positions tended to be fixed;

(*b*) it should enable us to make a subjective and objective assessment of the tolerability of postures; an objective assessment would be made by using criteria which had already been established in the literature and practice of industrial medicine or, failing these, which had been proposed but still needed further verification;

(*c*) it should provide a clinical description of the type and extent of somatic disorders and of the reduction in active and passive joint movements, by an analysis of their correlation with the specific postures as described in (*a*);

(*d*) the method should be quick and easy to use even by medical staff who are not specialists.

Initial experiments carried out in different commercial environments yielded sufficiently satisfactory results; the assessment of tolerability seems to be the most difficult task in the study of posture. This is due to the almost total lack of epidemiological studies which correlate types of posture and movements with the pathogenesis and development of specific disorders. However, the initial experiments we conducted indicate not only that this is possible, but that a careful consideration of the different parameters is enough to give us a sufficiently structured assessment of posture tolerability.

As far as the visual aspect is concerned, our opinion is that all the eye tests listed in table 4 should be carried out, both in short- and long-term monitoring of exposed workers. In fact the first two tests give us the possibility of evaluating the synergic relationship between accommodation and convergence (Borish 1970, Streff and Claussen 1971). This relationship is, in our opinion, precociously affected in the condition of forced close vision, because the fatigue generates an excessive abnormal convergence, mediated by a muscular hypertone of sympathetic nature and associated with an excessive accommodation

Figure 4. The old VDT workplace.

Figure 5. The new VDT workplace.

due to a reflex mechanism (Manas 1965). This condition is revealed by an increase of the exophoric tendency and of the refractive power of the crystalline lens (Borish 1970). In addition, for long-term exposure to this visual stress, it is likely that the possibilities of obtaining a complete recovery would decrease with time; the subject would then tend to acquire a permanent type of vision, in which the distant focal capacity is reduced in favour of the near one.

The eye tests (c), (d) and (e), therefore, are applied in order to find the amplitude of convergence and accommodation at the disposal of the subject, thus indicating the possibilities of a complete recovery (Skeffington 1969, Manas 1965).

The last two tests have been chosen to verify the results of the above-mentioned tests and for the early diagnosis of permanent visual impairment when monitoring working populations (Duke Elder 1973, Emsley 1972).

In conclusion, the methodology proposed aims at diagnosing early impairment and reversible signs of visual fatigue, that, if protracted, could create permanent visual impairment.

References

BEDFORD, T., 1948, *Basic Principles of Ventilation and Heating* (London: H. K. Lewis).

BORISH, I. M., 1970, *Clinical Refraction*, third edition (Professional Press).

CAKIR, A., HART, D. J., and STEWART, T. F. M., 1979, *The VDT Manual* (Darmstadt: Inca-Fiej Research Association).

DUKE ELDER, B., 1970, *System of Ophthalmology*, Vol. 5 (London: H. Kimpton); 1973, *System of Ophthalmology*, Vol. 6 (London: H. Kimpton).

EMSLEY, H. B., 1972, *Visual Optics* (London: Butterworths).

FANGER, P. O., 1970, *Thermal Comfort* (Copenhagen: Danish Technical Press).

GRIECO, A., OCCHIPINTI, E., BOCCARDI, S., MOLTENI, G., COLOMBINI, D., and MENONI, O., 1979, *Development of a New Method for Evaluation of Risks of Injury Induced by Working Postures*. Community Ergonomics Action DOC. N. 4832/78 e ACE.

MANAS, L., 1965, *Visual Analysis*, third edition (Société d'Optométrie d'Europe).

SKEFFINGTON, A. M., 1969, *Clinical Optometry: Behavioral Theory and Methods for Providing Successful Optometric Care* (Optometric Extension Program—Duncan —Oklahoma).

STEWART, T. F. M., 1978, *Meeting on Eye Strain and VDUs* (Loughborough University of Technology).

STREFF, J. W., and CLAUSSEN, V. E., 1971, *American Journal of Optometry*, **48**, n. 8.

User-adjusted VDU parameters

By C. R. Brown and D. L. Schaum

IBM System Communications Division, Kingston, N.Y., U.S.A.

One hundred users of the IBM 3277 Display Station adjusted the keyboard height and distance, the display height and distance, and the display tilt using commercially available adjustable furniture for purposes of this study. Initial adjustments and any subsequent adjustments made during a word guessing game were recorded photographically. Subjects were not photographed in any standard posture. However, a statistical subject with standard posture was constructed for each user according to his or her height. A variety of relationships between subjects and display unit are presented for both real and statistical subjects.

1. Introduction

The purpose of this study was to characterize human anthropometric variability found in display station use. The approach taken was to use subjects familiar with display units and display units familiar to the subjects. As a practical consequence, the adjustment mechanism was adjustable furniture designed to accommodate display units such as the IBM 3277 Display Station. Also practically, a large sample was available only if testing was contained within a half hour.

2. Method

Figure 1 shows the display unit and its range of adjustment diagrammatically. Initially, a subject began the experiment in one of two furniture configurations. For one, the keyboard and display were set at their lowest and closest positions (LOW-CLOSE). For the other, the keyboard and display were set at their highest and most separate positions (HIGH-SEPARATE). Half the subjects started with each extreme. The extreme setting was calculated to get subjects involved in the adjustment process. The tilt was demonstrated in a range from approximately 90 to 75°. The subject had wide latitude in the adjustment sequence and could, for example, ask the assistant to (1) raise the keyboard, (2) bring the keyboard closer, (3) raise the display, (4) bring the display closer, and (5) tilt the display. (The adjustment mechanism was operated by a research assistant, not by the subject.) Subjects were told that the object of the session was to find an arrangement comfortable to them. After the initial two

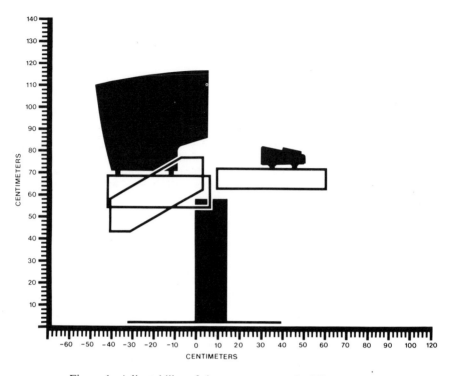

Figure 1. Adjustability of the components of a VDU work-station.

configurations, subjects played a word-guessing game. There were six words in the game. After each word, the subject could adjust any of the display unit components. All changes were photographed. Figure 1 shows the display unit in conjunction with the adjustability of the furniture. For the display unit, regions of adjustability are shown for the display perpendicular to the floor as well as 30° off the perpendicular. Measurements from photographs were taken with the floor and back leg of the furniture as axes. The data described here are for each subject's last configuration of keyboard and display.

3. Results

Figure 2 shows the results from the 100 subjects in terms of scatter plots. The plots are for the centre point of the display, the home row of the keyboard, the centre of the chair seat, the eye position of the subjects, and the eye position of the statistical subjects. The latter is obtained by constructing a figure with the subject's height but with a standard posture. The posture is hands on home

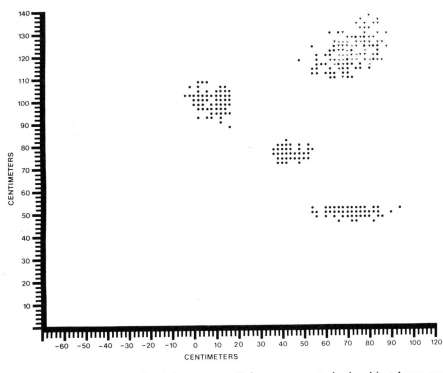

Figure 2. ● Subjects, ▼ Statistical eyes, × Points common to both subjects' eyes and statistical eyes.

row and arms parallel to the floor, back straight and head with 20 degrees forward tilt. These data were obtained from standard anthropometric tables.

Figure 3 shows the scatter plots from figure 2, with the adjustability envelope for the keyboard and display superimposed over the plots. The table gives the mean and standard deviation for each scatter plot. These statistics are given for both the X component and the Y component by initial condition.

3.1. *Procedural effects*

Initial condition did not result in any statistically significant difference in the Y components. However, differences between the two conditions were statistically significant for four of the X components ($p < 0.05$). These are indicated by an asterisk (*) in the table. Subjects who were in the HIGH-SEPARATE condition set the display some 6·6 cm further from the origin than those in the LOW-CLOSE condition. Additionally, they also moved their eye, chair, and keyboard further from the origin. The net result is very little difference in

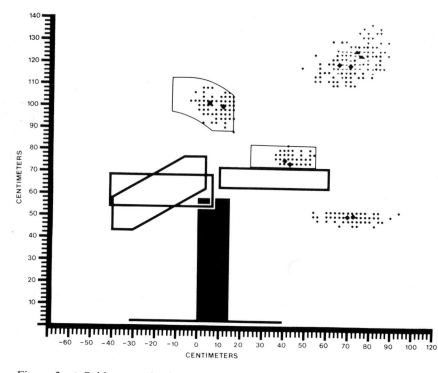

Figure 3. ● Subjects, ▼ Statistical eyes, × Points common to both subjects' eyes and statistical eyes, ▲ Statistical means, ◆ Subjects' means.

Means and standard deviations for figure 1.

| Component | | Initial condition | | | |
| | | HIGH-SEPARATE | | LOW-CLOSE | |
		X	Y	X	Y
Display*	Mean	11·8	98·7	5·2	100·1
	SD	3·2	3·9	5·5	4·3
Keyboard*	Mean	43·8	73·5	41·4	74·4
	SD	5·2	2·1	4·7	2·3
Chair*	Mean	73·7	49·9	69·7	49·7
	SD	7·5	1·8	7·9	1·6
Subject's eye*	Mean	70·4	118·6	65·3	118·4
	SD	7·6	4·7	7·0	5·0
Statistical eye	Mean	75·5	123·8	73·1	124·5
	SD	6·3	5·8	7·0	5·6

* Differences between X components of the initial conditions are statistically significant ($p < 0.05$).

relative position of components due to initial condition. The significant differences appear to be an artifact of the methodology.

3.2. *Adjustment variability*

The display and keyboard variability is quite large in both the X component and the Y component. For these data, accommodating a range of 4 standard deviations in product design or furniture is a challenge. Consider the Y component of the display. Four standard deviations is 16 cm or 6·3 inches. Yet the furniture limited the display adjustment at the high end and the keyboard adjustment at the low end. For a few subjects, these adjustments were set at the limit.

3.3. *Some correlations*

If subjects keep focal length constant, there should be a perfect correlation between the eye-to-keyboard distance and the eye-to-display distance. There is a correlation of 0·48 for the subjects and 0·61 for the statistical subjects. Our real subjects seem to differ from statistical subjects in posture and in the magnitude of the relationship. Subjects adjusted the display to be about 11 cm further from their eyes than the keyboard.

Other correlations indicate the reasonableness of the subject configurations. Eye height correlates with display height and keyboard height—both correlations are 0·48. Consequently, display height correlates with keyboard height (0·55). The eye and keyboard X components correlate (0·71). Keyboard and chair height correlate (0·43).

3.4. *Line of sight*

The subject's line of sight tends to be almost perpendicular to the display's front surface. The average is 82° with a standard deviation of approximately 6°.

3.5. *Angle of the display*

The average angle of tilt of the display was 9·7° from the vertical with a standard deviation of 3·5°.

4. Discussion

Some analyses remain to be done. What contributes to the variability? Do subjects within an anthropometric interval (height) have less configuration variability than subjects between anthropometric intervals? Some subjects modified the furniture several times. Others participated in only the two required configurations. Are these groups different? And, of course, are the preferences of male subjects different from those of female subjects?

4.1. *Adjustability evaluations*

The present study deals with preference within a loose psychophysical methodology. If the preference distribution is fairly flat for each of the adjustment parameters, fairly large ranges of variation are understandable. Nevertheless, considerations of both anthropometric range and range for line of sight suggest the usefulness of a range of vertical adjustment at least as large as that obtained in the present study.

4.2. *Related criteria*

Productivity is an important variable that was not examined in this experiment. It seems reasonable that preference, comfort and productivity are interrelated. Productivity increases may not be necessary to motivate the design of flexible display units although it is certainly reasonable to expect long term productivity in application environments to be related to comfort and preference.

5. Conclusions

Although the data show considerable height variability, the variability was constrained somewhat by the adjustment limits. Seventeen subjects set the display at the upper limit of 81 cm (31·9 inches). Nine subjects set the keyboard at the lower limit of 71 cm (28·0 inches).

The keyboard lower limit points up the usefulness of a thin keyboard. If the distance from table top to home row were reduced to 30 mm, the table top at the lower limit would increase from 62 cm (24·4 inches) to 67·6 cm (26·6 inches). The lower limit of the display was not tested by the 'application'—a simple word-guessing game. An application with frequent reference between keyboard and display would tend to generate lower settings.

The present study no doubt underestimates the range of useful adjustment in either furniture or VDU design.

Section 6.   Psychosocial aspects

Job stress in video display operations

By M. J. SMITH, L. W. STAMMERJOHN, BARBARA G. F. COHEN and
NINA R. LALICH

National Institute for Occupational Safety and Health, Center for Disease Control,
Public Health Service, U.S. Department of Health, Education, and Welfare,
Cincinnati, Ohio, U.S.A.

A questionnaire survey evaluation of job stress and health complaints in
VDU operators and control subjects was undertaken at three separate
facilities. The response from approximately 250 VDU operators and 150
controls indicated that job task demands interacted with VDU use to
produce an increased stress level and heightened health complaints in
VDU operators. Ergonomic solutions to reduce VDU operator health
problems should deal with job task demands in addition to work station
and VDU design features.

1. Introduction

Much attention has been paid to ergonomic design factors of visual display
units (VDU) and their relationship to operator health complaints, but little
has been directed to job design factors that may contribute to psychological
job stress. Some studies have examined the psychosocial stress aspects of
VDU work as secondary aspects of broader ergonomic evaluations. For example, Gunnarsson and Östberg (1977) found that in situations where operators
had little control over their job tasks, the majority complained of monotony,
while in situations where the job afforded some variety and control, only a
small proportion felt the work was monotonous. Cakir et al. (1978) found that
feelings of stress expressed by a group of VDU operators did not differ in
magnitude from other worker groups previously examined.

Cakir et al. (1979) found differences between hourly paid and piece-rate
paid VDU operators in sociability, frame of mind, state of stress, fatigue, and
inner security, with the piece-rate operators scoring poorer in all categories.
For a different group of VDU operators who previously did clerical work,
60% complained of monotony even though their present jobs were similar to
their previous clerical jobs in task requirements. The results indicated that the
jobs reporting the highest levels of monotony also reported the highest levels
of fatigue. All these studies have shown that the psychosocial stress aspects of
VDU work need to be considered in determining the impact of VDUs on
operator health.

M. J. Smith et al.

In the United States over the past few years, complaints about VDUs have been steadily increasing. The initial efforts of the National Institute for Occupational Safety and Health in this area were concerned with evaluating the possible health risks of VDUs regarding ionizing and non-ionizing radiation emissions. Some attention was also given to ergonomic factors including workplace, equipment and job-design features. However, it remained for the current study to offer the first systematic evaluation of psychosocial stress and health complaints of VDU operators in the United States.

2. Methods

A questionnaire survey was used to gather information about job demands, job stressors, psychosocial stress level, psychological mood, health complaints and working conditions for VDU operators and control groups at each of three study sites. Included in the survey form was a cover letter explaining the purpose of the study and instructions for filling out and returning the questionnaire. The questionnaires were handed out on-site to each participant, taken home and filled out, and returned to work the next day for collection by the research team. Participants could return their questionnaire by mail if they preferred. At the first site, 102 of the total 250 VDU operators at the facility were given a questionnaire, as well as 110 control subjects. The response rate was 73% for VDU operators and 38% for control subjects.

At the second site, 103 VDU operators were surveyed; this was virtually all employees who worked on VDUs. Ninety-three control subjects were also surveyed. The response rate was 48% for the VDU operators and 23% for the control subjects. At the third site, all VDU operators available on all shifts were given questionnaires for a total of 303 VDU operators. There were 212 control subjects surveyed. The response rate was 43% for VDU operators and 44% for control subjects.

3. Results

3.1. *Psychosocial job stress*

Various measures of psychosocial job stress were contained in the questionnaire. These included scales developed to compare the level of stress in different jobs (Caplan *et al.* 1975), standardized job stress scales (Work Environment Scale, WES) (Insel and Moos 1974) and selected questions on sources of job stress.

Table 1 shows the response means for VDU operators and control subjects at each site for the ten dimensions of the WES (Insel and Moos 1974). At all sites both the VDU operators and control subjects reported mean values for nine of the ten dimensions that were divergent from established normative values in an elevated stress direction. A Wilcoxon Two Sample test (Quade 1966) was used to compare the responses of operators and controls at each site.

Table 1. Mean responses for VDU operators and controls for WES† stress scales.

	Involve-ment	Peer cohesion	Staff support	Autonomy	Task orientation	Work pressure	Clarity	Control (by superior)	Inno-vation	Physical comfort
Site (1)										
VDU	1·04	1·08	1·41	1·23	2·12	3·35*	1·80	3·15	1·34	1·52
Control	1·25	1·80*	1·38	1·56	1·69	2·05	1·63	2·72	1·42	1·58
Site (2)										
VDU	1·64	1·73	1·92	2·00	1·95	2·68	1·46	1·90	1·29	1·24
Control	2·38	2·47	2·33	2·42	2·26	2·28	2·00	2·89*	0·79	1·00
Site (3)										
VDU	1·28	2·25*	1·71	2·13*	1·73	2·27	1·31	1·50	1·04	1·10
Control	1·19	1·63	1·46	1·46	1·60	2·16	1·50	2·21*	0·99	0·94
Norms	2·80	2·73	2·94	2·69	2·51	1·77	2·33	2·32	2·40	2·04

Stress scales

* Significant at 0·01 level using a Wilcoxon Two Sample test.
** Significant at 0·05 level.
† Work Environment Scale (Insel and Moos 1974) Form S.

Table 2. Mean responses for VDU operators and controls for job demands† stress scales.

	Workload dissatisfaction	Boredom	Role ambiguity	Quantitative workload —Q	Quantitative workload —E	Self-esteem	Role conflict	Workload variance	Job future ambiguity
Site (1)									
VDU	3·40**	3·43	1·86	4·19*	3·60**	12·77**	1·67	3·01	3·62
Control	2·62	3·14	1·97	3·25	3·32	10·84	1·92	2·53	3·78
Site (2)									
VDU	2·36	2·28	1·64**	3·46	3·40	9·41	1·89	2·79	3·26*
Control	1·78	1·82	1·23	3·63	3·67	8·25	1·61	2·97	2·46
Site (3)									
VDU	2·15	2·26	1·56	3·59	3·40	10·23	1·75	2·70	3·05
Control	2·27	2·40	1·76	3·53	3·59	9·96	1·99	2·86	3·14
Job demands and worker health									
High	2·90	3·37	2·41	—	4·06	—	2·01	3·51	3·61
Median	2·13	1·83	2·06	—	3·51		1·75	2·81	2·70
Low	1·66	1·34	1·31		3·24		1·36	2·43	1·82

* Significant at 0·01 level using a Wilcoxon Two Sample Test.
** Significant at 0·05 level.
† Scales taken from *Job Demands and Worker Health* (Caplan *et al.* 1975).

Operators at site (1) reported less peer cohesion and more work pressure; while operators at site (2) reported less supervisory control; and operators at site (3) reported more peer cohesion, more job autonomy, and less supervisory control. A Kruskal Wallis test (Quade 1966) was used to compare the VDU operator responses across the three sites. Operators at site (1) reported less peer cohesion, less autonomy, more work pressure, and more supervisory control than operators at sites (2) and (3).

Table 2 shows the response means for VDU operators and control subjects at each site for nine of the dimensions reported by Caplan *et al.* (1975). At site (1), operators reported more workload dissatisfaction, quantitative workload, job future ambiguity and higher self-esteem than the control subjects. In comparing the responses from this study to the Caplan *et al.* (1975) study, both operators and control subjects reported greater workload dissatisfaction, boredom, and job future ambiguity than the median Caplan group. In fact, the VDU operators at site (1) reported higher values on these three dimensions than any of the Caplan groups.

At site (2), the VDU operators reported more role ambiguity and job future ambiguity than control subjects. However, both operators and controls reported lower role ambiguity than the median Caplan group. The VDU operators reported more boredom and job future ambiguity than the median Caplan group.

At site (3), there were no significant differences between the operators and control subjects for any of the Caplan dimensions. However, both operators and controls reported more boredom and job future ambiguity than the median Caplan group. The VDU operators reported less role ambiguity than the median Caplan group.

A Kruskal Wallis test was used to compare the VDU operators across the three sites. Operators at site (1) reported higher workload dissatisfaction, quantitative workload, more boredom, higher job future ambiguity, and greater self-esteem than the operators at sites (2) and (3).

Table 3 lists the specific stressors that contributed to the stress level of VDU operators and controls at each of the three sites. VDU operators at site (1) reported three times as many significant stressors as VDU operators at either of the other two sites. The most frequent stressors for site (1) VDU operators involved problems with workload, work pace, and boredom. VDU operators at site (2) reported only one stressor more frequently than controls, "little time to complete work". On the other hand, the controls at this site reported "less time to think", "less time to daydream" and "higher workload expectations". There were no differences for specific stressors between VDU operators and controls at site (3).

3.2. *Psychological mood disturbances*

Psychological mood was evaluated using standardized scales (Profile of Mood States, POMS) (McNair *et al.* 1971) and checklist questions about

Table 3. Percentage of VDU operators and controls reporting stressful levels of particular stressors.

Stressors	VDU	Control	Site
Work very fast	71*	29	1
Work very hard	61*	29	1
Little time	32**	7	1
Great deal of work	57*	22	1
Cannot set pace	34*	7	1
Cannot choose work	77**	50	1
Full attention	80*	52	1
Never workload slowdown	48**	25	1
Never time to think	12	40**	2
Workload high	39**	18	1
Workload expectations—others	47*	23	1
Workload expectations—others	18	50**	2
Little time to complete work	14**	0	2
Time to daydream	8**	20	1
Time to daydream	7	0**	2
Increased workload	20**	3	1
Increased concentration	23**	5	1

* Significant at 0·01 level using a chi square test for homogeneity.
** Significant at 0·05 level.

Table 4. Mean scale values for mood states for VDU operators and control groups.

	Mood states					
	Anxiety	Depression	Anger	Vigour	Fatigue	Confusion
Site (1)						
VDU	11·6	10·9	8·0	14·9	10·1*	7·0
Control	10·2	11·0	9·1	17·1	6·3	6·4
Site (2)						
VDU	8·7	8·8	8·8	16·8	6·4	5·6**
Control	6·5	7·2	7·1	16·0	5·5	4·0
Site (3)						
VDU	9·5**	9·4	8·7**	17·4	7·2	6·0*
Control	7·2	6·8	6·1	18·0	5·1	4·2
Norms for college students	13·5	14·0	9·7	15·6	10·6	11·0

* Significant at 0·01 level using a Wilcoxon Two Sample test.
** Significant at 0·05 level.

mental health status. Table 4 shows the mean values for each of the separate scales of the POMS for each site. For site (1), only the fatigue scale mean was higher for operators than controls. At site (2), operators showed more confusion than controls. At site (3), operators showed higher levels of anxiety, anger and confusion than controls.

3.3. *Health complaints*

Health complaints and disease states were collected using a self-report checklist. For the health complaints, the frequency of occurrence in the past year was recorded for 59 separate items, and for the disease states the presence or absence of a medical diagnosis in the past five years for 23 disease states was recorded. None of the disease states showed significant differences between the VDU operators and their controls at the three sites. Table 5 lists the health complaints for which there were significant differences between the VDU operators and control subjects for the various sites. As can be seen, a greater number of VDU operators than controls at site (1) reported the following health complaints: fever, eye strain, blurred vision, burning eyes, problems of colour perception, nervousness, fatigue, neck pain, neck pressure, neck pain into shoulder, sore shoulder, loss of arm strength, sore wrist, hand cramps, swollen muscles, numbness, pain in arms and legs, and pounding heart. At site (1), there were no health complaints for which control subjects reported more problems than operators.

Table 5. Percentage of VDU operators and control subjects with selected health complaints showing a significant effect†.

Health complaint	VDU	Control	Site
Eye strain	90	61	1
Eye strain	80	61	3
Blurred vision	75	52	1
Burning eyes	72	47	1
Irritated eyes	52	36	3
Colour perception	45	21	1
Fatigue	85	59	1
Irritability	79	41	2
Depression	64	26	2
Anxiety	56	21	2
Nervous	56	26	1
Neck pain	90	60	1
Sore shoulder	74	49	1
Sore shoulder	49	31	3
Pain in arms and legs	73	46	1
Neck pressure	67	39	1
Neck pain into shoulder	63	30	1
Swollen muscles	57	32	1
Sore wrist	57	19	1
Hand cramps	57	36	1
Numbness	54	25	1
Pounding heart	49	27	1
Loss of arm strength	42	18	1

† At 95 % level of confidence or greater using a Wilcoxon Two Sample test.

For site (2), a greater number of VDU operators than controls reported the following health complaints: irritability, depression, and anxiety. None of the health complaints had a higher frequency for controls than VDU operators at site (2). At site (3), a greater number of VDU operators reported the following health complaints: eye strain, irritated eyes and sore shoulder. There were no health complaints that were more frequently reported by controls than VDU operators at site (3).

Differences in reporting of health complaints for VDU operators across the three sites were evaluated using a Kruskal Wallis test (Quade 1966). Of the 59 health complaints, 28 were significantly higher for the VDU operators at site (1) than for VDU operators at sites (2) and (3). These health complaints were spread across many ailments including respiratory, gastro-intestinal, musculoskeletal, visual, and psychological mood problems.

4. Discussion

Two issues stand out when examining the results of this study. First, all worker groups including control subjects reported high levels of psychosocial stress when measured against comparison worker groups examined in previous studies (Insel and Moos 1974, Caplan *et al.* 1975). Such elevated stress levels may account for the lack of clear-cut differences between operators and control subjects at two of the three sites studied. Secondly, job demands, in the form of task requirements, appear to be responsible for a significant portion of the job stress and health complaints of VDU operators independent of their use of VDUs. This is reflected by the much higher levels of both job stress and health complaints reported by the VDU operators at site (1) over the VDU operators at sites (2) and (3).

The heightened stress level for both operators and controls suggests that comparisons between the operators and controls may not be the most satisfactory means for evaluating the impact of VDUs on worker stress level and health complaints. Logical comparisons may also be made with other occupations previously studied (Caplan *et al.* 1975, Insel and Moos 1974). This could be necessary due to organizational factors such as strained employee/management relations, which could have produced a heightened stress level for all employees in the organizations being studied, thereby washing out the impact of the VDUs. While this factor was not measured, such strained relations may have been produced by difficult labour negotiations in progress at all the sites. At site (1), many of the control subjects were aware that they might lose their jobs by the end of the year due to a business slowdown, and that those who would be retained would have to become VDU operators. Also, at sites (2) and (3), many of the control subjects knew that they would be converting to VDUs within the next few months. These factors undoubtedly contributed to the elevated stress levels of the control subjects.

Even with the elevated stress levels, VDU operators at site (1) showed increased stress and heightened health complaints over their controls and other VDU operators at sites (2) and (3). This illustrates the extreme influence that the VDU operation at this facility had on these employees. If we examine only the results from site (1), then the conclusion to be drawn would be that the VDUs were the primary cause of the operators' problems, since the job tasks of the operators and controls were almost the same, except that the controls used pencil and paper rather than VDUs to carry out their tasks. However, comparison of VDU operators at site (1) with those at sites (2) and (3) shows even greater differences than between the site (1) operators and their controls, with higher stress and more health complaints for site (1) operators. This would suggest that the VDU usage cannot be the only source of the operators' problems and that job demands in the form of task requirements and task control were important interactive factors in producing operator stress and health complaints at site (1).

The majority of VDU operators at site (1) held jobs that involved rigid work procedures with high-production standards, constant pressure for performance, very little operator control over job tasks, and little identification with and satisfaction from the end-product of the work activity. The impact of these working conditions is reflected in their reporting of high work pressure and workload, fast work pace, and boring and repetitive work tasks as their major sources of stress. On the other hand, the majority of VDU operators at sites (2) and (3) held jobs that allowed for flexibility, control, autonomy, and a great deal of job satisfaction and pride in their end-product. While these jobs also had high-production demands and tight deadlines, the operators had a great deal of control over how these demands would be met, which was reflected in their lower level of complaints about their job demands. Such flexibility probably allowed these operators to choose work strategies individually for minimizing stress while meeting the job demands. The greatest stress problems for these operators revolved around career development and future job activities as opposed to the job task demands for VDU operators at site (1).

Job demand factors also appear to have had an influence on the type of health complaints of the VDU operators at the various sites. At site (1), the significant health complaints of VDU operators dealt mainly with visual problems and musculoskeletal problems. These findings are in agreement with previous studies of VDU operators (Gunnarsson and Östberg 1977, Hollar *et al.* 1975) except that the relative frequency of complaints is somewhat higher in this group than in the previous studies. At sites (2) and (3), job demands in the form of job future and career growth influenced the type of health complaints of the VDU operators. In contrast to the visual and musculoskeletal problems of operators at site (1), operators at these two sites displayed psychological problems such as anxiety and irritability.

Overall, the study results suggest that there is an interactive effect between the type of work activity and the use of VDUs that is related to the level and type of stress and health complaints experienced by VDU operators. Ergonomic solutions that deal with the design of the work station and the VDU must be supplemented with proper job task design to maximize the protection of operator health.

Acknowledgments

The authors express appreciation to the following persons who contributed to the conduct of this study and to the preparation of this report: Lawrence Catlett, Kathleen Hicks, Joyce Fley, Dr. Wordie Parr, Gene Moss and William Murray of NIOSH; Mark Gottlieb and Drs. Steve Sauter and Robert Arndt, University of Wisconsin.

References

CAKIR, A., HART, D. J., and STEWART, T. F. M., 1979, *The VDT Manual* (Darmstadt: Inca-Fiej Research Association).

CAKIR, A., REUTER, H., V. SCHMUDE, L., and ARMBRUSTER, A., 1978, Untersuchungen zur Anpassung von Bildschirmarbeitsplätzen an die physische und psychische Funktionsweise des Menschen (Bonn: Federal Ministry for Work and Social Order).

CAPLAN, R., COBB, S., FRENCH, J. R. P., VAN HARRISON, R., and PINNEAU, R., 1975, *Job Demands and Worker Health*, Publication 75-160 (Washington: National Institute for Occupational Safety and Health).

GUNNARSSON, E., and ÖSTBERG, O., 1977, *The Physical and Psychological Working Environment in a Terminal-based Computer Storage and Retrieval System*, Report 35 (Stockholm: National Board of Occupational Safety and Health).

HOLLAR, H., KUNDI, M., SCHMID, H., STIDL, H., THALER, A., and WINTER, N., 1975, *Stress and Strain on the Eyes Produced by Work with Display Screens*. Report on a work-physiological study performed for the union of employees in the private sector (Vienna: Austrian Trade Union Association).

INSEL, P., and MOOS, R., 1974, *Work Environment Scale—FORM S* (Palo Alto: Consulting Psychologist Press, Inc.).

McNAIR, D., LORR, M., and DROPPLEMAN, L., 1971, *Profile of Mood States* (San Diego: Educational and Industrial Testing Service).

QUADE, D., 1966, On analysis of variance for the k-sample problem. *Annals of Mathematical Statistics*, **37**.

Investigations in operators working with CRT display terminals: relationships between task content and psychophysiological alterations

By R. Elias, F. Cail, M. Tisserand and H. Christmann

Institut National de Recherche et de Sécurité, Avenue de Bourgogne, 54500-Vandoeuvre, France

Two groups of women operators, engaged in either off-line data-acquisition or dialogue, were investigated. A lot of data concerning work analysis were collected by recording eye movements. A questionnaire involving four categories of symptoms, as visual strain, body pains, neuropsychical disturbances and job dissatisfaction, was administered to the two groups of operators.

The off-line data-acquisition group showed a significantly higher frequency of complaints for all the categories. These results are interpreted in light of the task contents. In comparison with dialogue, off-line data acquisition is characterized by a fragmented task with a higher frequency of sweeps between the visual display and documents, less degrees of freedom, less necessary learning and very short work cycles.

1. Introduction

The problems raised by work conditions concerning visual display are varied and complex; they involve the technology of visual display, the display work-station layout, the immediate physical and psychosocial environment as well as the task content. The influence of the latter factor on the ensemble of work conditions seems, to us, to be more and more important.

Visual display use can differ, depending on the nature of information to be treated, and the modalities of its use can have different implications on the operator's psychological or physiological strain. Three types of information are taken into consideration in this respect:

work output,

information-processing, and

work results or output.

Man–computer dialogue integrates all three types of information, whereas data-entry or data-acquisition is limited to work input. Our research is concerned with these two activities, that is, off-line data-acquisition in banking centres, and man–computer dialogue in a publishing house and a pharmaceutical distribution company.

2. Methods

Much of the data concerning the work analysis was collected by recording eye movements. We used an eye movement recorder (Nac Eye Recorder) which simultaneously records the subject's visual point of interest within his field of vision. This is achieved by reflecting an illuminated spot off the cornea which is superimposed into the field of view. Both the field of vision and the superimposed illuminated spot are then recorded on 16 mm motion picture film, closed circuit TV, or can be visually observed.

The visual exploration of the display is structured as a function of the task's demand and the perceptive activity depends on the nature of information to be treated (Guérin *et al.* 1979). The results of eye movement recordings were computed, to evaluate the length of uninterrupted looks for each of the two activities (data-acquisition and dialogue) and the frequency of sweeps (displacement of look from the visual display, to documents or the keyboard).

Two sample groups of women operators (89 and 81), 20–39 years old, corresponding to off-line data-acquisition and dialogue, were investigated by means of a questionnaire. The questionnaire included four categories of questions relative to: visual strain, body pains, neuropsychical disturbances and job satisfaction. The neuropsychical troubles were divided into three sub-groups: psychosomatic disorders, nervous disturbances and inadequate sleep patterns. Significance of the responses for each category and subcategory of items was tested (χ^2 test between the two groups of operators).

3. Results

(1) There is a large difference in length of uninterrupted looks between the two activities (figure 1). The time is much shorter for data-acquisition than for dialogue. For the five subjects studied, the average length is about 1 second in data-acquisition, whereas for the dialogue, the average length varies between 6 and 8 seconds for A and is 135 seconds for B (pharmaceutical distribution).

(2) The frequency of sweeping looks is much higher (12–18 regard displacements per minute) for data-acquisition, than for dialogue (figure 2).

(3) As concerns the responses from the questionnaire we mention the following:

  (*a*) 70 % of data acquisition operators and 28 % of dialogue operators reported that they are dissatisfied with their job (figure 3).

  (*b*) The chronic neuropsychical disorders were more frequently found in data acquisition operators than in dialogue (figure 4). For 8 out of 10 items concerning psychosomatic disorders, nervous disturbances and inadequate sleep patterns, the difference between the two groups was statistically significant.

  (*c*) The visual strain symptoms most often indicated by all the subjects were: discomfort glare, headaches, prickling sensation, blurred vision and visual acuity weakness. Each one of these symptoms was found in a significantly larger number for data-acquisition than for dialogue operators (figure 5).

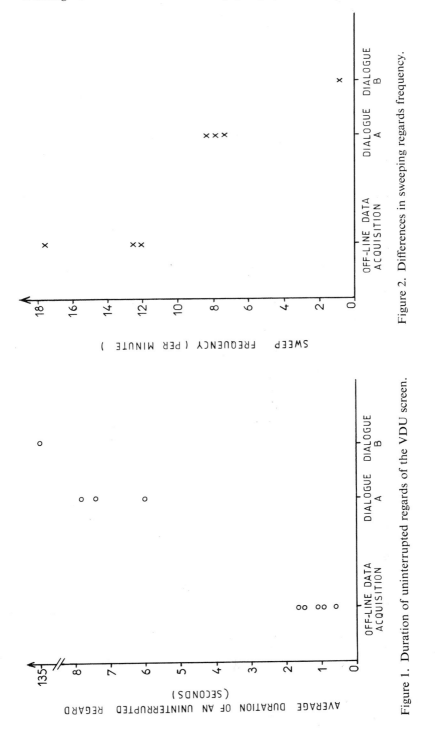

Figure 2. Differences in sweeping regards frequency.

Figure 1. Duration of uninterrupted regards of the VDU screen.

R. Elias et al.

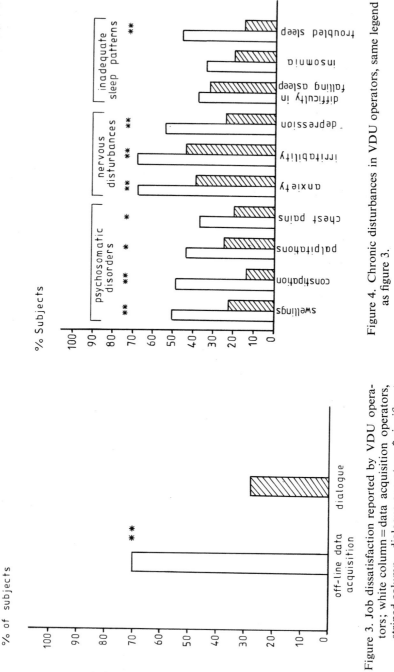

Figure 4. Chronic disturbances in VDU operators, same legend as figure 3.

Figure 3. Job dissatisfaction reported by VDU operators; white column = data acquisition operators, striped column = dialogue operators. * significant at $p < 0.05$, ** significant at $p < 0.01$.

% Subjects

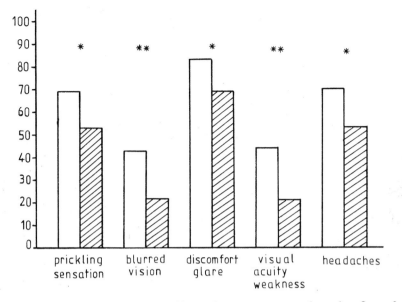

Figure 5. Visual strain symptoms in VDU operators, same legend as figure 3.

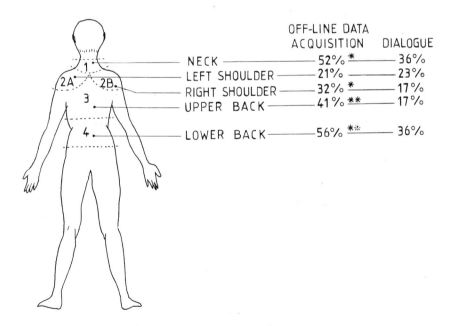

	OFF-LINE DATA ACQUISITION	DIALOGUE
NECK	52% *	36%
LEFT SHOULDER	21%	23%
RIGHT SHOULDER	32% *	17%
UPPER BACK	41% **	17%
LOWER BACK	56% **	36%

Figure 6. Sites of body pains in data acquisition and dialogue operators. * significant at $p < 0.05$, ** significant at $p < 0.01$.

(*d*) Figure 6 indicates the body pains most often mentioned by the operators. Out of the five sore spots mentioned, four were noted with a significantly higher frequency for the data-acquisition group: neck, right shoulder, upper back and lower back.

4. Discussion

The duration of uninterrupted regards in data-acquisition operators, in comparison with dialogue operators, corresponds, in fact, to different levels of information-processing. The shorter duration for data-acquisition activity, with an average length of one second, is determined by a fragmented task with a poor cognitive content. Also, the increased frequency of sweeps between the visual display and documents is consistent with the job characteristics of data-acquisition operators.

Consequently, the increased frequency of sweeps between objects with very different luminance levels contributes to inducement of great visual strain. On the basis of eye movement data, verbal reports and job analysis of both categories of operators, we may schematize the principal characteristics of these activities. They correspond in general to the 'repetitive' and 'non-repetitive' work characteristics formulated by Udris and Barth (1977). In our case, data-acquisition is characterized by: (*a*) executing function without decision-making; (*b*) fewer degrees of freedom; (*c*) less necessary learning; (*d*) very short work cycles. The man–computer dialogue is characterized by: (*a*) routine decision based on general regulations; (*b*) more degrees of freedom; (*c*) more necessary learning; (*d*) longer work cycles.

The elements of work analysis, along with the questionnaire answers, indicate a relation between specific task content on the one hand and the job satisfaction and the pattern of symptoms on the other. The results indicate that, by comparison with the dialogue activity, data-acquisition work has a negative effect on working life quality.

Simple, repetitive work, lacking interest and full use of the operator's capabilities, and its psychosocial consequences explain in large part the job dissatisfaction expressed by the majority of operators. They also explain the higher frequency of psychosomatic disorders, nervous disturbances and inadequate sleep patterns. These same relations were found by Caplan *et al.* (1975), MacKay and Cox (1979) and Broadbent and Gath (1979) for repetitive manual work or assembly-line work.

Our data concerning other apparently distinct dimensions, such as the symptoms of visual strain or body pains, have to be considered from a holistic point of view of the operator and his job. In this paper, we have not dealt with problems pertaining to office environment, technology of visual display or the display work-station, which certainly influence the operator's visual strain and body pains. Nevertheless, we think that the qualitative and quantitative aspects of these dimensions can be determined, in large part, by the specific contents of the task. For instance, posture problems could be more important for the data-acquisition group (fewer degrees of freedom, piece work, long periods of work seated).

For visual strain, the lighting of the workplace and visual exploration characteristics play an essential role. We have shown before, in measuring luminance, that all the workplaces investigated had inadequate lighting (Elias *et al.* 1979). This fault is amplified in data-acquisition offices by the large banks of windows which let in a large quantity of daylight and by the increased frequency of sweeps between objects with disparate luminance levels. Furthermore, work using a terminal involves accommodation, convergence and pupillary diameter changes, all of which are controlled by both the parasympathetic and the sympathetic nervous systems. As the activity of the latter is involved in the psycho-affective state of the operators or in their psychosomatic disturbances, it is possible that a disturbance of the sympathetic nervous system activity could be associated with changes in visual function.

References

BROADBENT, D. E., and GATH, D., 1979, Chronic effects of repetitive and non-repetitive work. In *Response to Stress*, edited by C. MacKay and T. Cox (London: IPC Science and Technology Press), pp. 129–141.

CAPLAN, R. D., COB, S., FRENCH, J. R. P., JR., VAN HARRISON, R., and PINEAU, S. R., JR., 1975, *Job Demands and Worker Health*, NIOSH Research Report, HEW Publication 75-160 (U.S. Dept. of Health, Education and Welfare).

COX, T., and MACKAY, C., 1979, Introductory remarks: occupational stress and the quality of working life. In *Response to Stress*, edited by C. MacKay and T. Cox (London: IPC Science and Technology Press), pp. 1–9.

ELIAS, R., MAYER, A., CAIL, F., CHRISTMANN H., and BARLIER, A., 1979, Conditions de travail devant les écrans cathodiques. Problèmes liés à la charge visuelle. *Cahiers de Notes Documentaires*—Paris, Institut National de Recherche et de Sécurité, 4ème Trimestre N° 97, pp. 577–583.

GUÉRIN, F., PAVARD, B., and DURAFOURG, J., 1979, *Le Travail sur Terminal à Ecran dans les Imprimeries de Presse*. (Paris: Collection de Physiologie du Travail et d'Ergonomie du Conservatoire National des Arts et Métiers).

UDRIS, I., and BARTH, H., 1976, Mental load in clerical work. In *Proceedings of the 6th Congress of the International Ergonomics Association*, University of Maryland, College Park, pp. 192–197.

Study on subjective symptomatology of fatigue in VDU operators

By S. Binaschi, G. Albonico, E. Gelli and M. R. Morelli di Popolo

Institute of Preventive Medicine for Workers, University of Pavia, Italy

In the investigation of subjective symptomatology of fatigue, the authors used the F scale of the Japan Industrial Fatigue Research Committee, based on multidimensional analyses on a sample of 52 VDU operators (data entry) and two control groups (54 bank clerks and 66 city bus drivers). The F scale has been filled up by the workers, and the following indices have been taken into account: frequency of affirmative answers to all items (T) and to items of each of the three internal components (A–B–C) of the scale; Student's 't-test' value for 'work load degree' and for 'fatigue accumulation degree'.

From our results we can infer that high eye strain, diffuse attention and work posture in particular greatly influence the subjective feelings of prolonged fatigue in VDU operators.

After discussion of the significance of the subjective symptoms of fatigue divided into A–B–C groups, the authors conclude that the neurophysiological conception of fatigue is validated by the F scale, and especially by group A items, which are the most important and significant of the whole scale.

1. Introduction

Fatigue is a universal phenomenon; it is an objective reaction as well as an experiential pattern (Bartley and Chute 1947), that is to say a subjective experience of someone wholly reacting to conflict situations; fatigue is therefore to be studied integrating the person with his own environment (Andreani 1962). Adequate measurements and graduation techniques for subjective fatigue are problems generally worked out using scales, assigning numbers of significance to objects or events in order to quantify subjective feelings of fatigue (McNelly 1954, Pearson 1957). We can mention non-dimensional, single point scales (McGrath *et al.* 1954, Hemphill *et al.* 1952); unidimensional scales (Borg 1972, Bujas *et al.* 1965, Gross and Bartley 1951); multidimensional analyses, aimed to point out categories of subjective symptoms, and to evaluate their internal correlation (Kinsman *et al.* 1973, Wijting *et al.* 1970, Wolf 1967). The last make a kind of link with the clinical method, because, as in a clinical diagnosis, concise conclusions are drawn on the basis of several implicitly related converging factors (symptoms).

2. Methods

We decided to use the F scale of the Japanese Industrial Fatigue Research Committee (Saito *et al.* 1970). As the relevant researches report (Kogi *et al.* 1970, Yoshitake 1971a, b, 1977), the items of the F scale—which were first conceptually chosen and then validated—can be grouped into three components:

(*a*) drowsiness and dullness, which shows decreased activation of the central nervous system;

(*b*) difficulty in concentration, due to mental fatigue;

(*c*) projection of physical disintegration.

In our research we adopted the questionnaire and methods illustrated by Yoshitake (1971 a) (table 1). The questionnaire (F scale) was filled up by the workers at the beginning and end of the work shift on the first work day (first and second test), at the beginning and end of the shift on the last work day, in the same week, before the day off (third and fourth test). To evaluate subjective fatigue the following indices have been taken into account:

(*a*) frequency of affirmative answers to each item (still being statistically calculated);

(*b*) frequency of affirmative answers to all items (T) and to items of each group (A, B, C);

(*c*) Student's '*t*-test' value for 'work load degree' (frequency of symptoms after work the first day of the week *minus* frequency of symptoms before work the same day) and for 'fatigue accumulation degree' (frequency of symptoms before work the last working day of the week *minus* frequency of symptoms before work the first working day).

3. The sample

Using the F scale, we studied 52 VDU (data entry) operators, and two control groups (54 bank clerks and 66 city bus drivers), 172 subjects in all. Five of the VDU operators were male, 47 female subjects, from 20 to 47 years old (mean age = 23 years). The bank clerks (BC) control group has been chosen because of the similar psychological and social aspects concerning the work environment, the city bus drivers (CBS) because of the high perceptual load and visual fatigue they usually experience.

4. Results

Sample analysis on the basis of different variables (job, age classes, and sex) has been made, and arithmetical mean, standard deviation, work load degree and fatigue accumulation degree have been calculated, for all the affirmative

Table 1. F scale: check items of subjective symptoms of fatigue.

Group A	Group B	Group C
1: Feel heavy in the head	11: Feel difficulty in thinking	21: Have a headache
2: Get tired in the whole body	12: Become weary of talking	22: Feel stiff in the shoulders
3: Get tired in the legs	13: Become nervous	23: Feel a pain in the back
4: Give a yawn	14: Unable to concentrate attention	24: Feel oppressed in breathing
5: Feel confused or muddled	15: Unable to take interest in things	25: Feel thirsty
6: Become drowsy	16: Become apt to forget things	25: Have a husky voice
7: Feel eye-strain	17: Lack of self-confidence	27: Have dizziness
8: Become rigid, or clumsy in motion	18: Anxious about things	28: Have a tic in the eyelids
9: Feel unsteady in standing	19: Unable to straighten up in posture	29: Have tremor in the limbs
10: Want to lie down	20: Lack patience	30: Feel ill

answers to the questionnaire (T) and for the three internal components (A, B, C) in each of the four tests. The results concerning the sample analysis on the basis of the 'Job' variable are reported here (tables 2–5).

Table 2. Sample analysis on the basis of 'Job' variable: mean, s d., fatigue indices for all the answers (T).

Job	1st test	2nd test	3rd test	4th test
VDU	$2\cdot7\pm2\cdot5$	$4\cdot7\pm3\cdot2$	$4\cdot2\pm4\cdot7$	$5\cdot8\pm5\cdot2$
BC	$1\cdot9\pm2\cdot1$	$4\cdot1\pm3\cdot5$	$2\cdot6\pm2\cdot4$	$5\ \pm3\cdot8$
CBD	$4\cdot6\pm5\cdot7$	$6\cdot6\pm6\cdot8$	$6\cdot1\pm6\cdot7$	$7\cdot6\pm7$

	Work load		Fatigue accumulation	
Job	t	p	t	p
VDU	7·62	$<0\cdot001$	3·19	$<0\cdot01$
BC	4·83	$<0\cdot001$	1·74	non-signif.
CBD	5·61	$<0\cdot001$	3·14	$<0\cdot01$

Table 3. Sample analysis on the basis of 'Job' variable: mean, s.d., fatigue indices for A-Group items.

Job	1st test	2nd test	3rd test	4th test
VDU	$0\cdot8\pm1$	$1\cdot8\pm1\cdot2$	$1\cdot9\pm2$	$2\cdot6\pm2$
BC	$0\cdot8\pm1$	$1\cdot8\pm1\cdot4$	$1\cdot1\pm1\cdot2$	$2\cdot3\pm1\cdot6$
CBD	$1\cdot6\pm2$	$2\cdot7\pm2\cdot8$	$2\cdot4\pm2\cdot7$	$3\cdot1\pm2\cdot9$

	Work load		Fatigue accumulation	
Job	t	p	t	p
VDU	5·52	$<0\cdot001$	3·63	$<0\cdot001$
BC	5·58	$<0\cdot001$	1·99	non-signif.
CBD	5·33	$<0\cdot001$	3·62	$<0\cdot001$

Table 4. Sample analysis on the basis of 'Job' variable: mean, s.d., fatigue indices for B-Group items.

Job	1st test	2nd test	3rd test	4th test
VDU	$1\cdot4\pm1\cdot9$	$1\cdot6\pm1\cdot7$	$1\cdot3\pm1\cdot6$	$1\cdot8\pm1\cdot9$
BC	$0\cdot7\pm1\cdot2$	$1\cdot4\pm1\cdot8$	$0\cdot9\pm1\cdot3$	$1\cdot5\pm1\cdot7$
CBD	$1\cdot6\pm2\cdot3$	$1\cdot9\pm2\cdot3$	$1\cdot9\pm2\cdot5$	$2\cdot2\pm2\cdot5$

	Work load		Fatigue accumulation	
Job	t	p	t	p
VDU	1·67	non-signif.	0·91	non-signif.
BC	2·50	$<0\cdot05$	1·01	non-signif.
CBD	1·96	non-signif.	1·46	non-signif.

Table 5. Sample analysis on the basis of 'Job' variable: mean, s.d., fatigue indices for C-Group items.

Job	1st test	2nd test	3rd test	4th test
VDU	0.5 ± 0.7	1.2 ± 1.2	1 ± 1.7	1.6 ± 1.8
BC	0.4 ± 0.7	1 ± 1.1	0.5 ± 0.9	1.2 ± 1.2
CBD	1.5 ± 1.9	2 ± 2.2	1.8 ± 2.1	2.3 ± 2.3

	Work load		Fatigue accumulation	
Job	t	p	t	p
VDU	6.65	<0.001	3.01	<0.01
BC	3.86	<0.001	0.68	non-signif.
CBD	3.81	<0.001	2.04	<0.05

5. Discussion

Mean values for subjective symptoms for VDU operators for the whole of the answers (table 2) are similar to BC control group, save for the answers to the third test. This result could suggest that the clear objective difference in visual strain does not make a clear subjective difference and that usually socio-psychological factors, due to work organization, are more important.

In regard to fatigue indices, the degree of work load and degree of fatigue accumulation are highly significant for the VDU operators, while the fatigue accumulation degree is not significant for BC. We could assume that the high perceptual load of VDU operators is significant for symptoms due to chronic fatigue because, as regards these symptoms, on the one hand they differ from BC, and on the other, they are similar to those for CBD who are also workers with high perceptual load. From our results, we can infer that especially high eye strain, requirement of diffuse attention and work posture greatly influence the subjective feelings of prolonged fatigue.

A second point in discussion is the significance of the subjective symptoms of fatigue divided into A–B–C groups (tables 3–5). Group A items are linked with 'weakened level of central nervous system activation' which causes these symptoms. It seems therefore correct to regard these items as an expression of "lowering CNS activation" (Saito *et al.* 1970) more than "drowsiness and dullness" (Yoshitake 1971 a) or "feeling of body physical inadequacy" (Yoshitake 1971 b). The constant non-significance of the index of fatigue accumulation degree relative to group B items does not agree with the hypothesis that group B only describes mental fatigue symptoms (Yoshitake 1971 b, 1977). In fact, symptoms due to mental work should chiefly appear as a chronic syndromic pattern; manifest analogies, moreover, can be found between group B items (table 1) and symptoms of depressive neurosis or symptoms of situational pseudo-neurosis, described by Bugard (1974) as "everyday-life psychopathology".

As group B items do not show statistically significant variations due to work load or fatigue accumulation, it seems more suitable to replace them with other equally handy, but far more sensitive and accurate psychodiagnostic means, such as Langner's scale of mental health (Langner 1962). Located symptoms, such as group C items, point out a factor of projection of physical fatigue (Saito *et al.* 1970). Our results do not validate the hypothesis (Yoshitake 1977) that group C items can distinguish jobs which require different physical strain; from this point of view, the whole number of affirmative answers is far more descriptive (table 2). In conclusion, the neurophysiological conception of fatigue (Grandjean 1979), based on antagonism between activating reticular formation and cerebral cortex inhibiting system, is validated by the F scale symptoms for subjective fatigue, especially by group A items, which are the most important and significant of the whole F scale. Thus, on the basis of our results, subjectiveness is directly linked to the suggested hypothesis for fatigue definition and ethology, that is to say neurophysiological and psychopathological theories; these theories, together with the experimental pattern, are synthesized in the central nervous system primary activation.

References

ANDREANI, O., 1962, Problemi e risultati sperimentali di ricerche psicologiche sulla fatica. In *Convegno Nazionale die Studio su Lavoro e Fatica Mentale* (Rome: Istituto Italiano di Medicina Sociale), pp. 30–50.
BARTLEY, S. H., and CHUTE, E., 1947, *Fatigue and Impairment in Man* (New York: McGraw-Hill).
BORG, G., 1972, Perceived exertion: a note on 'history' and methods. *Medicine and Science in Sports*, **5**, 90.
BUGARD, P., 1974, *Stress, Fatigue, Depression* (Paris: Doin).
BUJAS, Z., SREMEC, B., and VIDACEK, S., 1965, in *Psychological Aspects and Physiological Correlates of Work and Fatigue*, edited by E. Simonson and P. C. Weiser (Springfield: C. C. Thomas).
GRANDJEAN, E., 1979, Fatigue in industry. *British Journal of Industrial Medicine*, **36**, 175.
GROSS, I. H., and BARTLEY, S., 1951, Fatigue in house care. *Journal of Applied Psychology*, **35**, 205.
HEMPHILL, R. E., HALL, K. R. L., and CROOKES, T. G., 1952, A preliminary report on fatigue and pain tolerance in depressive and psychoneurotic patients. *Journal of Mental Science*, **98**, 433.
KINSMAN, R. A., WEISER, P. C., and STAMPER, D. A., 1973, Multidimensional analysis of subjective symptomatology during prolonged strenuous exercise. *Ergonomics*, **16**, 211.
KOGI, K., SAITO, Y., and MITSUHASHI, T., 1970, Validity of three components of subjective fatigue feelings. *Journal of Science and Labour*, **46**, 251.
LANGNER, R. S., 1962, A twenty-two screening score of psychiatric symptoms indicating impairment. *Journal of Health and Human Behavior*, **3**, 269.
MCGRATH, S. D., WITTKOWER, E. D., and CLEGHORN, R. A., 1954, Some observations on aircrew fatigue in the RCAF-Tokyo airlift. *Journal of Aviation Medicine*, **23**, 23.

McNELLY, G., 1954, *The Development and Laboratory Validation of a Subjective Fatigue Scale* (New York: Purdue University).

PEARSON, R. G., 1957, Scale analysis of a fatigue checklist. *Journal of Applied Psychology*, **41**, 186.

SAITO, Y., KOGI, K., and KASHIWAGI, S., 1970, Factors underlying subjective feelings of fatigue. *Journal of Science of Labour*, **46**, 205.

WIJTING, J. P., WOLLACK, S., and SMITH, P. C., 1970, A factor analytic study of the subjective components of activation. *Perceptual Motor Skills*, **31**, 635.

WOLF, G., 1967, Construct validation of measures of three kinds of experimental fatigue. *Perceptual Motor Skills*, **24**, 1067.

YOSHITAKE, H., 1971 a, Methodological study on the inquiry into subjective symptoms of fatigue. *Journal of Science of Labour*, **47**, 797.

YOSHITAKE, H., 1971 b, Relations between the symptoms and the feelings of fatigue. *Ergonomics*, **14**, 175.

YOSHITAKE, H., 1977, Trois patterns caractéristiques des symptomes subjectifs de fatigue. *Travail humain*, **40**, 279.

Collection of subjective opinions on use of VDUs

By L. Ghiringhelli

Via Schiaparelli 16, 20125 Milan, Italy

62 VDU operators were interviewed. Results, further to the already well known eye, back and head disorders, have emphasized the significance of mental discomfort. Causes are faults of the equipment or job organization. We think that VDUs add their particular problems to those common to every employee, but, above all, we suggest that they could become a symbol of mental discomfort to employees with the highest professional expectations.

1. Aim of the study

The main purpose of this study is to obtain the subjective opinions of operators about disorders probably induced by VDU work, either at the beginning of work with VDUs or after a long time of use; moreover, enquiring whether these disorders could be related to other variables, and which are the main sources of problems.

2. Description of the group

We interviewed 62 VDU operators, 47 of 'A' company (35 female and 12 male) and 15 of 'B' company (8 female and 7 male). The average age was $40\cdot5 \pm 7\cdot8$ years, average years in the studied task was $3\cdot9 \pm 1\cdot8$ and average years of study was $8\cdot75 \pm 3\cdot3$. The way of using the VDU could be considered the same, i.e. they did not 'speak' with the VDU. The time spent at the VDU varied from 1 to 8 hours a day. As control group we used 237 female employees of company B, of an age varying from 20 to 59 years, who had studied for 8 to 19 years, employed in different jobs not involving VDU use.

3. Methods

The operators were interviewed during working hours—always by the same person—in a separate room, using a questionnaire based on a previous study we made. Particular attention has been given to the troubles they had at the beginning of the work with the VDU and to troubles which could potentially be caused by VDU work and were present at the time of the interview. We have not considered troubles potentially related to previous medical history of which we became aware. Afterwards we asked for their opinion about their work. The data have been standardized and submitted to statistical analysis by χ^2-test. The sample has been divided in classes of variables (age, sex, job, work seniority, department, day average at VDU task, years of study). We compared the groups of the two companies. As we noticed no remarkable

Table 1. Subjective troubles referred by the operators at the beginning of work with VDU, as they remembered during interview.

	Number	%
Eye irritations	31	50·0
Headache frontal	18	29·0
Headache vertex	1	1·6
Headache occiput	1	1·6
Eye strain	15	24·2
Nausea	11	13·3
Anxiety	7	11·3
Myopia aggravation	4	6·5
Dizziness	3	4·8
Prostration	3	4·8
Reject sensation	2	3·2
Palpitations	1	1·6
Sexual disorders	1	1·6
Depression	1	1·6
Sleepiness	1	1·6
Back pain	1	1·6

Table 2. Subjective troubles related by the operators to daily use of VDU for a long time, i.e. troubles referred at the moment of interview not related to previous medical history.

	Number	%
Anxiety aggravation	27	43·4
Depressive disorders	25	40·3
Back pain	6	9·7
Neck pain	4	6·5
Dizziness	6	9·7
Impaired sight	21	33·9
Nausea	9	14·5
Eye irritations	28	45·2
Frontal headache	17	27·4
Dysmenorrhoea	2	3·2
Eye strain	12	19·4
Dyschromic vision	3	4·8
Total vision diseases	47	75·8

difference, we compared all the women of the two groups with the control group.

Some subjective disorders have been considered either individually (see table 1) or collectively in one single term (as for 'depressive disorders', see table 2), so looking for a statistical meaning. Moreover, it is worth remarking that the terms 'anxiety' and 'depression' do not have a precise and universal meaning and therefore have not been considered for the following statistical analysis (same as 'myopy' in table 1).

4. Results

By comparison of the operators of companies A and B, we have noticed two results with a statistical significance (both $p < 0.01$). In group B they suffer much more from troubles related to reflections and to bad functioning of the equipment.

In table 1 the main complaints at the beginning of work with the VDU are shown, as the operators remembered: we transcribed 'myopy increase' (impossible in a short time) to show the subjective sensation.

Table 2 shows the discomforts related to the VDU—in the operators' opinion—at the moment of the interview, i.e. several months after beginning of work. For both tables the remarks made in 'methods' are valid.

In table 3 the believed sources of troubles are listed. Psychotropic drugs are regularly used by 12% and occasionally by 8% of the interviewed operators. 24% of the operators answered that they wanted to continue their job, 14% were doubtful and 64% gave a negative answer. It must be said that 6.5% of the operators were close to the end of their career and had just switched over

Table 3. Main sources of troubles, as referred by the operators.

	Number	%
Equipment badly working	39	62·9
Reflections	27	43·5
Luminance	27	43·5
Colour	19	30·6
Postures	11	17·7
Flickering	5	8·1
Small letters	4	6·5
Monotony	4	6·5
To be at disposal of machine	4	6·5
Continuous concentration	3	4·8
Overwork	3	4·8
Eye movements	2	3·2
Lack of concentration	2	3·2
Isolation	1	1·6

from manual work in a factory. They gave positive answers to this and to the following question. Actually, when we asked an opinion about work, we got 22% positive answers, due to the definite decrease of the work load because of speed of equipment compared to manual operation (which usually is the case with operators working with long lists of clients or similar). Others say that work has been greatly facilitated by the use of VDUs (they are all working in the book-keeping department). Only one operator declares that his own work is better qualified by the use of VDU. Two operators—with troubles due to other reasons—gave a positive opinion owing to the possibility of being able to take breaks during working hours. 10% of the operators gave an ambivalent opinion: some of them—though taking advantage of it—are not able to use it for longer than a couple of hours owing to eye troubles or anxiety. Negative opinions (66%) are mainly due to mental discomfort (dependence on a machine, stupidity of work, disqualification, boredom, monotony, anxiety, irritation, stress, isolation, impossibility of having relationships, mental confusion) or to fear of organic troubles, as for eyes and back.

The following data are the only results we obtained with statistical significance:

(1) Eye diseases affect VDU operators more frequently than other clerks ($p < 0.01$).
(2) After 2 years of working, the majority of VDU operators say that screen light is unpleasant ($p < 0.01$).
(3) Though already accustomed, operators working longer than 3 hours a day are affected with eye strain ($p < 0.05$).
(4) Operators who have studied for more than 7 years (note that 36 out of 51 are younger than 35) more frequently:
   find faults with screen reflections ($p < 0.01$),
   have negative opinions about VDU work ($p < 0.05$),
   complain of mental discomfort ($p < 0.01$),
   show increased anxiety after more than 6 months work ($p < 0.05$).
(5) Operators who have studied more than 5 years more frequently find faults with bad functioning of equipment ($p < 0.05$).
(6) Operators younger than 35 (37 out of 38 have studied for more than 7 years) more frequently:
   give negative opinions about VDU work ($p < 0.01$),
   complain of mental discomfort ($p < 0.01$).
(7) At the beginning of VDU work, operators younger than 30 more frequently complain of headache ($p < 0.01$).
(8) Negative opinions are more frequently given by operators working less than 3 hours a day ($p < 0.01$), but only two operators in this group have studied for less than 6 years (8·3%, and they are also older than 35). The others vary between 8 and 13.
70·8% of these operators are younger than 35.

We can assume that people who have studied for a longer time could express themselves better and that young people were a more interesting sample because they are more sensitive and disposed to react.

5. Conclusions

The differences between the answers of company A and B groups could be related to bad location of VDUs in company B: sometimes near the windows and without any external glare shield. In fact both companies own IBM 3277 sets, the lay-out is a mixed open landscape space, even the lights are shielded by the same panels with vertical sheets. The only distinguishing factor between buildings A and B is that in building B the wall is almost completely made of glass while building A has ordinary windows. With regard to bad functioning, we can remark that in company B the computer is 200 km away from the seat of the company and the connections to it are linked to telephone lines.

From the results we notice that—as everybody agrees—eye troubles are a significant factor among VDU operators. Frontal headache and kinaesthetic troubles might have an ambivalent meaning. Beyond doubt are psychological troubles and back and neck disorders. We have already seen that some organic trouble would anyway show a generic state of arousal towards the VDU and maybe this is the meaning of some troubles that we could consider psychosomatic. The fact that the greatest discomfort is shown by younger and better educated operators, and the indicated discomfort sources, make us think that, further to the organic troubles, mental discomfort is particularly felt. Many interviewed operators—and other employees—found fault with artificial light, air-conditioning, open space: VDUs seem to add their own troubles and emphasize the usual problems of employees and we suggest that they could become a symbolic focus of discomfort.

Section 7.   Practical experiences

Practical experiences in solving VDU ergonomics problems

By T. F. M. STEWART

Butler Cox & Partners Limited, Morley House, 26–30 Holborn Viaduct, London EC1A 2BP, UK

VDU ergonomics problems have attracted considerable publicity in recent years. This has created a need for independent, realistic and practical evaluation of VDU problems followed by specific advice and recommendations. This paper reviews the author's experience of such assignments during 1979.

The conclusions suggest that VDU workplaces and environments are the main problems. Management and trades unions are encouraged to work together to apply existing ergonomics knowledge early in the system design process.

1. Introduction

VDU ergonomics problems have attracted considerable publicity in recent years. This has put pressure on users, trades unions, managers and computer suppliers to find out the facts and to act on them. Unfortunately, the research results are often difficult to interpret and may even appear contradictory. The researchers themselves are often unwilling or unable to commit themselves to specific recommendations. Some manufacturers offer advice but they are not unbiased.

Many organizations therefore need independent, realistic and practical evaluation of their problems followed by specific advice and recommendations. The topics covered in a typical assignment include the selection and/or the design of:

VDUs,

VDU workplaces,

visual, thermal, acoustic and social environment,

working methods and procedures,

work organization.

The purpose of this paper is to review our experiences in tackling these assignments for a number of clients during 1979.

2. Approach and methods

Butler Cox & Partners is a totally independent consultancy concerned with computers, telecommunications and office automation. My own background includes nine years of research and teaching in ergonomics at Loughborough University before joining the company as a specialist in the human aspects of information technology. The methods used for the investigations are based on research conducted throughout Europe and reported more fully elsewhere (see, for example, Cakir *et al.* 1979).

The methods included:

conducting detailed interviews with the relevant staff,
observing the working procedures and working environment,
measuring directly the workstation dimensions, illumination levels and so on as appropriate,
distributing and analysing brief questionnaires,
analysing existing company records and documentation.

The checklist in *The VDT Manual* (Cakir *et al.* 1979) was used as a basis for much of the measurement and assessment. However, the criteria were not regarded as rigid and considerable interpretation was necessary to establish the significance of the findings. As a consequence, this analysis deals only with the major problems encountered.

3. Sample of VDU ergonomics clients

The sample used for this review contains all our clients who commissioned VDU ergonomics assignments during 1979. How representative it is cannot readily be established, but in each case the organization at least had identified that it needed to prevent or reduce VDU problems. The sample composition is shown in table 1 and the types of application in table 2.

The role of trades unions in the assignments is shown in table 3.

Table 1. Survey sample.

11	Applications
5	Organizations
119	Users
80	VDU workplaces

Table 2. Applications surveyed.

Centralized data entry	3
Full time clerical operators	3
Intermittent 'professional' users	2
Tele-ordering operators	1
Machine operators	2
	11

Table 3. Trade union involvement.

Initiative for assignment	Reporting to union		
	Joint	Separate	None
Union	2	1	—
Management	1	—	2

4. Typical VDU findings

The two most important VDU features assessed were the quality of the displayed image and the characteristics of the keyboard. These are considered in turn below.

4.1. *Image quality*

The quality of the displayed image on a CRT-based VDU is a complex function of several parameters. Table 4 lists some of the most important and shows the number of VDUs which failed to meet an acceptable standard. Three of the ten models evaluated conformed to all the criteria and had completely acceptable image qualities for the tasks of their users.

Table 4. Typical VDU findings.

Image quality problems	%
Spacing	70
Shape	40
Stability	60
Resolution	50
Luminance	50
Contrast	10
	$N = 10$ models
Size, chromaticity	O.K.

Inadequate spacing between adjacent characters and between successive rows was the most frequently encountered problem (70%). In many cases, the system designer could only produce acceptable formats by introducing blank lines between rows, greatly and excessively reducing the capacity of the display.

Character instability includes flicker, swim and any other apparent movement in the displayed image. Despite the claims of virtually every manufacturer to produce 'flicker free' displays, distracting instability was a problem on six of the ten models.

Half the models had problems with the luminance and the resolution of the characters. Typically, on an inadequate display, one had to be traded off against the other. Individual operators varied in their response to this compromise and sacrificed whichever seemed less important to them.

The shape of the characters was not acceptable in four cases. These VDUs ignored typographic recommendations on the thickness of lines, the width/height ratio and the formation of individual characters.

4.2. *Keyboard*

The keyboards were assessed on a number of parameters and the results are summarized in table 5. The table shows that the majority of keyboard characteristics were acceptable. The most frequent shortcomings concerned the

Table 5. Typical keyboard problems.

	%
Non-detachable	50
Too thick	60
Shiny keytops	30

$N = 10$ models

Angle, colour, key spacing, feel, travel—all O.K.

keyboard thickness and its detachability. Both of these were observed causing constrained and awkward postures in the users. In some situations, the users had attempted to lower the keyboard by cutting a hole in the desk. However, this made it impossible to move and reduced the leg-room underneath the workplace.

The layout of the keyboards was assessed in relation to the specific task of the user. In many cases the layout of function keys could be improved but the existing layout could not be considered a major problem. One exception to this occurred in a data entry application where there were 11 variations of layout and function among 14 apparently identical keyboards. Such attempts to confuse the operators seem almost deliberate.

5. Typical workplace findings

A total of 17 different designs of workplace were evaluated and the results are summarized in table 6. The most frequent problem was lack of adjustability in the workstation. The majority of the chairs had some adjustability but it was usually difficult to use. Typically it involved getting off the chair and exerting considerable force on a knurled knob. As a consequence, these chairs were seldom adjusted. Only one type of workplace had a gas-lift chair action and these were fully exploited by the users.

Table 6. Typical workplace problems.

	%
Too few surfaces	35
Too small	30
Keyboard too high	67
No adjustability	94
Insufficient leg room	59
No chair adjustability	27
Poor chair adjustability	95

$N = 17$ types

Few of the workplaces were designed for VDU use and hence in many cases the keyboards were too high (up to 810 mm in some cases).

Leg-room was insufficient in many workplaces (59 %) due to obstructions under the desk or to the desktop being too thick.

Many of the workplace problems were aggravated by the design of the VDUs as mentioned above. Thick fixed keyboards made the shortcomings of the workplaces more critical.

6. Typical environment findings

The environments of all but one of the different types of workplace were assessed and the proportion where there were problems is shown in table 7.

Table 7. Typical environment problem.

	%
Poor thermal environment	100
Too much noise	63
Wrong illumination	56
Glare	71
Reflections	83
	$N = 16$ locations, 80 workplaces

In all cases the thermal environment was reported as causing problems. In some locations direct measurements were made but in the rest, the staff and management evaluations were noted. The introduction of VDUs and ancillary equipment added considerably to the heating and ventilating problems in some organizations. However not all the complaints can be attributed to this. The sedentary nature of VDU work may make some of the users more aware of deficiencies in the environment. The environment may also be a convenient scapegoat for other complaints related to the VDU or computers in general. None the less, the heating and ventilation systems evaluated were seldom capable of controlling the temperature, airflow and humidity to an adequate degree even when operating perfectly (which was seldom the case).

The next most frequently encountered problem concerned reflections and glare from windows and luminaires. The illumination level itself was less of a problem. Just under half the workplaces had an illumination level on the desk surface of between 300 and 500 lux (which is suitable for screen and document reading). Most of the problems concerned excessive illumination (up to 2500 lux in some cases), although the opposite extreme also occurred (100 lux).

Noise from the VDUs themselves was only a problem in a few cases (typically from the cooling fan) although some younger operators reported being distracted by the high-pitched whine from the electronics. Printer noise was frequently disruptive. Typically, it was not at a high enough level for major complaints but it often interfered with communication or concentration.

7. Other findings

In the organizations studied there were a number of other problems which were often as important as the more traditional ergonomics issues. These included personnel and supervision problems, difficulties in monitoring and controlling workflow and unfriendly or awkward man–machine dialogues.

Similarly there were organizations where potential problems had never materialized because these other issues had been handled successfully. For example, where VDU work was only a part of a well designed job, problems with the hardware were seldom significant.

8. Recommendations for solving these problems

The purpose of the above studies was to solve or prevent problems. A total of 11 sets of recommendations was made and the most common types of recommendations are summarized in table 8.

Table 8. Recommendations.

	%
Improve workplaces	64
Replace chairs	45
Modify lighting	45
Make minor VDU change	27
Make major VDU change	27
Reposition VDUs	27
Conduct operator eye tests	27
Modify ventilation	27
Modify organization	9
	$N = 11$ reports

The recommendations had to be practical and realistic. Regrettably in some cases this meant that there was little that could be done about some of the problems. There were many occasions when we would ideally have liked to recommend that the VDUs were scrapped for a particular reason but could not justify that action even to ourselves. None the less, there were three occasions when the evidence justified major action of this kind.

More frequently we recommended improving the workplace and modifying the lighting.

Many of the modifications were relatively simple involving additional work surfaces or a different positioning of existing desks or luminaires. Sometimes specially designed adjustable VDU workstations were recommended, but only where there was little or no adjustability in the equipment itself. Few of the fully adjustable workplaces on the European market are entirely satisfactory. Most involve trade-offs between ease of use and stability (especially when loaded with heavy VDUs).

The most practical way to introduce some adjustability into the workplace is often through the chair. Well designed, easily adjustable, stable chairs are widely available. The adjustability is more likely to be used than the nominal adjustability in expensive VDU desks.

Modifications to the lighting involved both changing luminaires and repositioning although in some office designs this is impractical. Simply removing excess fluorescent tubes results in uneven light distribution, but can be an acceptable compromise. One effective way of reducing illumination on source documents is to provide a document holder. Holding the documents at an angle also improves the keyboard/screen/document relationship. However, over-elaborate holders tended not to be used and we found simple lecterns most effective. Natural lighting was made more suitable by recommending blinds or curtains although this was not always satisfactory. When the visual environment could not be made satisfactory various filter attachments were recommended. The various types available all have their disadvantages (in terms of reduced resolution, luminance or high cost).

Modifying the ventilation usually meant providing some additional control over ineffective automatic systems. Most of the solutions were far from perfect, since many of the defects were basic design faults and would have involved major changes.

Where there was still doubt about the ergonomics of the workplace or where the planned use was particularly intense, we recommended operator eye tests (VET Advisory Group 1980).

9. Conclusions

It is difficult to decide whether this sample is at all representative of other VDU users. Someone at each location believed that they had or could have problems. It could be argued that most places are therefore not that bad since most people do not call in consultants to help them out. Equally it could be argued that if they care enough to call in consultants, then they are more aware of ergonomics than other people and may have avoided many obvious problems.

My own view is that the problems we find are common to many VDU users, although some are better off and some are worse. There are several conclusions which we believe can be drawn from our experience.

(1) There are many problems which can be solved with existing ergonomics knowledge—provided that it is applied.
(2) VDU manufacturers are beginning to improve the ergonomics of their products. The recommendations are gradually being applied.
(3) Workplace and environment design lags behind and is the cause of many VDU problems.
(4) Applying ergonomics need not be very expensive or very difficult but it helps if it is applied early.
(5) Joint VDU ergonomics initiatives by management and trades unions prevent subsequent recrimination and suspicion.
(6) Ergonomics advice must be practical and realistic if it is to be taken seriously.

References

CAKIR, A., HART, D. J., and STEWART, T. F. M., 1979, *The VDT Manual* (Darmstadt: Inca-Fiej Research Association).
VET ADVISORY GROUP, 1980, *Eye Tests and VDU Operators*. Final Report (London).

Trade union aspects and experiences with work on VDUs

By F. MARGULIES

Austrian Federation of Trade Unions, Deutschmeisterplatz 2,
A 1015 Wien, Austria

The paper describes how the Austrian trade union movement started to deal with the social impacts of automation as early as 1959, developing an approach, which can be summarized as saying 'yes' to the development of technology, '*but*' on the condition that measures are being taken to avoid negative impacts on employees while making the best of potential benefits.

This general approach to technological innovation has been applied to many real instances such as the installation of VDU systems in offices and workshops. Systematic research, initiated by the unions and carried out by university institutes led to interesting results and important conclusions, which are reported in the paper.

Provisions for ergonomic considerations, implementation of time limits for VDU-work, job rotation, etc. are not considered sufficient, as long as the problem of work content is being neglected. To achieve VDUs being applied in a humane, non-Tayloristic, interactive mode, methods of participative decision-making and of participative systems design will have to be implemented.

Austria is only a small country, her applied technology changing more slowly and less spectacularly than in other countries. Yet her trade union movement, comparatively strong and influential, has been alert to the impacts of automation for more than twenty years. We have dealt in detail with these problems as early as 1959, at our fourth national congress. At that time computers had only begun to be used in Austria and experts tried to convince us that automation would never have any meaning in a country as small and poor as ours.

Time has proved that the experts were wrong. The policy we adopted in 1959 has remained our fundamental guideline since. "Trade Unions are not opposed to technological progress" we said in a resolution, and we have never since left any doubt that no modern trade union can abstain from modern technology. There never was and never will be room for any kind of Luddite thought.

On the other hand, technology must not become an end in itself, but has to be seen in the human context. It can be justified only by its service to man, by its contribution to the improvement of the quality of life and in providing the chance of self-realization to the individual. That is why we wish the application of science and technology to be planned and controlled and why we demand the full participation of the workers and their representatives in all relevant decisions. We strive for the worker to change from a spectator to an actor in technological change, to turn from its victim to its master in order to ensure that technological progress shall become human and social progress as well.

And we strive to make managers, experts and designers realize that the more sophisticated their systems become, the more dependent they are on knowledgeable, motivated, active operators and users.

Humanization of work, to our mind, can be achieved not *for* the people, but only *with* the people.

This general approach to technological innovation finds its full application with respect to VDUs in offices and workshops.

It started as usual with all the nice stories about the advantages of VDUs, about the pleasure and relaxation experienced by operators in comparison with punch-card machines and so on. But soon reports came in about all sorts of complaints. It was in early 1973, when a lady called at my office, very nervous and desperate, telling me about a most peculiar experience she had just had. When she looked out of the window after some hours of intensive VDU-work, the snow on the opposite roof seemed all pink to her. Nobody would believe her and not only the managers of her firm, but also her colleagues and her shop steward called her a grumbler or even a hysteric.

On that we started some investigations which eventually led to the research mentioned here by Professor Haider, and in 1975 to the publication of the brochure on eye-stress caused by VDU-operating. But this event also taught us the lesson that complaints always have a very real background and should never be dismissed as insignificant grumbling.

A great deal of similar and additional research has been carried out since and even VDU producers like IBM, Siemens, Nixdorf and ITT made it a point to advise their customers and the public on the ergonomic aspects to be considered when setting up VDU workplaces. It seems, however, that resistance to this advice was too strong or pressure behind it was too weak. Anyhow, our experience shows that only in very few instances are human aspects really being considered by employers or their managers. Though these people ought to be used to exact and detailed cost/effectiveness calculations, they are obviously unable or unwilling to include in their calculations factors like better health, job satisfaction, frustration and personnel turnover.

Our answer as trade unions is to increase the pressure from the employees' side. Professor Haider's brochure, although giving pure facts without any bias or evaluation, has alerted VDU-users and their shop-stewards; lectures, courses, articles and other information sources have added to that. It is gradually being accepted that there is no 'one best way' when applying VDUs or any other technology. Alternative solutions have to be found, discussed and selected in a participative mode of design and decision, *and implemented*!

I am all in favour of continuing research, finding more facts and more accurate details. But the reports at this Conference have been full of facts and figures about the adverse effects of VDU work. The mere fact of people complaining about such effects should, I believe, be quite sufficient to make us think about changes and implement improvements. If employers or producers do not accept this, they should not blame the unions if this becomes yet another area of industrial disputes. Saying this, I should inform you, that Austria's strike statistics show 7 man/seconds per head for 1979 with similar figures for the years before. But both agreements and disputes have two parties.

Our trade union, at any rate, has advised employees not to wait until the VDU installation in their office has been completed, let alone until all researches have been carried out, but to take the initiative at the earliest possible moment. As soon as they hear any rumours about VDU plans, the works council should contact the management in order to obtain complete information and to start negotiations about all the relevant details. Our Work Constitution Act entitles the works council to obtain all information available on major technological or organizational changes and to negotiate agreements to avoid any negative impact of such changes.

A check-list has been set up by the union containing the main ergonomic factors to be attended to in these negotiations such as the qualities of the screen and the keyboard, possible movement of the VDU, adjustability of table and seats, positioning of the operator, working area, light, climate, noise, reflection and several other items of that kind. The check-list of BEA is a very valuable addition. However, we consider it a major issue to ensure time limits for VDU-work. In our opinion, *no more than four hours per day and no more than one hour without a break* should be worked on the screen.

A more complete list of ergonomic factors giving details and figures on all these points is now being prepared and will be published together with the report on our second research about the colour effect, which Professor Haider has just finished and on which he reported in his paper.

At the same time, representatives of our union, supported by university experts, are at the disposal of all the works councils to be called upon for advice, suggestions, and even assistance in negotiations with management. We are very happy to say that we can register a change of attitude taking place slowly and gradually. The increased activity of our colleagues helps achieve improvements more frequently and with rather satisfying results.

Yet we feel that fitting a VDU workplace with even the best of ergonomic arrangements will solve only part of the problem. The problem of work content still remains to be solved. If VDU-terminals are applied within a Tayloristic work organization, based on division of work, they will be used for further division of work and the effect on the operator will necessarily be that of more monotony, more frustration and less job satisfaction with all their consequences. But VDUs can be applied in an entirely different way. In a non-Tayloristic organization, the VDU would be used to supply a wide range of knowledge and information, thus enabling the user to deal with a wider and integrated range of tasks, enriching his work content, providing more flexibility, more challenge in his work and more possibilities of personal identification and realization.

There are instances in our country, and to my knowledge to a far greater extent in other countries, where this kind of work organization has been implemented or is subject to experiments. It has as a rule yielded excellent results, but it is far from general acceptance, let alone general application.

I certainly admit that a new type of work organization is more complicated and more risky to implement than a new piece of furniture. It implies fundamental changes in the hierarchical structure of a firm and in the long run probably a change in social structure as well. Yet I maintain that these changes are inevitable if serious technical, economic and human setbacks are to be avoided. And I further maintain that to achieve satisfying changes of that kind, it will be inevitable to grant employees and their trade unions full rights of participation. I hope that the valuable work done by the Permanent Commission and the International Association on Occupational Health and by the many experts dealing with VDU work, will be extended to include matters of work organization, of job content, and of self-realization in one's work—not to replace and not to reduce ergonomics, but rather to supplement it and to progress towards the human use of human beings of which Norbert Wiener, the father of cybernetics, wrote and dreamt some 30 years ago.

References

HAIDER, M., SLEZAK, H., HÖLLER, H., KUNDI, M., SCHMID, H., STIDL, H. G., THALER, A., and WINTER, N., 1975, *Arbeitsbeanspruchung und Augenbelastung an Bildschirmgeräten* (Wien: Vlg. des Ö.G.B., Automatisationsausschuß der Gewerkschaft der Privatangestellten).

HAIDER, M., KUNDI, M., and WEISSENBÖCK, M., 1980, Worker strain related to VDUs with differently coloured characters. *Ergonomic Aspects of Visual Display Terminals* (this volume), p. 53.

CRT-keyboard VDUs—implementing the solutions that already exist

By D. Doran

British Airways, Heathrow Airport (London), Hounslow TW6 2JA, UK

This communication supports the message delivered by the opening speaker (Professor E. Grandjean, Chairman of the Scientific Committee), that "Therapies are useful only if they are applied". The content of this communication is based not on scientific research but on practical experience; examples drawn from 12 years' experience and thousands of CRT-keyboard VDUs demonstrate that many therapies already exist —and the message is that these therapies should be applied immediately, without waiting for theoretical perfection, so as to reduce unnecessary discomfort to operators.

1. Introduction

Advertising hoardings, direction signs, information boards, printed books— all these are covered, in the English language, by the words 'Visual Display Units'. It can be argued that the visual display units of primary concern at this international meeting should be described as CRT-keyboard visual display units—not merely for the sake of precision in the use of the English language but more to draw attention to the cathode-ray tube (CRT) and the keyboard as two of the distinguishing features which contribute to making this type of VDU a Visual *Discomfort* Unit.

One of the earliest large-scale applications of CRT-keyboard VDUs was for airline passenger reservations, and British Airways (the amalgamation of the former BEA and BOAC) was one of the first airlines to introduce VDUs for this purpose—in 1968. Since then British Airways has introduced several types of VDU for numerous types of operation—some involving 'continuous use' and some involving 'intermittent use'. The number of VDUs in British Airways in early 1980 was about 3900, and the number of staff using a VDU in their work, either continuously or intermittently, was about 10 000.

British Airways therefore has a long and wide experience of the discomfort aspects of CRT-keyboard VDUs. In this short communication it is possible to offer, from this experience, only two main points: one is a plea and the other an idea.

2. The plea

Many years ago, when CRT-keyboard VDUs were the latest novelty, there was some toleration of the inherent imperfections in the postural and visual characteristics of the equipment. Indeed, much effort was devoted to adapting the lighting (natural and artificial) of the workplace to compensate, so far as possible, for what was sometimes described as a 'difficult visual task'.

But in more recent years solutions, either complete or partial, to many of the problems have been fairly well established; most of these solutions are design solutions capable of easing substantially the 'difficult visual task', but these solutions are still not sufficiently often incorporated into the design of new equipment.

The following are examples of problems for which solutions already exist.

Integral keyboard. A keyboard rigidly attached to the CRT unit, instead of being linked by means of a flexible cable, means that the operating distance for the hand and the viewing distance for the eye must be in a fixed relationship —for all operators! Those manufacturers who are still selling integral keyboards are therefore selling *unnecessary* discomfort.

Combined brightness/contrast control. The operator needs to be able to adjust both the brightness and the contrast on the CRT screen according to circumstances, and to adjust each independently of the other. Yet some manufacturers still provide only a single adjustment control, and thus still provide *unnecessary* discomfort.

Difficult character colours. Researchers continue to debate the relative merits of various green, green–yellow and yellow phosphors, to any of which the eye is much more sensitive than it is to blues and reds. Meanwhile a few manufacturers continue to use phosphors which generate displays in blue or red and which thus generate *unnecessary* discomfort.

Flicker. Because the phosphor refresh rate on most CRT screens is virtually coincident with the frequency of the electricity supply (50 or 60 Hz according to country) some operators under some conditions will perceive flicker. Yet flicker can be eliminated, at minimal cost at the design stage, by merely doubling the refresh rate so as to exceed the critical flicker fusion frequency of all operators under all circumstances and thus to eliminate another *unnecessary* discomfort.

Specular reflection in screen. Specular reflection of light sources, which obscure parts of the display, can certainly be reduced at the design stage. Increasingly this has been done by some manufacturers (with judicious adjustment of concomitant factors), but nothing has been done by others, so that the result once again is *unnecessary* discomfort.

These are merely a few examples. The plea is that all such solutions as already exist should be more widely adopted by VDU manufacturers at the design stage. A major obstacle however would seem to be that the known design solutions are almost unknown to VDU customers, namely the managements of organizations purchasing VDUs; in consequence many VDU

Visual environmental considerations (monochrome displays) starting from the centre of the visual field (the CRT screen) and working outwards.

Screen	(1) Screen shape/size (convexity/distortion)
	(2) Screen brightness (and brightness range)
	(3) Screen ⎫ contrast (and
	    Character ⎬ contrast range)
	(4) Screen ⎫
	    Character ⎬ colours
	(5) Character construction/form/stroke-width
	(6) Character size (height : distance)
	(7) Character proportion (width : height)
	(8) Character critical-detail size
	(9) Character resolution/sharpness
	(10) Character brightness fluctuation ('wander')
	(11) Character vibration ('jitter')
	(12) Character drifting
	(13) Flicker
	(14) Smear
	(15) Ghost images (phosphor wear)
	(16) Space between characters
	(17) Space between lines
	(18) Specular reflection in screen
		Visual discomfort from any of these considerations is *entirely* the responsibility of the manufacturer
		—
		the customer cannot improve
		—
		but the customer can specify
		—
		so the customer *must* specify
		—
		and must know what to specify

Surround	(19) Screen edge-trim (gloss/reflectance) (20) Fascia surface (gloss/reflectance) (21) Fascia edge-trim (gloss/reflectance) (22) Signal-lights (glaring/winking) (23) Keyboard fascia (gloss/reflectance) (24) Specular reflection in keys	Likewise the responsibility of the manufacturer — but the customer may be able to improve

Background	(25) Reference documents ⎫
	(26) Surface (horiz.) of desk-top ⎬ Reflectance
	(27) Surfaces (vert.) of other ⎬ and
	    furniture ⎬ bright-
	(28) Surfaces of wall, ceiling, ⎬ ness
	    floor
	(29) Light sources, natural
	(30) Light sources, artificial
		The customer can improve to compensate for residual discomfort

Note: For multicolour displays several additional considerations must be added.

manufacturers have no incentive to adopt these known solutions and can continue to sell VDUs solely on their technical capabilities.

This international meeting, through its various national connections, should convey the message to all intending VDU customers

(*a*) that many of the problems are *unnecessary* because design solutions, either complete or partial, already exist, and

(*b*) that the VDU customer must put the primary onus on the VDU manufacturer by specifying optimum environmental standards.

This implies that the VDU customer must know what to specify. This can be done by means of systematic check-lists, with known supporting standards. The first example above, the integral keyboard, would appear on a check-list of postural considerations, and the other four examples on a check-list of visual considerations. As a specimen of this approach the table reproduces the list which the author has developed over many years in British Airways as a basis for checking the *visual* considerations for ordinary *monochrome* displays. It will be seen that this list follows a logical sequence starting from the centre of the 'difficult visual task'. More detailed lists, with more detailed supporting standards, have been developed subsequently, notably by the Universities of Berlin and Loughborough (Cakir *et al.* 1979) and by the German Federal Republic which is preparing mandatory requirements (*Sicherheitsregeln für Bildschirm-Arbeitsplätze im Bürobereich*).

Even a simple list, with basic known solutions, would help intending VDU customers to avoid much unnecessary discomfort.

3. The idea

The human eye can adapt to widely different values of brightness (or luminance) *successively*, but *not simultaneously*.

In an ordinary working situation (i.e. without a CRT-keyboard VDU) it is generally accepted that the task in the centre of the visual field should have the highest brightness, that the brightness of the immediate surround should not be less than about one-third of this, and that the brightness of the general background should not be less than about one-third again:

$$\text{Task : Surround : Background} :: 9 : 3 : 1.$$

Other ratios are sometimes recommended (e.g. $5 : 2 : 1$), but the essential principle is that the change in brightness should be a *progressive* change from the centre of the task outwards. If the task involves work with ordinary (usually white) paper—and if the immediate surround is a desk-top in a light-coloured wood finish—and if the general background is that of an ordinary office—then the progressive change in brightness (task : surround : background) either already exists or can be achieved.

In this case the progressive change is a progressive *decrease* in brightness.

A similar progressive *decrease* in brightness could probably be applied to the case of a light (positive image) CRT screen, but of course such a display produces other problems.

The idea here proposed, and already proved in practice, is that for the usual dark (negative image) CRT screen the application of the principle of progressive change in brightness (task : surround : background) is progressive *increase* instead of progressive *decrease*:

Therefore

Ordinary task : Surround : Background : : 9 : 3 : 1

But

CRT task : Surround : Background : : 1 : 3 : 9.

This idea, successfully implemented in British Airways, is offered as another solution that should be more widely implemented. It has the advantage that if it is ignored by the manufacturer (e.g. by supplying a black fascia, and perhaps also a white casing) it can be implemented by the customer (items 20 etc. of the table).

4. Conclusions

The discomfort created by many VDUs can cause (for the operator) resentment, complaint, eye-strain, etc. and (for the employer) restrictions on use, lack of performance, claims for concessions, etc. and, perhaps, largely abortive expenditure on piecemeal palliatives.

The discomfort is the cumulative, perhaps synergistic, effect of several problems. But there already exist solutions, either complete or partial, to most of these problems.

Exchanging experience and perfecting knowledge is certainly important, but it is equally important to devise means of informing VDU customers that many of the problems are *unnecessary* so that they can persuade VDU manufacturers to put theory into practice by adopting known solutions to unnecessary environmental burdens.

Reference

CAKIR, A., HART, D. J., and STEWART, T. F. M., 1979, *The VDT Manual* (Darmstadt: Inca-Fiej Research Association).

Practical implications of the interest in ergonomic aspects of VDUs

By D. J. Wheatley and B. M. Drake

ITT Human Factors Group, Harlow, UK

This paper discusses the problems encountered when information and data currently existing are put to use in solving practical problems relating to visual display units. Much detailed information is available and the major problem we are now facing is the problem of communication; the research has been done and we have at least some of the answers, but can we communicate them to the people who really need them?

Our approach to this situation has been to establish exactly who needs the information and also what they need and then to tailor its presentation to the specific needs of each group. Our audience within ITT consists of three main groups: systems designers, quality assurance personnel, and thirdly, most important of all, the users of VDUs. It was apparent that not only did each group have different information requirements but that the most effective means of communication was different in each case.

The information for systems designers was produced as a text containing detailed technical information, emphasis being placed on a simple but effective cross-referencing system to make the information more accessible. A check-list was developed for the second group, summarizing the desirable characteristics to look for in VDUs and work-stations. The needs of the VDU user, however, were more for explanation and advice on how to avoid problems. The result was a concise brochure relying heavily on illustration as a means of communication.

In order to ensure that we reach the right people and that each gets the information they require, the documents will be supplemented by a tape/slide presentation covering the major problems connected with VDUs and making it easier to isolate the real problems. Site surveys are recommended in each case to enable specific requirements to be taken into account.

We hope this approach—tailoring information and its presentation to the specific situation and the specific problem—will enable us to use the information we now have more effectively to solve real problems in practical situations.

1. Introduction

During the last decade, visual display units have become widely accepted throughout industry and the initial concern shown for the possible hazards has been sustained to the present day. There is general agreement that problems exist, but their exact nature is still somewhat elusive. Although many problems have been solved there is one major factor still confronting us (especially those of us who are practitioners). That is the problem of interpreting these solutions and communicating the essential message to our real audience: the designers, purchasers and most importantly, the users of visual display units.

This paper describes how the problem presented itself to us as the ITT Human Factors Group and how we have attempted to meet that challenge.

2. The communication problem

We have had numerous enquiries from medical, marketing and industrial relations groups, as well as designers and users—enquiries about the potential hazards of using VDUs, and requests for advice on the setting-up of terminal installations. As a result of this sort of widespread concern, ergonomists, psychologists and industrial hygienists have been able to meet the challenge, to study and investigate reports of eyestrain and similar problems and to propose solutions. Consequently, there is now a large body of information available relating to the ergonomic aspects of VDU design and usage. The main problems we face now are those of interpretation and of putting this information to effective use—in other words, the classic problem of communication, the research has been done and we have at least some of the answers, but can we communicate them to the people who really need them? This is an area which merits as much effort as the research.

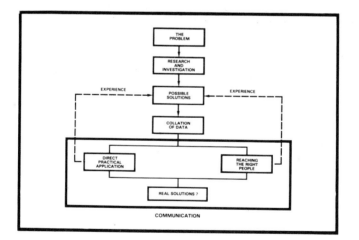

Figure 1. The communication problem: much research has been done but can we use it effectively?

3. The solution

One of the first things to be established is exactly who needs the information. The enquiries we had indicated that there was a wide range of people and professional groups interested in this area and also that each group had its own specific needs. The designers of VDUs, for example, have different problems and therefore different information requirements from the users of a system. Our response to this was to collect together the available information relating to the ergonomics of VDUs, and information relating to their design, installation and everyday use.

This formed a sizeable document, thorough and detailed, but this is where the communication problem arose—the data were comprehensive but were they comprehensible? Were they accessible? In fact did people really need all this information and data?

Our audience consisted of three main groups of people:

(a) systems designers involved in the design of ITT VDUs and computer systems,

(b) quality assurance personnel and those who choose to buy VDU equipment, and

(c) the users of visual display units.

Having identified those groups who needed information, we continued by determining what information they needed. We did this by conducting an internal survey of all interested people using questionnaires and interviews. Our problem then was to structure this in such a way that it would be of maximum benefit to them (figure 2).

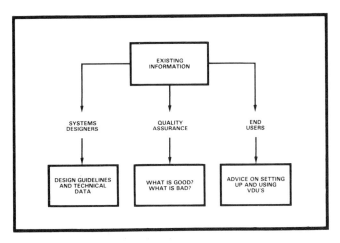

Figure 2. Information requirements of the three main groups making up our audience.

It was clear that not only did each group have differing information requirements, but that the most effective way of communicating it in each case was equally varied. We therefore set about the task of tailoring the information to the individual needs of each group and producing concise documents containing the relevant information in a form which was easily comprehensible.

3.1. *Manual of design guidelines*

We found that systems designers—a group which included industrial designers, software, hardware and electronics designers—needed detailed information relating to the ergonomic implications of the terminal design. This was produced as a text containing design guidelines. However, to make the facts more accessible, emphasis was placed on the use of a simple but none the less effective cross-referencing system within the text. This indicated the complex interdependence of various factors, guiding the reader through the text as well as through all the arguments relating to his topic of interest— an important issue which is the essential message of ergonomics, especially with regard to the presentation of information for designers.

3.2. *Checklist for VDUs and work-stations*

Discussions with the second group of people—the quality assurance personnel —enabled us to develop a check-list. This summarized the important ergonomic aspects of both VDUs and work-stations in such a manner that alternatives could be directly compared on various criteria in a consistent and structured way.

3.3. *User guide/brochure*

The requirements of the user were not so much for detailed technical information, but more for explanation and advice on how potential problems can be avoided through careful arrangement of the work-station and attention to the general working environment. The result was a clear and easily readable brochure, relying extensively on illustration as an effective means of communication. We particularly hope to reach a wide audience by integrating this brochure with the usual support and marketing documentation accompanying VDUs, enabling the users to avoid problems from the beginning, particularly visual and postural problems, and leading to a more rapid acceptance of VDUs into the working environment.

Producing such documents is, however, only one step towards bridging the communication gap. A further problem arises because people sometimes cannot identify exactly where the difficulties lie. As emphasized above, not only do we need to reach the right people, but we have to ensure that each gets the relevant information to solve his particular problems and therefore we need to identify these specific problems. We have approached this aspect of the situation in two complementary ways.

4. Identifying the problem

Firstly, a tape/slide presentation is being developed, covering most of the problems associated with the use of VDUs. This aims to clarify the major issues, enabling those directly concerned with VDUs to establish the problem areas. Thus, the most appropriate solution, whether it be in the form of documentation, or a study of the specific system or installation, can be more accurately determined and steps can be taken towards alleviating the real difficulties.

5. Site surveys

The second factor to be considered is to what extent the information can be generalized. The requirements and limitations of specific situations must also be taken into account, especially the environmental conditions and task requirements. We therefore consider that the information provided has to be supplemented by a study of the specific situation or installation in order to achieve the necessary accuracy. Specific advice can then be provided on the siting of terminals and the suitability of the work-station and environment (see figure 3). Additionally, the psychological benefits to be gained from this involvement should not be underestimated, and by helping to overcome natural resistance to change, can achieve more to smooth the implementation of new systems than the indirect provision of impersonal data.

Figure 3. Each individual installation has to be studied to permit specific factors to be considered.

The Human Factors Group has so far carried out four studies of specific VDU installations, three within the ITT Group and the fourth for an ITT customer, providing advice and recommendations both on the siting of terminals and on the environment in which they will be used, paying particular attention to the immediate work-station. We consider that this is particularly important and frequently has more influence on the incidence of visual fatigue than is often realized.

Fortunately, furniture manufacturers (particularly in Europe) are now responding to the demand for adjustable work-stations specifically designed for use with VDUs. They provide work-surfaces, lecterns and a wide range of adjustment for height and angle of the keyboard and display unit, allowing the operator to tailor the work-station to his own specific requirements and avoiding the fatigue which can arise through postural factors. We are currently conducting a survey of the furniture which is on the market.

6. Conclusions

The major problem we are facing is to communicate the information we have to the right people. This involves isolating the real causes of difficulty in a VDU installation: our tape/slide presentation is intended to clarify these issues and will help in this process. We can then determine the most appropriate solution, which could be detailed technical information, a check-list or a brochure, supplemented almost invariably by a site survey to enable specific factors to be taken into consideration.

We hope that our approach, that of tailoring information and its presentation to the specific situation and to the specific problem, will enable us more effectively to use the information we now have to solve practical problems, in the process increasing people's understanding both of ergonomics in general and the hazards (or non-hazards) of using VDUs.

To help achieve this, there are three golden rules to remember:

(1) Treat each installation as an individual problem, considering fully the job specification.
(2) Always use a check-list when selecting and installing a VDU or work-station.
(3) Demand flexible and easily adjustable work-stations from the furniture manufacturer or terminal supplier. Better still, if at all possible, have it custom built for the specific VDU and the specific task being performed.

New technologies can be introduced quite painlessly if attention is paid both to the human factor in the design of the equipment, and to the needs and expectations of the people who have to use and work with the equipment in the long term. They are our audience, they are the people we need to reach and they are the people we at ITT are trying to reach.

NCR: From the first computer in Italy to the 1980s Research and development on VDUs connected to EDP systems

By G. Bassani

NCR Corporation, Viale Cassala, 22, I-20143 Milan, Italy

This paper deals with three general areas of display characteristics which affect readability:
(1) Character definition: physical dimensions, shape, style, etc., of display characters including recommended font.
(2) Light conditions, colour, viewing angle, etc.: brightness, contrast, colour contrast, glare, horizontal and vertical viewing angles, flicker.
(3) Format definition: factors relating to how information is presented (capital letters versus lower case, numbers of characters per line, etc.).

1. Introduction

At the Institute of Electronics—Milan's Polytechnic—the first computer installed in Italy can still be seen. NCR installed it in 1953–54. It was a first-generation computer using vacuum tubes and no VDUs were connected to it. A few years later the second generation of computers started to use VDUs and many efforts have been made since, in order to ensure maximum safety to the users.

Today's generation of computers makes extensive use of VDUs and NCR has set Engineering Standards to influence the design of VDUs. VDUs are being increasingly used in offices, factories and other premises throughout the world, mainly to display information held in computers or generated by them and also as an integral part of word processing systems.

Are there health problems in connection with the use of VDUs? A two-year investigation recently completed by IFRA (International Research Association of Newspaper Technology) concludes that "despite a considerable amount of research, there is at this time no evidence to suggest that using VDUs is likely to damage eyes or eyesight". It also rules out radiation dangers from VDUs on the ground that this (at normal operator distance) is no greater than background radiation. In England, Dr. Gilbert, Principal Medical Officer of the Post Office Telecommunications Occupational Health Service, reported that the Post Office had monitored large numbers of VDUs for both ionizing and non-ionizing radiation with 'nil-detected' results.

Three general areas of display characteristics affect readability:

(1) Character definition: physical dimensions, shape, style, etc., of display characters including recommended font.
(2) Light conditions, colour, viewing angle, etc.: brightness, contrast, colour contrast, glare, horizontal and vertical viewing angles, flicker.
(3) Format definition: factors relating to how information is presented (capital letters versus lower case, number of characters per line, etc.).

2. Character definition

Character height is specified according to the range of visual activities of intended users and the viewing distance required for a specific display. Character height is always referenced to numerals and upper case letters.

The character height should subtend 12 minutes of arc at the greatest anticipated viewing distance for those people who are expected to use the display in the normal course of their work. The vision of these operators is expected to be near normal. The preferred character height for operator viewing is as follows:

minimum height = either 0·0035 × view distance (in millimetres) or
2·54 millimetres (whichever is larger).

Casual users of a display, such as store customers, are not expected to have near-normal visual acuity. Consequently, those displays which are to be read by casual users should have a character height subtending 24 minutes of arc at the casual user's greatest anticipated viewing distance. This preferred character height is determined as follows:

minimum height = either 0·007 × view distance (in millimetres) or
5·08 millimetres (whichever is larger).

Character height to width ratio is that value obtained by dividing the character height by the character width (H/W).

Height to width ratios (H/W) of 1/1 to 1/0·7 are acceptable for letters, and 1/0·7 to 1/0·5 for numbers. Displays used at large horizontal viewing angles (over 60°) should have the acceptable range of H/W decreased as follows:

$$H/(W + W \sin (\text{viewing angle}-60)).$$

Character height to stroke-width ratio is that value obtained by dividing the character height by the character stroke-width (H/SW).

Height to stroke-width ratios of 10/1 to 20/1 are acceptable for light characters on a dark background, and 5/1 to 15/1 are acceptable for dark characters on a light background.

Space between characters is the distance between the outside edges of adjacent characters and should be no less than 0·8 times the character stroke-width. The recommended distance is 1·0 to 1·3 times the character stroke-width.

Space between lines is the distance between the lower edges of the capital letters on one line and the top edges of capital letters of the next line down. The space between lines should be between 0·4 and 1·0 times the height of capital letters. The maximum of the range may be exceeded due to format requirements.

Font is the overall specifications of the shape and style of a character set (letters, numbers and symbols). Helvetica Medium (or equivalent) is recommended as the standard font for displays. Helvetica Bold Condensed (or equivalent) is acceptable when display area limitations prevent the use of Helvetica Medium.

Note: This recommendation is not applicable for CRT or plasma display terminals.

3. Light conditions, colour, viewing angle, glare, etc.

Brightness contrast. Adequate brightness contrast is mandatory for distinguishing display characters from the background (excluding colour effect). If the brightness contrast is too small, the display characters will blend into their background. If the brightness contrast is too large, the display characters will appear blurred.

Brightness contrast is the ratio of the difference between the luminance of an object and its background to whichever has the greater luminance. The equation for brightness contrast is expressed as either a ratio or percentage:

$$\text{brightness contrast ratio} = (B - D)/B$$
$$\text{percentage brightness contrast} = 100 \times (B - D/B)$$

where B is the greater luminance (brighter) and D is the lesser luminance (dimmer).

Brightness contrast should be between 60 and 95%. Ambient light conditions and display character and format variables affect the acceptable range. High ambient light conditions restrict the range from 40 to 70%. Very low ambient light conditions restrict the range from 60 to 90%. Displays with ideal display character and format dimensions may have the lower limit of the acceptable range lowered to 80% of the lower limits listed above. Brightness is measured with a laboratory grade photometer. The ambient light conditions under which the measurements are taken must represent both the typical and extremes of ambient light conditions anticipated in the use of the display.

Colour contrast is not typically required to achieve good displays. However, colour may be used to enhance a display by either improving legibility (by adding colour contrast to brightness contrast), or by providing display coding.

Colour contrast is the difference in hue and saturation between an object and its background. Although there is no applicable equation for colour contrast, there are some rules which may be used as guides if colour contrast is to be employed in a display. Colour matching is the most practical approach to making colour measurements.

Do not use complementary colour for characters and their background (complementary colours are visually disturbing). Do not exceed the brightness contrast range presented above. Follow traditional uses of colour when colour coding is required, such as green for go, 'OK', good events; yellow for caution event; and orange or red for stop, danger or hazardous events. Do not use red and green or blue and yellow for colour contrast. Many people are either red–green or yellow–blue colour deficient.

Viewing angle. Many displays are designed to be read by other than the device operator. These people will be standing to the side of the operator and consequently, will have some horizontal viewing angle to the display. Also, the operators of some equipment will not be standing in front of the display when they are using the system, and their horizontal viewing angle will have to be taken into consideration.

The vertical viewing angle must be taken into consideration for three reasons. First, not all operators are the same height (whether standing or sitting). Second, some displays will be inclined to induce a vertical viewing angle so that ambient light source will not be reflected back to the operator. Third, some devices may be used in both the standing and sitting position.

Viewing angle is the angular measure of how far from normal (perpendicular to the display surface) a viewer's eyes are expected to be positioned while required to read the display. The limits of acceptable viewing angle are a direct function of the display's ability to maintain contrast with increased viewing angle. The design application of a display should not require the user of a display to view it at a horizontal viewing angle of more than 75° from normal. This maximum viewing angle is only acceptable under ideal display conditions (i.e. with no loss of contrast as a consequence of viewing angle). It must be noted that displays which are to be viewed at large viewing angles should have their character dimensions adjusted to help compensate for those dimensions which are perceived smaller because of the viewing angle. (See above for specific recommendations.)

Maximum viewing angle required for a specific display should be specified prior to selecting the display generator. Many display generators are not acceptable at large viewing angles.

Glare adversely affects the legibility and readability of displays and is considered annoying and undesirable. Glare can be measured with a laboratory grade photometer and evaluated in accordance with the 'brightness contrast' requirements.

Glare associated with displays is divided into three categories. The first is unwanted light reflected from the display which reduces the contrast of the display. The second is a condition of light contrast between the display and its surroundings, such as bright display in a dark bar or restaurant which causes the display characters to blur together. The third condition is a very bright light source adjacent to the display which reduces the contrast of the display within the eyes of the person trying to read it. The first type of glare should conform to the 'brightness contrast' recommendations given above. Brightness contrast for the second and third types of glare should not exceed:

67% between the display and its surroundings,
90% between the display and remote surfaces,
85% between display and adjacent luminaires,
98% between any objects of the visual field of view.

Flicker. Flickering displays are annoying to read. The only acceptable type of 'flickering' display is one that flashes on and off to alert the user.

Flicker is said to occur whenever a light source turns on and off at a rate at which the human eye can perceive that the light is not continuously on. The cycle rate of a rapid-decay display medium should be about 60 Hz. It should be noted that there are two circumstances in which the eyes are particularly sensitive to flicker. The first is when the display is composed of text which must be read by the user. The user's rapid eye movements while reading the text enhance his ability to detect flicker. The second is where the light to dark ratio for each cycle is around 0·03 (97% of the cycle in darkness) with a bright display. Under these conditions, the user's ability to detect flicker is maximized. Slow-decay display media may be refreshed at a slower rate. The human eye is the best meter for determining whether there is any perceptable flicker in a display. The evaluation should be conducted as described under 'brightness contrast'.

4. Format definition

The format of how information is presented relates to such aspects of displays as how many characters should be placed on one line, which words should be capitalized or in lower case, what size borders (if any) should be used, and the message content being displayed.

Number of characters per line. Number of characters per line has been demonstrated to affect reading speed.

The number of characters per line is the number of characters acceptable on one line of display and is relevant to displays of text. It should be between 40 and 80.

Use of upper and lower case letters. Upper and lower case letters convey different information to the reader. In some display situations, upper case letters read better than lower case, and in other situations, the opposite is true.

Upper case refers to capital letters and lower case refers to small letters with ascenders and descenders. (Ascenders are the lines of some letters which extend up above the top of the small letter 'o', whereas descenders are the lines of some letters which extend down below the bottom of the small letter 'o'. Upper case letters should be only used for indications, such as 'ON-LINE', or 'POWER ON'. Upper case letters should also be used when appropriate in upper and lower case text. Lower case letters should be used in displays which are narrative, such as 'Enter your account number', or 'Start when green light comes on'.

Border size. Displays with properly dimensioned borders have been found to be more attention-getting than borderless displays.

Border size is the distance between the peripheral characters of a display and the edge of the display. (It is only applicable when there is a difference between the display background and the display surroundings. When the background and surroundings are the same, there is no border.) When borders are present, they should be between 0·5 and 1·5 times the height of capital letters.

Certainly many other factors are taken into account when researching and developing VDUs, like environmental design, temperature, humidity and barometric pressure; acoustical noise for printing devices connected to VDUs, etc., but to discuss these would take much longer.

Can VDU operation cause dermatitis?

By H. Tjønn

Directorate of Labour Inspection, Oslo 1, Norway

Ten cases of dermatitis in the faces of VDU operators were recorded in Norway. No physical or chemical cause could be detected. The problem will have to be given further attention.

During the last 12 months, the Medical Department of the Norwegian Labour Inspectorate has received some reports of exanthema in the faces of some VDU operators.

The number of reported cases is ten. All reported cases have been suffering from exanthema in the face and some suspected that the exanthema was caused by their operating VDUs. The cases are now being explored; they are spread throughout the country. All reported cases are female except one.

The subjects complained of itching and/or rash developing after half an hour up to some few hours of work. The rash began to disappear a few hours after leaving the workplace, and it was always gone the next morning.

Description of the exanthema

The exanthema developed most frequently over the cheekbones, was symmetrical and had a butterfly localization. Some of the cases also reported developing exanthema on the forehead. The exanthema was mostly numular with a relatively sharp border to normal skin. The affected areas showed redness and some minor desquamation. Some cases also showed small papulae.

Provocation tests were carried out with VDU operators who were known to react with exanthema when operating a VDU, by exposing them to the screen.

One operator developed during a provocation test a grave exaggeration of perioral dermatitis after few hours' work, and had to have sick leave and also tetracycline treatment. No special idiosyncrasy had been previously known by the cases, and no known light-sensitizing drugs were recorded as having been used.

Measurements of ionizing radiation as well as UV radiation have been made without any unwanted findings. The relative humidity as well as the general illumination were measured, but no unwanted findings were observed. One common environmental factor was found in all workplaces where cases developed, i.e. nylon-felt carpets on the floors.

We have searched the literature but did not succeed in revealing any description of dermatitis among VDU operators. Some different hypotheses have been made as to finding the mechanism of the observed exanthemas, but we still do not know what the cause is.

Section 8. Ergonomic design and guidelines

Ergonomic design principles of alphanumeric displays

By H. SCHMIDTKE

Institut für Ergonomie, Technische Universität München, Munich, F.R. Germany

This paper deals with design principles of alphanumeric displays. The dynamic range of symbol luminance control must be large if the displays are to be used in dark and light rooms. Luminance distribution within a symbol or between two symbols is highly important for legibility of signs. For an average reading distance of 50 cm a symbol height of 4 mm is recommended.

1. Dynamic range of symbol luminance

The necessary dynamic range of symbol luminance control depends upon the variability of brightness within the environment. It is a basic ergonomic requirement that modulation of the tube must be possible, in general from the threshold of visibility to the threshold of glare. Figure 1 shows the pattern

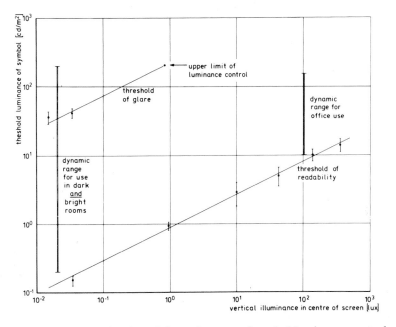

Figure 1. Determination of dynamic range of symbol luminance control.

of the two thresholds in relation to the brightness of the screen due to the level of illumination in the working room on the basis of subjective evaluation by 53 subjects. If, for instance, the display is used in a normal office environment with a band-width of illuminance 1 m above floor level from 100 lx to 1000 lx one can calculate the vertical intensity of illumination on the screen according to Lambert's cosine law as 26 to 260 lx, if the angle of adjustment of the screen is about 75°. In this case a dynamic range of symbol luminance control from approximately 10 cd/m² to 150 cd/m² (min. 100 cd/m²) is necessary. In several circumstances—for instance the bridge of ships—alphanumeric displays are used in a dark environment as well as in a very bright one. Therefore, the dynamic range must be adapted to these conditions. According to figure 1, the dynamic range has to be enlarged for displays used in dark and bright rooms approximately from 0·2 cd/m² to 200 cd/m².

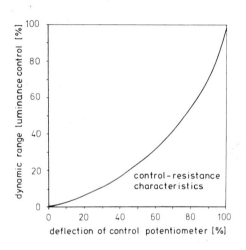

Figure 2. Determination of resistance characteristic of the potentiometer for luminance control.

The symbol luminance is controlled by a potentiometer. If the control-resistance characteristics of the potentiometer are linear as usual, a very little deflection of the control potentiometer will brighten the screen to such an extent that the level of adaptation of the operator can be disturbed if the display is used under dark conditions. Therefore, it is another ergonomic requirement to apply a non-linear control-resistance characteristic to the dimmer, as shown in figure 2. This characteristic will lead to a small increase of symbol luminance under dark conditions, and to a much higher one under daylight conditions, by the same movement of the dimmer.

2. Luminance distribution within the symbol

Measurements of luminance distribution within a symbol or between two symbols have shown that the resolution is highly dependent upon the method of generating symbols. Even when the modality of generating symbols is not an ergonomic problem, the result as visible on the screen is of high relevance. Figure 3 demonstrates the legibility of signs generated by two different tubes according to the level of luminance. It can be seen in the left part of the figure that even under the rather low luminance condition of 16 cd/m^2, the sign is nearly unreadable and it gets worse as luminance increases. Figure 4 shows the luminance distribution between the vertical lines of the letter M. The mutual interference is so high that the luminance between the two vertical lines drops under normal modulation only to approximately 30% of the maximal luminance. That means that a contrast between these two vertical lines of only 3 : 1 can be reached where one of at least 10 : 1 is required. Under bright modulation ($L = 23$ cd/m^2) with this tube, a contrast of no more than 1·4 : 1 is

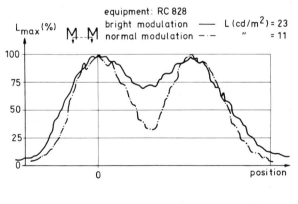

Figure 3. Legibility of signs generated by two different tubes according to the level of luminance (Cakir *et al.* 1978).

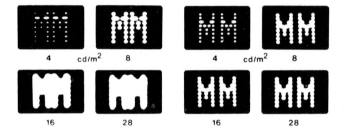

Figure 4. Luminance distribution between two vertical lines in the centre of image (Cakir *et al.* 1978).

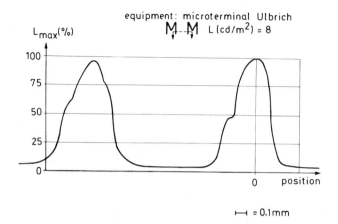

Figure 5. Luminance distribution between two vertical lines in the centre of image (Cakir *et al.* 1978).

possible! Figure 5 refers to the right part of figure 3. Here we see no mutual interference at all. From this example we can derive a third ergonomic demand: if the mutual interference of luminance of signs under normal modulation is higher than 5% of the maximal luminance of the sign, the distance between the signs must be enlarged to such an extent that the interference value falls below the critical value of 5%.

3. Symbol height

The requirement on symbol height depends upon the reading distance, the luminance contrast between symbol and background, the symbol luminance under normal modulation in relation to average illuminance of the working area, and the visual acuity of the operator. Because of the fact that the visual acuity of many operators even when corrected is less than normal and the conditions of room illumination and its installation are in many cases not optimal, the height of symbols determines to a great extent the usability of alphanumeric displays. Even though a symbol height below 2 mm is unusual, values between 2·5 and 3 mm can be found quite frequently, because with such a small symbol height the producers of VDUs are able to bring a whole page of text on the screen. This height might be sufficient for a reading distance of 30 cm. But because the luminance-gradient of electronically generated symbols is flat and the dot-or-dash raster technique does not lead to a homogeneity of the symbol comparable to printing, it is advisable to demand a symbol height of ca. 4 mm for an average reading distance of 50 cm. In figure 6 the results of reading experiments are demonstrated which were obtained

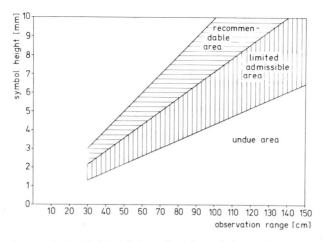

Figure 6. Symbol height as a function of observation range.

under identical conditions with the same alphanumeric display but changeable symbol height. According to speed and accuracy of reading in these experiments, we can differentiate between three areas of reading performance relative to reading distance, namely a preferred, a limited admissible, and an undue range of symbol heights. In view of ergonomic requirements, the symbol height should be chosen from the preferred range.

As a matter of fact there are several other ergonomic design aspects of alphanumeric displays, as well as workplace arrangements, which have to be taken into consideration. But within the limits of this article I have tried to focus attention on a few points which have been less frequently discussed in the past.

References

CAKIR, A., REUTER, H. J., VON SCHMUDE, L., and ARMBRUSTER, A., 1978, Anpassung von Bildschirmarbeitsplätzen an die physische und psychische Funktionsweise des Menschen. *Forschungsbericht der Humanisierung des Arbeitsleben* (Bonn: Der Bundesminister für Arbeit und Sozialordnung).
HARTMANN, E., 1979, Lichttechnische und physiologisch-optische Probleme bei der Arbeit an Datensichtgeräten. *Arbeitsmedizin, Sozialmedizin, Präventivmedizin*, **14**, 182–186.
SCHMIDTKE, H., 1975, Datensichtgeräte. In *Handbuch der Ergonomie*, edited by BWB, C-7.1.1 (Steinebach).

Visual display units: present status in ergonomic research and applications in the Federal Republic of Germany

By G. W. RADL

Technischer Überwachungsverein Rheinland, Cologne
and University of Trier, F.R. Germany

The present status in application of VDUs in the Federal Republic of Germany is described and the main reasons for the poor image of VDUs are discussed. On the basis of some theses from the standpoint of ergonomics, the needs and some facts in the areas of research and applications of the present results are reported.

1. Present status in application of VDUs

Today approximately 250 000 VDUs are in use in the F.R.G. (Diebold 1978). The category of VDU means CRT-displays for presentation of data and text information. Approximately 80 000 of these VDUs are used, mainly continuously during the daily working shift, for data input into electronic data-processing systems. Approximately 120 000 are employed with computer systems and are in use either continuously or intermittently for dialogue with technical information-processing systems. Approximately 12 5000 units are installed in offices for word-processing. A small number of them are in use for text communication. Approximately 35 000 VDUs are used in industry and in research and development areas. If the analogue TV-monitor is also included within the definition of VDU, a number of 300 000 or more TV screens must be added, which are installed in industrial television systems.

2. The image of the VDU at the workplace

The image of work with VDUs is generally bad in the F.R.G. The causes are complex, but it seems to be possible to point out the following main factors (Cakir *et al.* 1977, Peters and Radl 1980, Picot and Reichwald 1979, Weltz *et al.* 1978):

(1) To date, many of the screens and keyboards are badly designed. The most unsatisfactory points are: low luminiscence level on the display, low contrast between characters and background, flicker of the display,

reflections on the screen, and the design of the whole box in such a way that it is often impossible to use in a man-adapted position. In many cases keyboards are connected with the display box and are unnecessarily high and produce light reflections, mainly on the surfaces of the keys.

(2) Relatively poor workplace design and bad positioning, including mistakes in the illumination, can also be found at many of the present workplaces. The F.R.G. has good and strict regulations for workplace design, but there have been no specific regulations for workplaces with VDUs until now, except the recommendations of the Bundesanstalt für Arbeitsschutz und Unfallforschung (which has the function of an ergonomic board), valid since 1979.

(3) Also, the illumination conditions at most VDU workplaces are unsatisfactory. German standard prescribes 500 lx for office workplaces (German Standards). But there are only general recommendations to avoid glare. Information on how to avoid glare and reflections on the screen is not disseminated. The existing illumination problems are caused by daylight as well as by artificial lighting.

(4) Eye defects are often the reason for increase in workload of many persons working with VDUs. These eye defects are not caused by VDU use. Field studies have shown that more than 50% of all German adults have non-corrected eye defects (Peters 1975, Peters and Radl 1980, Radl 1980) and this is an important loading factor, when these persons work with VDUs. The F.R.G. has good employment laws with many detailed regulations about medical service for the employee (Peters 1975), but to date none of these specifically covers methods of eye-testing and consequences of their results for VDU workers. It is only recently that opticians and medical officers have begun to understand this field.

(5) In many cases the use of VDUs has forced an increase of information transmission rates between man and technical information-processing systems. Normally a new technical and more computerized system with VDU workplaces is installed for economic reasons. Most manufacturers promise in their advertisements to reduce costs by increase of performance of the man–computer system. Therefore all activities during the introduction phase as well as later are concentrated on bringing a higher output (meaning an increase of symbols per minute, data per hour or other number of working units per day and employee (Radl *et al.* 1980). It is difficult to explain that the main effect of the use of computer and VDU technologies should be to increase not primarily the quantity of information rates at the man–technical information-processing system interface, but the quality of the whole system performance, e.g. through better information selection and handling, through more flexibility of the organization, through better written output and through better and more adaptive reactions of the offices—and last but not least through more humanity at the workplace in the office.

(6) Many arguments in the discussions about VDU workplaces are emotional. This is understandable, because the VDU has become a negative symbol for anxieties of the employee in the office: anxiety about the technical and organizational changes in the white collar area, anxiety about mass unemployment by the rationalization effects, anxiety about dequalification and anxiety over more control from the computer (Peters and Radl 1980, Radl *et al.* 1980). It is important to know and to try to solve these social problems. But it is also important to separate the ergonomically caused and the socially caused problems in the discussion of the acceptance of VDUs, because each kind of problem needs different measures to be solved.

(7) VDUs have very bad publicity in the German newspapers. If a problem of their use is discussed in a research report or at a congress, the papers will generalize it for all sorts of VDU workplaces and they will once again point out how unhealthy and dangerous work with VDUs is.

The existing problems in VDU workplaces should not be hidden. The other papers and the discussions during this workshop have demonstrated the present problem status. But the problems should also be solved, and this can be done step by step. It is important to accept that ergonomics has not only the function of analysing and discussing the problems of man at the workplace but also of creating practical, usable solutions! What practical solutions should be found, what is going on in this field in the F.R.G.?

3. Some basic theses

The following theses express the present basis for ergonomic activities in the field of VDU workplace design and of VDU use:

(1) Eye discomfort and workload in VDU workplaces can be reduced to or below the level at workplaces without VDUs but with similar tasks. The condition: screen, presentation mode, VDU box, keyboard, the whole workplace and the environmental factors have to be designed as well as possible by existing technologies and following existing recommendations which are the results of ergonomic research and practical experiences.

(2) It is not generally in question whether to use a VDU or not. But there are many questions and also practical answers on how to design a specific VDU workplace and its environment with respect to man and his specific task at this workplace. Manufacturers and users do not only need our criticism on VDUs and workplaces. They need detailed information on how to make it better.

(3) Work-time limitations and special break-time regulations for VDU workers are not the optimal way to solve the existing problems. It should not be the main target of ergonomics to compensate high workload,

which is caused by poor working conditions, only by time limitations or by additional break-times. The better measure consists in avoiding the loading factors by man-adapted workplace design and by an interesting, non-monotonous task.

(4) An ergonomic optimally designed VDU workplace is necessary but not enough. The social aspects of VDU use—and this means for most people the increase of computerization in the office—are as important as the ergonomic aspects.

4. Present status of ergonomic activities in the F.R.G.

In respect of this thesis, until now the following activities characterize the present status in ergonomic research and application of ergonomic knowledge on workplaces with VDUs.

Research work has been, and is being, carried out in many institutes at universities and research organizations. Most investigations are involved with special problems, e.g. visual presentation (Cakir *et al.* 1977, Moog 1975) or optical problems (Krueger and Müller-Limmroth 1979). A few projects were done as field studies also pointing out the social aspects (Weltz *et al.* 1978). Some research projects are financed by the government programme, 'Humanization of Worklife'. The Federal Ministry for Research and Technology is also trying to bring research work into the area of the social aspects of new technologies for information processing and information transmitting in the office (Picot and Reichwald 1979).

The sensitivity of some of the manufacturers towards better ergonomic product design has increased not only in their advertisements but also in their products. Positive examples are VDUs with higher refreshment rates than 50 c.p.s. to avoid flicker, the presentation in a mode with dark symbols on a light background on the screen, to adapt the illumination level of the display to the illumination level of data sheets or paper manuscripts, and, to avoid light reflections on the screen, flat keyboards with non-reflecting surfaces, and VDU units which are better adapted to ergometric measures as well as to different needs of special use. Also ergonomics is applied more and more in office furniture for workplaces with VDUs.

The dissemination of the knowledge that VDU units should be installed and used at ergonomically designed workplaces also increases. Positive examples are the operating recommendations given by the Bundesanstalt für Arbeitsschutz (Handlungsanweisung) and the brochures edited by the Bavarian Ministry for Labour and Social Affairs (Krueger and Müller-Limmroth 1979) and by some computer manufacturers (IBM 1979, Radl 1979/80, 1980, Siemens 1979). A positive factor for dissemination of ergonomic knowledge is the information seminars arranged for managers and VDU users by scientific organizations, the trade unions and many companies for their employees (Radl 1980).

In the near future Berufsgenossenschaften (work-accident insurances) will publish ergonomic and medical requirements at VDU workplaces (Verwaltungs Berufsgenossenschaften 1980). Also German standards for adaptation of VDU workplaces to man are in preparation (DIN 66 233 and DIN 66 234).

Positive, also, is the beginning of eye-testing for VDU workers with a two-step system. The medical officer will apply a first scanning test. When this scanning test shows that an employee has an eye defect he is sent to the ophthalmologist, who will decide what to do after a second exploration. In most cases the eye defect can be corrected totally by glasses. In a few cases the ophthalmologist will recommend that VDU work and other work which can generate eye strain should not be done during the whole shift, or not at all (Peters and Radl 1980, Verwaltungs Berufsgenossenschaft).

So human factors are being more and more regarded when VDUs are established and used in the F.R.G. If ergonomic activities are continued, VDU workplaces in the future could become a positive example demonstrating that new technologies and new organizational forms of work can improve not only economic aspects but also the quality of working life.

References

CAKIR, A., REUTER, H.-J., SCHMUDE, L. von, and ARMBRUSTER, A., 1977, Untersuchungen zur Anpassung von Bildschirmarbeitsplätzen an die physische und psychische Funktionsweise des Menschen. *Forschungsbericht der Humanisierung des Arbeitsleben* (Bonn: Der Bundesminister für Arbeit und Sozialordnung).

DIEBOLD Management Report, 1978, *Der Markt für Informationstechnologie.*

German Standards DIN 2137 (Alphanumerische Tastaturen. Tastenanordnung, Belegung mit Schriftzeichen); DIN 2139 (Alphanumerische Tastaturen. Tastenanordung fuer Dateneingabe); DIN 2449 (Bueromoebel. Schreibtische, Schreibmaschinentische); DIN 4551 (Bueromoebel. Buerodrehstuhl mit verstellbarer Rueckenlehne mit und ohne Armstuetzen); DIN 5035 (Innenraumbeleuchtung mit kuenstlichem Licht); DIN 33 400 (Gestalten von Arbeitssystemen nach arbeitswissenschaftlichen Gesichtspunkten); DIN 66 233 and DIN 66 234 (Kennwerte fuer die Anpassung von Bildschirmarbeitsplaetzen an den Menschen— in preparation).

HAEUSING, M., 1975, *Gestaltungsrichtlinien fuer Bildschirmarbeitsplaetze mit Rastersichtgeraeten. Research report No. 26* (Meckenheim: Forschungsinstitut für Anthropotechnik).

Handlungsanweisung fuer Arbeitsplaetze mit Datensichtgeraeten. Edited by the Bundesanstalt für Arbeitsschutz und Unfallforschung in Dortmund (Wilhelmshaven: Wirtschaftsverlag Nordwest).

IBM, 1979, *Ergonomische Faktoren der Bildschirmarbeit.* IBM Form GE 12-1500-1 (Sindelfingen: IBM Deutschalnd GmbH).

KRUEGER, H., and MÜLLER-LIMMROTH, W., 1979, *Arbeiten mit dem Bildschirm—aber richtig* (Muenchen: Bayrisches Staatsministerium fuer Arbeit und Sozialordnung).

MOOG, R., 1975, *Codierung von Informationen auf Sichtgeraeten. Empfehlungen zur Dimensionierung.* PDV Report No. KFK-PDV 61 (Karlsruhe: Gesellschaft für Kernforschung).

PETERS, TH., 1975, *Arbeitswissenschaft fuer die Bueropraxis. Handbuch der Buero-medizin und -ergonomie* (Ludwigshafen: Kiehl Verlag).

PETERS, TH., and RADL, G. W., 1980, *Ergonomie am Bildschirmarbeitsplatz* (Ludwigshafen: Kiehl Verlag).

PICOT, A., and REICHWALD, R., 1979, *Untersuchungen der Auswirkungen neuer Kommunikationstechnologien im Buero auf Organisationsstruktur und Arbeitsinhalte* (Eggenstein-Leopoldshafen: Fachinformationzentrum Energie, Physik, Mathematik).

RADL, G. W., 1979/80, *Ergonomie. Grundlagen der Arbeitsplatzgestaltung. Arbeitsplaetze mit Bildschirmgeraeten* (Paderborn: Nixdorf Computer AG).

RADL, G. W., 1980, *Ergonomische und arbeitspsychologische Fragen bei der Textverarbeitung mit Bildschirmterminals* (Koeln: CPT Text-computer Vertriebs GmbH).

RADL, G. W., REICHWALD, R., SCHELOSKE, G., SCHREIBER, R., and WELTZ, F., 1980, *Akzeptanz neuer Buerotechnologien. Bedingungen für eine sinnvolle Gestaltung von Arbeitsplatz, Organisationsstruktur und Mitarbeitsbeteiligung* (Düsseldorf: Akzente, Studiengemeinschaft 'Akzeptanz neuer Bürotechnologien').

SIEMENS, 1979, *Ergonomie am Bildschirmarbeitsplatz* (Erlangen: Siemens AG).

VERWALTUNGS BERUFSGENOSSENSCHAFT, Sicherheitsregeln fuer Bueroarbeitsplaetze. In preparation (Hamburg).

WELTZ, F., JACOBI, U., LULLIES, V., and BECKER, W., 1978, *Menschengerechte Arbeitsgestaltung in der Textverarbeitung.* Research Report HA 79-06 (Eggenstein-Leopoldshafen: Fachinformationszentrum Energie, Physik, Mathematik).

Ergonomic and medical requirements in VDU workplaces and corresponding rules within the Federal Republic of Germany

By K. Buhmann

Verwaltungs-Berufsgenossenschaft, Überseering 8, 2000 Hamburg 60, F.R. Germany

In the Federal Republic of Germany the unions and the employers' associations have called for the elaboration of binding regulations for VDU workplaces. These regulations are intended to provide for uniform criteria though well-proven research results are not yet completely available. The regulations so far drafted for VDUs in offices try to take account of general requirements. They regard the VDU workplace as a system comprising several parts which are closely connected to each other. The regulations try to formulate well founded knowledge in order to make them known to the manufacturers and applicants. Thus it is intended to avoid uncertainties in shaping VDU workplaces in future.

1. Introductory remarks

The world-wide commitment of scientific research in this field and the thorough discussion of its results at national as well as at international level show that health effects and damage possibly caused by the utilization of video display units (VDU) cannot yet be totally evaluated. But this international workshop has shown that there are solutions, and many problems of shaping VDU workplaces have been fairly well established.

On the other hand, as Professor Grandjean said, there is a large difference between the workplaces he had found and those you can see in his published book *Fitting the Task to the Man*.

According to serious estimates, up to 1·5 million VDUs will be operating during the next few years in offices in the Federal Republic of Germany. This development not only raises problems concerning ergonomics and occupational health but social and socio-political problems as well. Therefore, the unions and the employers' associations alike have called for the elaboration of binding regulations, though well-proven research results are not yet completely available. The regulations so far drafted for VDUs in offices try to take account of general requirements. They regard the VDU workplace as a system comprising several parts which are closely connected to each other:

the shaping of the workplace;
the organization of job contents and job techniques; and
health precaution measures.

2. The shaping of the workplace

The shaping of the workplace and the working environment has to be based on a comprehensive adaptation of the working equipment to the ergonomic requirements of the employee.

This means that the work-surface height, the seat height and the foot rest height should be sufficiently adjustable to meet individual requirements. Figure 1 shows the adjustability suitable for Central Europe. Under-table installations must not prevent the employee from adopting an individual body posture. Figure 2 shows the minimum leg-room which must be guaranteed. Working equipment can only be arranged in a flexible way if the table is sufficiently large and plain. A separation of the table would lead to pinpointing individual working equipment, and thus changes individually required or determined by changing job techniques would not be possible to the degree required by ergonomics.

This means that the arrangement of the parts of the main working equipment, i.e. screen, keyboard and document holder, must be independent of each other. The arrangement of working equipment must be made in a way to guarantee that it meets ergonomic requirements even when a plain table is used. The measurements of the screen must allow for the required adjustability as to height and inclination. A keyboard height of 30 mm ensures that not too large a difference between seat surface and the horizontal forearm occurs if a normal body posture is adopted. As for the measurements, an exclusively vertical arrangement of working equipment maintaining at the same time the viewing distances would be the most extreme but useful situation. Therefore,

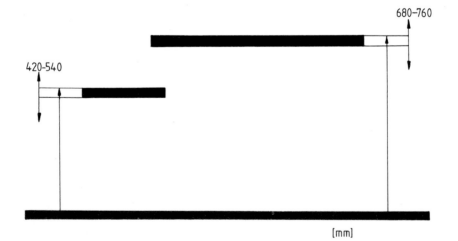

[mm]

Figure 1. Proposed ranges of adjustability for seat and work surface heights suitable for Central Europe.

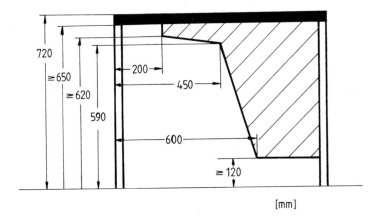

Figure 2. Proposed dimensions for VDU workplaces.

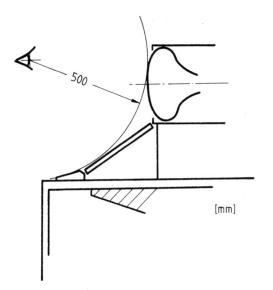

Figure 3. Proposed design for maintaining the same viewing distance to screen, source document and keyboard.

such arrangements have to be possible in general if normal sizes are used, even if they can only partly be applied due to job techniques (figure 3).

The visual requirements of display workplaces, their working equipment and their working environment have been fully covered by Professor Schmidtke, Dr Krueger and Mr Stewart elsewhere in this volume.

3. Organization of job contents and job techniques

If ergonomic aspects alone were taken into account in shaping display workplaces, this would still not lead to workplaces adapted to human needs. Personal factors have to be recognized, too. Organization in the office must in any event prevent employees from becoming socially isolated. If possible, work has to be organized in such a way that the whole job is done at one and the same workplace. Only by doing this can the employees be motivated, their efficiency increased, and deficiencies as well as the number of faults caused by monotony be limited.

As far as social aspects are concerned, each reorganization has to be based on existing structures. An arbitrary separation of existing connections is difficult to compensate. In order to limit the degree of automatic psychological functions, thinking processes have to be included in job techniques. Further development work has to be carried out in order to guarantee that no jobs have to be done by the employee which cannot—or can only at uneconomical cost—be pursued by the technical system. A flexible time structure has to be chosen for job techniques. Deadlines should not be set by the system but, if possible, by the individual employee himself.

Peaks of efficiency and persistence differ from employee to employee. The same applies to the wish for rests. Inflexible rest regulations cannot, therefore, solve the problem.

From the point of view of occupational health, it is undoubtedly recognized that several short rests guarantee a better effect than a small number of long rests. Work interruptions which are due to the system may not, however, be regarded as rests, since the employees are under stress to fulfil their set tasks and are waiting for an available system.

Organizers should have recognized that high efficiency and, therefore, an effective utilization of the system having only a minimum rate of faults, can only be guaranteed by sufficient and suitable rests. This method, and not working according to fixed time rates, is really suited to raise efficiency. Time stress is a considerable challenge for the employee, and it would be false to believe that efficiency can thus be increased. In particular, when high quality is required the increased rate of faults constitutes an additional psychological stress. As far as possible, employees should be made familiar with new working methods and new technologies. This includes comprehensive instruction and education. It is not sufficient—as is often done today—just to show them how things work, since objections against the new system will undoubtedly remain and may possibly lead to the above-mentioned difficulties.

4. Health precautions

Compared to present office workplaces, VDU workplaces are characterized by the fact that even well-proven persons have to constantly change between watching the different working equipment: screen, keyboard and document.

In order to harmonize the viewing distance with the working equipment in an ergonomically useful manner, the viewing distance to the keyboard must be about 500 mm. But this viewing distance does not mean that no stress remains for any employee. Depending on the intensity and the duration of work at the VDU, asthenopic discomforts such as headaches, burning eyes, or eyes running with tears may occur. If eye correction is lacking, or if it is insufficient or not sufficiently adpated to the VDU workplace, it may lead to a wrong body-posture, and may thus lead to health impairments, even if the workplace is shaped according to ergonomic needs.

Therefore the future principles for health precaution measures for employees at VDU workplaces provide for general health examinations to study whether an eye correction should or should not be made with regard to the workplace. Experts are of the opinion that these examinations should be carried out by screening tests. In these the following characteristics will have to be examined:

long-distance acuity;
short-distance acuity;
stereoscopic viewing capability and heterophoria;
fusion;

and for corresponding requirements,

colour acuity;
mesopic acuity.

If any objections against work are raised by the physicians, an expert optician has to carry out an eye correction. This also applies if employees claim certain discomforts though the screening test has shown no medical evidence. Regular further examinations according to the above scheme have to be carried out in order to detect changes of acuity due to work or due to ageing.

5. Conclusions

The above-mentioned requirements for VDU workplaces adapted to human needs go far beyond existing measures of accident prevention. Binding regulations are only possible for ergonomic and safety measures and for required precaution measures.

DIN regulations as an addition to existing accident protection regulations called *Safety Regulations for VDU Workplaces in Offices* are at present being elaborated within the Federal Republic of Germany. They are binding for applicants. It is intended to make manufacturers observe them by means of legislation on equipment safety. Measures for adapting job contents to human needs can only be taught to applicants by giving advice.

All expert bodies share the opinion that these regulations are adapted to recognized requirements of ergonomics, safety and occupational health, as well as to future developments.

Ergonomic design of a workplace for VDU operators

By L. Bandini Buti, F. De Nigris and E. Moretti

Società di Ergonomia Applicata, Milan, Italy

and G. Cortili

Institute of Human Physiology, University of Milan, Italy

A workplace for VDU operators has been designed and verified with the direct participation of the workers and technicians working with the VDU. The main requirements for the supporting set of the VDU and its keyboard are the following:
> they must be independently and easily tiltable;
> the height of the supporting set can be fixed at 72 cm;
> a curved footrest must be placed on the base of the supporting set.

1. Objects and methods

The scope of the research was to design a workplace for VDU operators working in the photocomposition of newspapers by adopting the ergonomics methodology we have widely employed during the last ten years in many practical investigations in different kinds of industries (Grieco *et al.* 1974, Odescalchi *et al.* 1976).

This methodology is based on:

the interdisciplinarity of the technicians of industries and of the researchers not merely as a sum of different contributions, but as a synergic interaction of a well trained group;

the global aims and scopes of the researches and/or interventions. For example, to eliminate noise from the workplace, it is not enough to concentrate attention only on the sonic waves, but it is also necessary to study the work organization, the lay-out of the whole section and the way to perform the job;

the direct participation of the workers. They participate both in making the economic decisions and in setting the scale of priorities related to the ergonomic interventions; as a part of the enterprise dialectically confronting the management, and, as technicians, with their own kind of knowledge.

The objects of the present research were:
the design of a supporting set for a VDU and its keyboard;
the definition of the characteristics of a more suitable chair for this kind of job;
the identification of the requirements to have the most flexible workplace, either for adoption in different jobs or for introduction of different lay-outs.

The research has been carried out in the factory of a company in Milan, located in the centre of the city, which employs 350 persons. The company carries out contract printing for newspapers.

At the start of the research our ergonomic group had already been working in this factory for two years in air purification and in noise reduction of the rotatives section. For this reason the ergonomic methodology was widely known and accepted at all company levels: management, technicians, work-shop committee and representatives of the homogeneous workers' group.

The research has been developed through four successive steps which had been previously discussed with the management, the company's technicians, the workshop committee and the homogeneous workers' group of linotypists, and we have had, both at the beginning and during the research, an active and continuous participation of the company's personnel.

The four research steps were:

(1) An introductory analysis to identify the basic elements needed to realize a prototype workplace.
(2) The design and realization of the prototype.
(3) The experimentation of the prototype and the evaluation of results.
(4) The industrial design of a workplace that would:
    meet ergonomic requirements,
    have a low cost without harming its industrial production,
    dispose of all technical attachments (e.g. cables) for VDU and keyboards.

The introductory analysis was carried out in a section where 30 VDUs were working, which had been temporarily set-up by the company since our research was concomitant with the conversion from text-editing by linotypes to photocomposition.

Objects of the introductory analysis were: the characteristics of the source documents both with regard to the formal aspect (typed texts, typed texts with hand-made corrections, photocopies, agency texts) and to the contents (normal texts, texts with a considerable amount of names and/or phrases in a foreign language, classified advertising, tables of numbers and/or names); the mode of distribution of the source documents; the characteristics of the workplaces, which had been realized with common tables and chairs normally used for the linotypes; the physical environment; the work shifts. One of the most important was from 9.30 p.m. to 3 a.m.; the work load: 7 hours of work with 30 minutes of rest. The National Labour Contract provides for 8500 types/hour inclusive of spaces and printing codes. The company contract is not very different: 48 000 effective types/work shift, and the ability to learn the typing techniques on the new keyboards as a function of the two training methods experienced by the operators. Some operators were trained by direct reading of the text, i.e. the same situation as the linotype job. Others were trained by using head-phones and dictating texts at increasing speed. The best results were obtained with the first training system.

Some of these objects were examined not only for design purposes, but for a better interpretation of the subjective judgements of the job expressed by the workers.

The objects were studied by means of:

an objective evaluation of the source documents and job performance and a measurement of the workplace and physical environment;
a series of case studies during five collective sessions of about $1\frac{1}{2}$ hours each with 5–6 keyboard operators at a time.

2. Results

The results of the introductory analysis directly used in the prototype design can be summarized as follows:

(a) The keyboard must have more inclination than keyboards available on the market. This depends either on habits acquired when working on the keyboard of linotypes or on individual differences: postural attitude and size of the body, ability in performing the job and visual acuity.

(b) The possibility of tilting the VDU and moving it freely a few centimetres on its support to avoid glare from the screen. It is practically impossible to ensure a controlled lighting in a room with windows during the whole year and all the day. The tallest operators may want to tilt the VDU to have the visual axis normal to the plane of the screen.

(c) The text must have different positioning: over the VDU, at the side of the VDU, between VDU and keyboard.

(d) A very important need is a footrest. Many operators utilized as footrests various gadgets they had found around.

(e) The source documents flow does not require a collection point for the texts. Therefore a service table is used by the operators only for their small personal belongings. In actual fact the size of a service table is aimed only at spacing out the workplace. A few operators complained that typing method and movements of the other operators near them influenced their work.

(f) The chair must be: revolving, without wheels or with self-blocking wheels, without arms, and with an easily adjustable height.

Some of the main results, related to the job as a whole rather than to the design of the workplace, were focused on the great relevance of formal aspects of source documents and on the necessity of a standardization of printing codes on source documents.

This is a serious problem, particularly for a company that effects contract printing since the texts are prepared by employees of another company and, for this reason, it is impossible to improve the situation through informal and personal contacts.

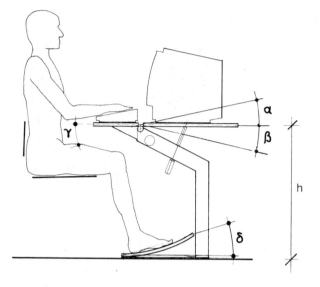

Figure 1. Lateral section of the prototype of the VDU set. The angles and the height vary: α, from $0°$ to 15; β, from $0°$ to $20°$; γ, from $0°$ to $20°$; δ, from $14°$ to $24°$; h, from 66 to 82 cm.

Figure 2. Prototype workplace for testing.

Figure 1 shows a lateral section of the prototype and the values of the angles to test. The footrest is curved to follow the rotation of the lower leg. The VDU set was equipped with a rear panel adjustable in height and with a service table.

The workplace so realized was located in a section (figure 2) where 12 VDUs were working, for trial purposes. The tests were carried out on 19 operators with height ranging from 1·60 to 1·92 m and weight from 59 to 104 kg. All groups were composed of former linotypists. At the beginning of the test, the operators adjusted their workplace with the assistance of a researcher. The test lasted approximately 30 minutes for each operator and consisted in the actual composition of different texts. A questionnaire was filled in by the researcher during and after the test.

The experimental results that were more relevant for the final design of the VDU set were:

The keyboard supporting table must be very easily and gradually tiltable. Also the VDU supporting table must be tiltable, although its adjustment is much less frequent. The variation of the angles α, β and γ (see figure 1) was judged enough.

The height of the VDU set supporting table can be fixed at 72 cm.

The front part of the footrest must be reduced in order to allow postures very close to the keyboard, while the rear part should be extended to allow sloppy postures. The inclination δ can be fixed at 14° (see figure 1).

A rear panel 100 cm high allowed operators to see their colleagues and at the same time excluded any moving background.

The text holder must be freely movable and fixable in any position.

By accepting the above findings we were able to design a VDU supporting set suitable for different jobs and/or lay-outs (figure 3). Further improvements were:

The wires are placed on the base of the rear panel.

To facilitate cleaning, the footrest can be lifted and the rear panel does not reach the floor.

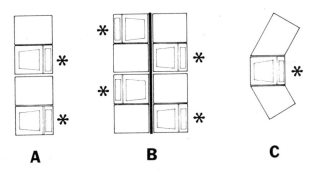

Figure 3. Schema of different utilization of the VDU set as a function of the job and/or of the lay-out.

The shape of the support of the VDU set is such as to allow the legs to be freely placed on the footrest.

Acknowledgment

We thank the management, the technicians and the workshop committee of the S.A.M.E. s.r.l. of Milano for their active cooperation, and useful suggestions.

References

GRIECO, A., CORTILI, G., BANDINI BUTI, L., and ODESCALCHI, C. P., 1974, Medicina preventiva ed ergonomia. *Le Scienze*, **73**, 124–131.

ODESCALCHI, C. P., BANDINI BUTI, L., CORTILLI, G., and MORETTI, E., 1976, *La Concezione Ergonomica, le Condizioni di Attuazione, il suo Contributo alla Prevenzione*. Azione Comunitaria Ergonomica. Doc. n. 1654/75 i ACE.

Ergonomics in the design, evaluation and application of the Philips PTS 6000 terminal system

By N. Claridge

Ergolab, Renstiernas gata 12, S-116 31 Stockholm, Sweden

Ergolab was responsible for the ergonomics behind the design and evaluation of the Philips PTS 6000 terminal system. The first of four stages was to define the user population and the work tasks, from which present-day and future demands were established. Information was obtained not only from Sweden but also Western Europe, America and Australasia.

The second stage was, according to ergonomic principles, to develop individual modules for the system. As a result, two keyboards, a plasma display, and a printer were designed.

The third stage was to design 'mock-up' workplaces which resulted in a *sitting workplace* being recommended, and two standing workplaces being acceptable.

The theme of this work has been user involvement throughout, and constant re-evaluation is essential. As the demands change so must workplace design alter to accommodate them.

1. Introduction

Ergolab is an independent ergonomic consultancy organization based in Stockholm, Sweden. During 1976–78 a series of investigations was carried out for Philips Elektronikindustrier AB by Ergolab. This presentation is a summary of the work.

The Philips PTS 6000 terminal system was originally designed for application to banking systems within Europe. As the market for this system expanded, it became apparent that it must be able to cater for varying customer requirements from all over the world, In 1975 Philips decided to develop new modules to the 6000 system and, as a result of customer demand, include ergonomic criteria and recommendations in the design stages.

During this period the project was effectively divided into four main stages:

Definition of the user population, and establishing their individual demands upon the system.

Design and evaluation, using ergonomic criteria and recommendations, of the individual modules of the PTS 6000 terminal system.

Development of 'mock-up' workplaces using the modules designed as a result of the previous stage.

Implementation of the selected modules into the working situation, and subsequent evaluation.

2. The user population

The 6000 system has potentially a wide range of applications. To date, it has been used mainly within the area of banking and it was from here that information about users' present-day and future demands were obtained. Data were collected through interviews and questionnaires with both cashiers and customers not only from Sweden but also Western Europe, America and Australasia.

Compared to the present day, future bank work routines will be increasingly computer-terminal oriented, especially when such an 'intelligent' system will be coupled with equipment such as cash-dispensing machines, inherently reducing counter work. However, one aspect highly valued by cashiers is contact with customers. Excellent employee–customer interaction is often the pride of many banks and any improvement to the modules or changes in workplace design should not interfere with this.

Customs and workplaces vary not only from country to country but also bank to bank. Three basic types of workplace were established: a workplace where the cashier sits; one where the cashier stands; and one where two cashiers share the same equipment.

Further aspects, such as tradition and capital investment, reduce the willingness of banks to redesign existing workplaces. Consequently the new modules of the PTS 6000 must be flexible enough to cater for wide variation between old existing workplaces and modern, newly designed, ones.

3. Design and evaluation of the component units

The next stage, having established the demands of the user population, was to design and evaluate possible modules according to ergonomic specifications. The units involved were four alternative printers, with recording journals, two keyboards and a data screen.

3.1. *The printer*

Four printers were presented for evaluation. Three printers were designed to be placed upon the work-surface, two having a vertical feeding method and one having a horizontal. The fourth printer was a free-standing unit with a vertical feed.

During the evaluation stage emphasis was given to unit size and flexibility. Smaller, easily placed units were preferred. Considering a user population, ranging from fifth percentile woman to 95th percentile male, the units were evaluated by sketch drawing according to two main principles:

Arm movement of a cashier should not extend above shoulder height while adopting a correct sitting or standing working posture at a workplace including a printer, and using A4 paper.

Printer size should be as small as possible enabling maximum flexibility. Noise emitted should not disturb cashier–customer conversation (45 dBA).

Initially the horizontal feeding method was preferred but its size and disruption of keyboard usage made it unacceptable. Consequently the vertical feeding printer was selected (without an inbuilt display) which could either be lowered into or placed on top of the work-surface.

A journal should be included in the printer unit as a recording system and, if required, could be a readable source of information for the cashier. Its location was not critical, but it should be within 'optimal viewing angles' for a cashier at a correct working posture. Because most 'feeding' was done with the left hand the journal was located on the right side of the printer unit.

3.2. The data screen

Feedback about the work task indicated that the data screen would *not* be the primary source of information, although a display was necessary to provide data required for customer service, i.e. customer credit situation. Its size could therefore be significantly smaller than a traditional screen and could be either in the form of a separate display unit or inbuilt into a printer unit. The former suggestion was developed as the latter resulted in several workplace design problems.

After a series of smaller experiments and with consideration to ergonomic variables, a plasma display, containing six lines of red text on a black background, was designed. An attractive aspect of this unit is that the filter in front of the display is angled, thus reflecting unwanted light onto a black surface and preventing distracting glare.

3.3. The keyboard

Information indicated that the prime task would be numeric, although alpha keys would occasionally be required. A numeric together with an alphanumeric keyboard should be located at the workplace. Design of the keyboard focused heavily upon keyboard profile, i.e. thickness and angle. The aim was to design a thin keyboard, which did not need to be lowered into the work-surface, or require a hand rest. The resultant flexibility would enable operators to position the keyboard to personal satisfaction and comfort. Other aspects considered were keyboard angle, key characteristics and colour.

A possible solution was a module system whereby a unit of alpha keys could be attached to the right of a numeric keyboard. This was not economically possible at the time and two units, a numeric keyboard and an alphanumeric keyboard, were designed. As a result of this work Philips produced a new 'slim-line' keyboard, fulfilling all ergonomic criteria and which permitted maximal flexibility of keyboard positioning during workplace design.

The design and evaluation stages resulted in four units to the PTS 6000 system:

one printer unit, *without* an inbuilt display;
two keyboards, one numeric and one alphanumeric;
one plasma display.

4. Workplace design

The next stage was to build mock-up workplaces using the above modules. It was important to consider the needs of both the cashier and the customer. Handicapped people who fell into these categories were also considered but required a separate project and were not included.

Considering a user population from big males to small females, mock-ups of workplaces were constructed for the following situations:

a workplace with a sitting cashier;
a workplace with a standing cashier;
a shared workplace with two cashiers.

Some of the workplace design criteria included were:

optimal and maximal reach distances—all units, including the customer counter, should be within maximal reach distance from the cashier (optimal, 350–450 mm; maximal, 550–650 mm);
arm movement should never be above horizontal from the shoulder;
horizontal and vertical viewing angles—the positioning of primary and secondary sources of information without causing undue head movement;
customer counter heights—a trade-off between writing levels for a standing customer and maximal arm movement for a sitting cashier;
easy access, maintenance and service of hardware units.

The mock-up study resulted in three designs being chosen, one workplace for sitting cashiers being *recommended*, and two workplaces for standing cashiers being acceptable.

The designs were subsequently tested in a real banking situation with cashiers and customers under working conditions. It is hoped that feedback from this application will, if necessary, lead to modifications and improvements to the design. Constant re-evaluation by both designers and everyday users is extremely important. Subjective comments often reveal small everyday problems overlooked in earlier design stages. As the cashiers' job or the customers' demands change, so the design of the workplace and system must change to accommodate them.

The theme used during all stages of this work has been user involvement. Involving actual or potential users in the design process helps to provide the designer with detailed knowledge of the users' requirements, helps to train the users to appreciate, understand and use the system, and helps to ensure that the final system will be both useful and used.

Name index

Subject index